AN ANTHROPOLOGY OF WAR

AN ANTHROPOLOGY OF WAR
Views from the Frontline

Edited by

Alisse Waterston

Berghahn Books
NEW YORK • OXFORD
www.berghahnbooks.com

First published in 2009 by

Berghahn Books

www.berghahnbooks.com

© 2009 Berghahn Books

Originally published as a special issue of *Social Analysis*, volume 52, issue 2.

Library of Congress Cataloging-in-Publication Data

An anthropology of war : views from the frontline / edited by Alisse Waterston.
    p. cm.
  Includes bibliographical references and index.
  ISBN 978-1-84545-622-1 (pbk. : alk. paper)
    1. War and society. I. Waterston, Alisse, 1951–.

HM554.A68 2009
303.6'6—dc22

                                      2008042875

British Library Cataloguing in Publication Data

A catalogue record for this book is available from the British Library.

Printed on acid-free paper

CONTENTS

To Partners In Health
a solidarity movement
a vision for social change
a blueprint for action

ACKNOWLEDGMENTS

I am deeply grateful to Carolyn Nordstrom, Brian Ferguson, Steve Reyna, Jose Vasquez, Avi Bornstein, Lesley Gill, Beatriz Manz, and Paul Farmer, the intellectually and morally brave contributors to this volume. They are among the leading chroniclers of war for our times, anthropologists who serve as witnesses with honesty and integrity. They have braved the field to bring back raw truths about war—its precursors, its causes, its aftermaths, its effects on human lives and on the future of humankind. Notwithstanding the field-level, local focus of most of the chapters, the global reach of US imperial ambition becomes strikingly apparent in this collection. The authors transport us from Colombia and Guatemala to Israel and Palestine, Iraq, Afghanistan, Haiti, and elsewhere—sites of direct and indirect US military and economic intervention and occupation, political influence, and authority.

I am indebted to Ellen Weinstein for so generously allowing us to use her artwork for the cover of this book. Artist Mark Vallen describes *Camouflage* as "a close-up portrait of an American soldier … Such images are always tragically the same, a gallant warrior in uniform imbued with the virtues of service and self-sacrifice … But Weinstein's artwork looks beyond facile patriotism to expose an unsettling reality. The soldier's portrait … and the American flag back-drop are entirely composed of snippets of tabloid press reports trumpeting … inconsequential celebrities … Does the camouflage hide a thoroughly narcissistic and debauched society—or does a manufactured culture of distraction mask a deep-rooted militarism?" (Foreign Policy in Focus Web site, 12 March 2008). *Camouflage* visually captures both the anthropological approach to understanding war and a key mechanism that makes war possible.

I am grateful to Bruce Kapferer and Vivian Berghahn for their enthusiastic support of this important collection. I thank Berit Angelskår for her gracious assistance at a critical stage in the process, and Shawn Kendrick for her sharp eye and careful editing. I would like to extend special thanks to the Executive Program Committee of the American Anthropological Association for sponsoring the 2006 panel, "War," on which this collection is based.

My deepest appreciation goes to Howard Horowitz for his help, encouragement, inspiration, and love. For their support and guidance, I am grateful to Maria D. Vesperi, Barbara Rylko-Bauer, Carolyn Nordstrom, Paul Farmer, and Zoe Agoos. I also thank Matthew Zuckerman and Leah Horowitz, my wonderful children, who are so loving, caring, and committed, my mother Louise M. Waterston, and my siblings David Waterston, Jessica Waterston, Linda Waterston Justiniano, and Adrienne Waterston. I thank Linda for referring me to Jean Ziegler's work. I extend special thanks to Adrienne for designing the original mock-up (a collage of a collage) for the compelling cover that graces this book.

My goal in putting together this collection is to undermine war, to help bring an end to war. Toward that purpose, the editor's royalties from this book will go to the non-profit organization Partners In Health, Paul Farmer's direct-action response to war. I dedicate this book to Partners In Health—a vision, a movement, a blueprint for change.

Alisse Waterston
New Rochelle, NY

PRELUDE
An Accountability, Written in the Year 2109

Carolyn Nordstrom

An Archaeology of the Future

Did scholars at the dawn of the twenty-first century recognize that their work not only illuminated the past and shaped the present but also produced the future? Did they see in their analyses the harbingers of new kinds of wars, unprecedented forms of violence, undeveloped potentialities? What outcomes did they purposefully or unintentionally contribute to through the cacophonous poetry of their theories? What responsibilities did they shoulder for the legacies they imparted?

Thus begins *An Accountability*, written in the year 2109. It stands as an archaeology of the future and a reflexivity that ponders how we, as scholars and anthropologists, will be read—and judged—by future history.[1]

Notes for this section are located on page 11.

For much of the first decade of the fledgling twenty-first century, anthropologists in the United States have been producing academic scholarship while at war. With Iraq, certainly. With each other, undeniably. With themselves, perhaps. With lethal inequalities, hopefully. What intellectual and moral bearings animate the heartbeat of their epistemologies as they ripple across and interact to configure, in however large or small a way, our emergent tomorrows?

* * *

An Accountability © 2109

A Future of a History

Overview: 100 Years, from the Past to the Present

Anthropology committed suicide in the mid-twenty-first century. It was a death both epistemological and ontological.

This came to pass as:

The new millennium saw war become a growth industry,[2] and post-national twenty-first-century non-state hyper-financial giants—economic and political powerhouses—flourished. These organizations resembled reticulated net formations that maximized cross-border linkages (thus avoiding state-based legal systems) to create massive and largely impenetrable webs of ownership across resource extraction, industrial production, global transport, distribution, banking, and security institutions.[3] Legal and illegal, state and extra-state were heuristic definitions used by analysts. To these reticula, the distinctions were largely irrelevant, employed only when productive. The state was reduced to another out-competed power regime.

Scholars did not foresee these emergent futures. Universities, grounded in nation-state structures, crumbled.

* * *

Twentieth-century anthropology demanded accountability for its discipline's harmful actions in the colonial era. Yet was anthropology at that time aware that it stood in the same relationship to a history of the future? Did anthropologists craft their knowledge knowing that they would be held accountable for both the constructive and destructive impact their work would have in shaping global events to come?

It is not a failure that anthropologists on the cusp of the twenty-second century want to repeat.

As anthropology sought to re-establish its ethical tradition—indeed, itself—at the end of the twenty-first century, two events transpired:

first, the discipline accepted as foundational that 'theory is ontological', that is to say that theory has a being as well as a knowledge. It exists only by virtue of being produced, consumed, performed, and interacted, and therefore it can be said to be invested with reflexivity. Thus, as we will conclude, '*theory is theoretician, is*'.

second, the idea of anthropology as both account and accountability emerged—the idea that our accounts are not merely voices of the world, but ways of creating the world.

An Account's-Ability

An example of the vast repercussive inter-linkages of a single act helps illustrate the roiling realities of the twenty-first century we speak of here:

In the first decade of the twenty-first century, a bullet is fired in Iraq.

How did anthropology see this? And how did this act of viewing bring us to the world we occupy a hundred years later?

At that point in time, the discipline provided excellent analyses of 'nation' and its 'isms' (nationalism, reificationalism, racism, perspectivism, etc.), inequalities and power, gender and personhood, complex belief systems, non-state networks, and the lived realities of violence and peace.

Anthropology wove these together to stand at the leading edge of theories of globalization. It was the most sophisticated among the disciplines at understanding the relationships among the visible and invisible facets of human experience: social, intellectual, experiential, econo-political, emotive, phantasmagorial.

But the field was less successful at seeing linkages throughout global experiences as they move across, and configure, for example:

- the global economic flows foundational to hyper-placed beyond-state powers;
- the ironies that as they wrote against oppressive power hierarchies they worked in academies defined by such inequalities, and that these *were* nationalisms of the state;
- and that these inequalities were experientially related to those arising in war, and simultaneously in domestic realms.

Emergent tomorrows.

We look back at that time and wonder if scholars saw these deep global connections yet found it difficult to publish their findings in a state-based system given to obscuring the subterranean webs of power that the industrial elite depended on. Or perhaps these questions were 'taught out' of academic cognition—invisibilities crafted so successfully by the power brokers of the time that average intellectuals learned to 'not-see'. Were early twenty-first-century researchers sitting in coffee shops across the United States discussing the future repercussions of what and how they wrote and did not write? Did they realize that they defined themselves (and no one else) as *the* theoreticians, even though they produced literature having little impact on the world by virtue of writing style and publishing venues? Did late-night discussions link war, the topics they chose to study, child and labor abuses, and the control of financial empires? Did classroom conversations explore the fact that they would be held liable, not by their own standards of the day, but by emergent future epistemes—ones crafted by the very trajectories that they helped set in motion?

Few formal public presentations dug deeply into the fact that the ontological life of theories was generated in institutions shaped within the confines of state ideologies based on hierarchies of job and representation, individualism as success, limited good, aggressive competition, and theoretical wars. Few publications from the United States exist, for example, asking, as Albanian scholars did in the early 1990s, "How many among us will become human rights violators, will become not merely complicit but pro-active in political oppression when our universities crumble on the frontlines of war and we are handed guns?"

Emergent Hyper-Placed Non-State Powers in the Early 2000s

To situate this discussion, it is important to note the kinds of state and extra-state power regimes that were consolidating at that time. And to show that these were far more sophisticated and complex global entities than any of the multi-national corporations, pan-national religious and identity associations, non-state paramilitary and terrorist groups, non-governmental organizations, and criminal networks then in existence.[4]

Wars yielded immense profits. Everything necessary to outfit and sustain fighters, their governments, and their populations flowed from cosmopolitan centers of production. Vast resources (from laboring bodies through the minerals fueling the industrial centers to the luxury items such as diamonds and kidneys that marked inequalities) poured back from the war zones into industrial centers, usually in peace locales, to pay for these costs. Most of the exchanges were trans-state. A significant percentage were extra-legal.

Those who were the most successful at this were business, military, and government leaders who saw the world as a vast web of exchanges in which the state and state-based laws were of only minor importance.

As the twenty-first century progressed, such people harnessed not only the commodity-resource cycles of profit but the means of moving these. International transport adhered only in the loosest of terms to state law and control. With fluid, constantly changing, and multiple countries of registry, incorporation, ownership, and oversight, shipping was itself sovereign. As businesses manipulated multi-country bases, they transferred people, goods, and monies between physical states with sovereign impunity. Profits from the legal and the extra-legal were difficult to unravel, thus making it possible for businesses to invest unrecorded (extra-legal) monies in ways that invisibly maximized their economic and political power. Extra-legal money flows could rival legal ones. Industries bought their own offshore banks and consolidated financial empires. In the early 2000s, a bank could be bought for as little as $25,000, and an island to serve as its sovereign base for perhaps $1 million.[5]

The manipulation of unrecorded finances, invested strategically in the world's stock markets, businesses, and financial institutions shaped these institutions. These vast interrelated networks—legal, extra-legal, undefined—and not the state, were what such leaders saw. It was here economics, politics, identities, and sovereignty were crafted for many.

In the First Decade of the Twenty-First Century, a Bullet Is Fired in Iraq

This bullet situates two trajectories illustrating the points being made here.

TRAJECTORY #1: The bullet was a singular object and event. It was locatable in time and space, thought and emotion. The person it hit was a vital compendium of life—a unique body animated by a vibrant personality and situated amid a living history, an irreplaceable present, and a creative interplay of cultures.

Simultaneously, the bullet was part of a vast set of economic and political transactions. The war zones of the early twenty-first century were not isolated nation-state events but interrelated processes spanning the globe that far surpassed the reach of wars. Such 'trans-actions' were defined by movement, not set valuation. They constituted fluidity, and economic empires were created not only *within* but *as* flux. Power, said at the time to be 'located', was in fact honed in this hyper-placed flux.

The multi-state economic transactions (from military expenditures through defense contractors to development systems) in which the bullet took 'life' ran in the trillions of dollars. Yearly.

Arms industries, generally situated in peacetime centers, were linked to others that provided life's necessities: food, medicine, communications, transport, energy, hope, and aid. In embattled zones where transport and industry were the first casualties of violence, everyone still had to eat. Had to buy antibiotics. Had to sell themselves for the money to obtain these necessities. Sometimes these links were associative, for example, arms businesses partnering with energy and transport ones. Other times, diverse goods and services were all part of a single transnational corporation—one that could broker oil deals, supply the weapons to the militaries presiding over the deposits, and provide life's necessities to workers and troops alike. Determining where a state began and ended in these transactions—much less its complicity in extra-legal actions and the exploitation of desperate labor—was formidable at best, if not impossible.

War and reconstruction had to be purchased. The payment exacted by peacetime locales (the valuable raw resources fueling global cosmopolitan politico-market hegemony) gutted the countries at war of the very means to reconstruct.

Unaccountability was strategic.

A difficulty in untangling all this was that both a racketeer in forced child prostitution and the 1991 Nobel Peace Prize Laureate Daw Aung San Suu Kyi, who stood against oppressive rule in Myanmar, were painted with the label 'criminal' in formal legal terms.

A contradiction was thus embedded in the very core of the state. Great fortunes and great cruelty thrive in the realm of the unregulated. But ironically, the realm of the unregulated was also where the average person turned for survival in an unsure world. It was here that ordinary citizens could gain the currency to buy industrial necessities, agricultural supplies, and development goods. Such (illicit) goods purchased hard currency, helped broker power, and allowed investments in land, legal industries, and political partnerships for the disenfranchised and desperate. These spawned and supported subsidiary industries, both legal and illicit. Daily necessities followed these same development trajectories. When government frameworks are in flux, non-state networks are often the only support and supply systems functioning.

It is in this vast extra-legal domain that power regimes are contested, where new forms of capital, access, and authority arise, some crumbling before they master any real influence in global affairs, others supplanting old regimes with new. It is this very paradox—the extra-state abusively wild-catting outside legal controls, yet affording development for people with few means of survival—that made the extra-legal such a powerful force of change in the 2000s.

What responsibility did US scholars at this time, as citizens in a country at war, take for addressing such phenomena as represented in the following examples:

extra-legal profits were invisibly laundered into political power and had an impact in shaping emergent national economies.

A weapon sold is a sale, whether it is legal or not. Perhaps the unrecorded sales were more attractive, especially for legal national and multi-national businesses. Laundering untracked monies into legal economies (through legitimate businesses, stocks and bonds, and financial institutions) could offer significant control of those markets. The elite of the extra-legal controlled more money than the gross national product (GNP) of many of the world's countries. This could be called a twenty-first-century form of global warlordism, much of it rooted in peacetime cosmopolitan-center businesses.

uncharted economies were beyond law, beyond accounting.

The key question, of course, is why these extra-legal economies were not recorded. It is hard to fathom how economic indices based solely on formally recorded monies and economies were accepted universally when massive flows of extra-legal commodities, services, and monies were fundamental in defining political processes and economic health worldwide. Gross domestic product (GDP) calculations were in actuality far from being 'gross' in that they considered only the legal. No economic indices for calculating a GDELP (gross domestic extra-legal product) existed. Simply put, there was no way, for example, to find data on the entire extra-legal profit in Europe in 2010, or how laundering it into the legal economy affected stock, interest, and currency rates.

The answer rests in the fact that those seeking to control vast financial empires eschewed transparency. Virtually all of the trillions of dollars that moved across the boundaries of legality ultimately passed through formal (legal) economies in ways that proffered forceful zones of profit and power. The excesses and abuses of war were linked to global systems of exchange that were deeply woven into the fabric of everyday life and formal institutions.

> *severe financial collapses resulting from global-level profiteering destroyed entire economies by the mid-twenty-first century, fanning the flames of war and repression yet again.*

These were foreseeable events based on historical precedents, the most obvious being the collapse of the colonial world, the cycles of economic depressions and failed states, and, centuries earlier, the disintegration of kingdoms and regional empires against the ascending supremacy of the Enlightenment state. Merchants in the Middle Ages developed international commerce systems intended to stand apart from kingly rule. These actions, extra-legal to monarchic law, were often deemed criminal. They presaged the development of the state just as the extra-state networks of modernity later foreshadowed post-state politics. Power by definition is not a teleological process.

> *states eroded under the weight of emergent forms of economic and political suzerainty;*

> *and what academics 'saw'—what they made visible and invisible in theory—helped set these realities into motion.*

We now know to ask: if analysts cannot see the full compendium of economic, political, and social forces defining the evolving twenty-first century, yet those controlling the intersections of the extra-legal and legal across war and peace can, who defines power?

It seems self-evident that those forging suzerainty both inside and outside the state and its laws knew that economics at that time was a *pas de deux* of the il/legal. They were aware that these constructions heralded new post-state powerhouses partaking of state institutions when convenient and forging non-state ones when necessary. But publications by many of the economic and political analysts of those days demonstrated that an understanding of these complex extra-state realities all too often faded into incomprehensibility. Removed from global understanding, isolated tales of warlords, terror, crime, and corruption were shot through with myths and assumptions.

The explanation for this may rest with the fact that from the Enlightenment to the early twenty-first century the sciences took shape and structure within the confines of the state. Research knowledge was begot in the womb of the state and delivered by the midwife of modernity. Academics came of age embedded in state institutions, and thus they privileged it. 'State' is a conceptual category, not an objective entity. It exists only because people believe in the laws, geographical designations, and imagined communities that designate the flow and flux of humanity and space into discrete parts. It is an abstract notion given substance by virtue of being recognized as substantive. A state needs academics to theorize it into being. Academics need institutions to recognize them and financially support them to bring them into being.

From a state-centered perspective, anything outside the state is seen as less substantive, less powerful, less dynamic. And is less studied. Unable to 'see' (in theory, data, analyses, and policy) non-state actualities, state-based institutions were blind-sided by these actualities.

Reality was the weapon that toppled state supremacy.

TRAJECTORY #2: As the bullet was fired in Iraq, other forms of violence simultaneously increased. The bullet, although unique, was also embedded in a vast generalized pattern of violent societal acts:

> *the rise in political violence correlated with a rise in domestic, gender, sexual, and criminal violence.*

Crises were embedded in crises. Profits were layered in profits. Abusive practices were hidden in proclaimed social values. Intertwined, overlapping, and interpenetrating contexts rippled across the world's continents.

When the pathologically abusive—that which violates human rights and endangers lives—was inculcated into social systems, the values attaching to it came to have a far broader impact. The lines of il/legality were strongly blurred for populations in general: average businesses used undocumented labor and offshore accounts; average citizens more frequently raped (or battered or killed) or were raped (battered, killed); average 'patriots' turned to illegal profiteering.

> *wars' end did not signal an end to these higher levels of violence.*

Statistics worldwide suggested that at the turn of the twenty-first century roughly one-third of the global population experienced domestic/interpersonal violence, although individual countries varied from far less to more than two-thirds of the population. People then were just beginning to explore the correlation: if trauma from political violence impairs societal recovery, trauma from any violence will have the same effect. Popular culture had long offered the image of military leaders presiding over a desolate pile of rubble—the kingdom that they had decimated in order to wrest control of it. But another reality was less easily captured by the popular imagination or academic investigation: the political leader presiding over a broken and maimed society, a shattered cultural stability, a wounded daily reality.[6]

> *linkages among differing forms of violence extended across both time and space.*

For example, by the advent of the twenty-first century, a large percentage of prison populations in the United States had suffered from domestic, sexual, and/or interpersonal violence growing up. Crime in post-war conditions did not fall, and in a number of cases it increased.[7]

Several interconnected factors brought about this rise: devastated post-war economies remained unable to provide the essentials for populations; war profiteers shifted not to legal pursuits but to new lucrative ventures; unscrupulous military and political actors sought to maximize their power through corrupt earnings. As the Mozambicans explained at the time, people had learned violence but failed to *un*learn it. Violence had become an institutionalized habit across the terrains of crime, security, business, and home.[8]

> *while all of these realities were evident to twenty-first-century anthropology, it tended to characterize correlations between contemporary war, long-term domestic and civil violence, complex extra-state networks, and the temporary demise of the field 50 years later as problematic at best, ridiculous at worst.*

Epistemological Suicide?

In the subsequent 100 years, an epistemic change has taken place that renders it impossible *not* to see the ways in which these various trajectories unfold and define one another within larger universes of human meaning and interaction. In watching the nation-state unravel and collapse, theoreticians have been able to discern how emergent forms of power politics and its related economies come into being. It is said colloquially that the ashes cannot recognize the phoenix rising from them.

While these futures were not woven into the theoretical todays of the early 2000s, it is important to recognize that anthropology at that time helped set the stage for the deeply reflexive definition of ontological theory that emerged. It pushed the limits of these inquires further than any other field with the exception of theoretical physics. At the same time, anthropology struggled within a larger pan-state epistemological system that failed to recognize that as we create knowledge, we create our nascent selves. We now conclude: given that epistemology is knowledge, it appears that anthropology did not recognize itself.

If the scholars in the first decade of the twenty-first century had created theories fully engaged with the truths of their world and their place in it—past, present, and future—would this century have suffered such severe repressions, economic collapses, power abuses, and social crises?

We now wonder: did anthropology commit suicide?

Ontological Reflexivity

Time corrects.

Anthropology was not dead. It reanimated itself with the idea that not only people but also the theories they 'live' can be considered reflexive. Theory ceased to be seen as a product or a performance enacted by the academic 'ego as I'. It became imbued with the same complex of interactions—cognitive, existential, phenomenological, emotive—that define theoreticians, that is, humankind, and their productions within the larger world.

Today we know that the theories we create and employ are generative. The Cartesian dichotomy between producer and product, between subject(ivity) and object(ivity) has been laid largely to rest: *'theory is theoretician, is'*.

The way we explain our todays creates our tomorrows. We are as accountable for what we choose not to see and address as we are for what we do. We are as responsible for the existential and emotive content of our epistemologies as we are for the cognitive. Any notion of 'theoretical' and 'applied' today seems barbaric, a way of perpetuating meaningless yet divisive large-scale (intercontinental) political agendas. We expect anyone writing on power and inequality to explore the ways that working in a university or organizational system based on hierarchies of inequality (tenure systems, grant and publishing gate-keeping, zero-sum competition, theoretical wars, etc.) shapes their epistemologies.

Writing *An Accountability* today also embraces the recognition that we can read the interrelated trajectories of our world. Theory oftentimes is habitus—a straightjacket into which we confine ourselves. Accountability, like reflexivity, carries the premise that we can know more than we know. Epistemology is vibrant, unfolding, emergent.

Rather than trying to see theory as a dispassionate way of looking out on the world in an attempt to explain it, theory is now seen as part of life's engagement in the world. Theory—produced, performed, enacted, engaged—is intrinsic to being, and to being human.

Recognizing this, we must then ask in our theoretical work: how do we want to be human?

* * *

Postscript from 2009

Where have these rules of what and how we research and write come from? How do we confer power on our gatekeepers? And why in our academic lives do we follow the patterns of power that our work decries? Those who benefit from war zone violence seek to silence social scientists who have the courage to speak to the future of power. Those who benefit from global war today seek the same silencing. And social science seems to have obliged by producing theories that—due to writing style, publication venues, jargon, arrogance, fear, and uncontested rules—extend little beyond the narrow confines of the subdisciplines of the field.

Will this be judged in the future as complicity with dangerous forms of hegemonic power?

Will the poor starving peasant woman who finally fights back against an abusive solider or the actively oppressed artists who take their critiques to the streets to educate or the children who ask for and expect engaged scholarship from their teachers be seen by future generations as more courageous—both intellectually and personally—than today's 'cutting-edge academics'?

Notes

1. This discussion points to North American scholars because it is my academic home and because I do not think it is appropriate to critique those of other countries. However, this is not meant to imply a North American–centric perspective. On the contrary, this essay is concerned with that which ripples across the terrains of space and time.
2. Most analysts considered only the visible. For example, the top ten global defense contractors (curiously calculated without considering countries like China) in 2006 alone made $200 billion in defense revenue and $415 billion in total revenue (http://www.defensenews.com/index.php?S = 07top100byrevenue). Only 26 countries that year had gross domestic products over that sum (http://www.imf.org/external/pubs/ft/weo/2007/01/data/index.aspx). Further hundreds of billions were made yearly in extra-legal arms sales (see Nordstrom 2004).
3. See Naím (2006), Naylor (2005), and Nordstrom (2007).
4. The formation of these hyper-placed non-state powers followed a trajectory similar to that of the 1600s, when the phoenix of the newly born state rose from the ashes of kingdoms and regional empires. By the 2000s, it was the state that was the old man of politics. The familiarity of the process should have been more apparent to those conducting analyses.
5. See Naylor (2005).
6. See Das (2006), Das et al. (2000), Kaldor (2007), and Zizek (2006).
7. See Darby (2005) and Nordstrom (2004).
8. See Nordstrom (1997).

References

Darby, John. 2005. *Violence and Reconstruction.* Notre Dame, IN: University of Notre Dame Press.

Das, Veena. 2006. *Life and Words: Violence and the Descent into the Ordinary.* Berkeley: University of California Press.

Das, Veena, Arthur Kleinman, Mamphela Ramphele, and Pamela Reynolds, eds. 2000. *Violence and Subjectivity.* Berkeley: University of California Press.

Kaldor, Mary. 2007. *New and Old Wars: Organized Violence in a Global Era.* Palo Alto, CA: Stanford University Press.

Naím, Moises. 2006. *Illicit: How Smugglers, Traffickers, and Copycats Are Hijacking the Global Economy.* New York: Anchor Books.

Naylor, R. T. 2005. *Wages of Crime: Black Markets, Illegal Finance, and the Underworld Economy.* Ithaca, NY: Cornell University Press.

Nordstrom, Carolyn. 1997. *A Different Kind of War Story.* Philadelphia: University of Pennsylvania Press.

———. 2004. *Shadows of War: Violence, Power, and International Profiteering in the Twenty-First Century.* Berkeley: University of California Press.

———. 2007. *Global Outlaws: Crime, Money and Power in the Contemporary World.* Berkeley: University of California Press.

Zizek, Slavoj. 2006. *The Parallax View.* Cambridge, MA: MIT Press.

INTRODUCTION
On War and Accountability

Alisse Waterston

My worry is that anthropology may have become too self-marginalized as a discipline, increasingly irrelevant to the big questions of the day in our world, content to snipe from the sidelines as soon as it seems safe … It would be nice if anthropologists could be among those leading this discussion, rather than merely following it at a safe distance. (Nolan 2006)

This book on anthropology and war is a direct product of … a crisis of conscience which has called into question the right of anthropologists to remain aloof from the great issues of our times. (Fried, Harris, and Murphy 1967)

… seeing *is* power. (Nordstrom 2007)

The 1967 volume, *War*, edited by Morton Fried, Marvin Harris, and Robert Murphy, grew out of an "unprecedented plenary symposium" of the 66th annual meeting of the American Anthropological Association. The symposium was

Notes for this section are located on page 28.

held, according to the authors, because one year earlier, 350 anthropologists attending the association's annual meeting had signed a petition declaring their "widely shared sentiment that anthropologists have both a moral and professional concern for the effects of war on the human species." The petition called for organized symposia to take place the next year that would counter the fact that only a "miniscule portion of the [1966] meeting's formal papers and symposia had displayed any concern for the critical issues of contemporary society" (Fried, Harris, and Murphy 1967: x).

Oh, how the times they have changed, and, oh, how they have not. The prospect for peace with justice looks bleak as we move deeper into the twenty-first century. The horrors of modern warfare—the deaths, mutilated bodies, dehumanization, destruction of social and material infrastructures—have not shocked the world enough to bring about an end to war. Instead, the arrogance of power marches on. In violence and with confidence, it creates and maintains conditions of scarcity while protecting private, concentrated wealth. "[W]ar is not sporadic anymore, it is permanent," claims sociologist Jean Ziegler. "It is not any more a crisis ... but normality" (Accardo 2005). In this time of permanent war, the US imperialist project takes center stage, the arrogance of its structural power marching on in active, interventionist warfare in Iraq and Afghanistan, and certainly more covertly elsewhere. Of course, this is not a brand-new development. Since the twentieth century, US power and wealth have greatly expanded, as Lesley Gill (2007: 142) puts it, "by killing, manipulating, and impoverishing the peoples who anthropologists traditionally study" (see also Dewey 1927).

Debates remain in US anthropology about whether the discipline, individual anthropologists, and the largest association of anthropologists in the world should remain "aloof from" or actively engage in the "great issues of our times" (Fried, Harris, and Murphy 1967: ix). Yet since 1967—over 40 years ago—more and more anthropologists have stopped believing that neutrality and objectivity are the values to which we ought to subscribe. Instead, they put a premium on ethics, responsibility, philosophical pacifism, and anti-war and anti-imperialist political activism (Gjessing 1968; Gough 1968; Hastrup et al. 1990; Holland et al. 2007; Jones 1971; Ortega 2006; Price 2004; Rylko-Bauer 2008; Rylko-Bauer, Singer, and Van Willigen 2006; Sanford and Angel-Ajani 2006; Singer 1990; Wolf and Jorgensen 1970). There are now many anthropologists who no longer believe in fairy tales, who do believe that "to say *nothing* is as much a significant act as to say *something*" (Berreman 1968: 392), and whose work and anti-imperialist engagements have been radical, revolutionary, and effective, even if not entirely transformative. For example, at recent annual meetings of the American Anthropological Association (AAA), anthropologists passed three important resolutions, in part motivated by the Pentagon's attempts to recruit anthropologists into US military initiatives: one resolution condemns and calls for an end to the US occupation in Iraq (AAA 2006); a second condemns torture and demands full US compliance with the UN Convention against Torture (AAA 2006); and a third opposes US military actions against Iran (AAA 2007).

As with the 1967 book, this edited volume, *An Anthropology of War: Views from the Frontline*, grows out of an important event at the 2006 AAA annual meeting—a presidential panel that drew an audience of approximately 500 anthropologists. For this collection, I asked the contributors, all of whom have been working in war zones, to make a clear and powerful statement concerning what they know about war: its precursors, its causes, its aftermaths, its effects on human lives and on the future of humankind. Each contributor has been a witness to war and can draw on examples of conflicts from various sites around the world. They tell stories, from their vantage point, of what they have seen, heard, smelled, read about, studied, analyzed, remembered—what they think and feel about war. They share with readers the big take-away messages from their years of research, activism, and experience in war zones. The reach of US imperial ambition is strikingly apparent as the authors transport us from Colombia and Guatemala to Israel and Palestine, Iraq, Afghanistan, Haiti, and elsewhere—sites of direct and indirect US military intervention and occupation, political influence and authority, and imperialistic economic undertakings and policies.

Reckonings

It has been a humbling experience for me to work on this special issue and this introduction. I am awed by the contributors, what they know and their intense experiences in war zones. I am also struck by the sheer quantity of literature on war by historians, philosophers, social critics, journalists, novelists, and anthropologists. It is overwhelming, as Brian Ferguson notes in "Ten Points on War," his chapter in this collection. Referring just to the literature in anthropology, Ferguson recalls the days when it was "possible to read practically everything that came out on the subject." There is no longer a way to offer a comprehensive work on the anthropology of war, and it is not the intention of this publication to do so. Instead, this collection takes up Carolyn Nordstrom's challenge: if we were to look back on the current moment from 100 years into the future, what would have been important to know about war?

Let me be blunt about the ambition here. My goal in putting together this collection is to undermine war, to help bring an end to war and the US imperial project. There are thousands of US anthropologists who, in Nordstrom's words, "have been producing academic scholarship while at war," whether or not war is the focus of their work. The whole world is living in a time of war—not just particular wars but continuous, imperial war, which has a tremendous, if differential impact, on the lives of most people everywhere across the globe.

I come to this project not as an expert on war but as a person living in a time of war who grew up in a century marked by war, has brought children into this war-torn world, and tries to teach young people about it. This collection is not just an intellectual exercise but a plea—desperate, frantic, anxious. Maybe this slight volume can find its way into the hands of the public and into global consciousness, so that we might find a way to end this insanity and be safe.

"How in your opinion are we to prevent war?—still unanswered ... let us make the attempt; even if it is doomed to failure," Virginia Woolf proposed

([1938] 1966). For us, it may be too late for prevention, but we can ask instead, "How in your opinion are we to bring an end to war?—still unanswered." In order to end war, we need to understand it. Even if our efforts are doomed to failure, with this collection we attempt this essential step.

In "Prelude: *An Accountability*, Written in the Year 2109," Nordstrom offers an insight that is also a charge: "The way we explain our todays creates our tomorrows." Inspired by this challenge, I present in this introduction a set of discussions on accountability as it pertains to war. First, there are the anthropological *accounts*, the stories that ethnographers tell about what they have seen, heard, and done on the frontlines. The contributors to this volume are among the leading ethnographers of war, braving the field to bring back raw truths. Then there is the *accounting for* war, explanations that help us understand causes, patterns, and practices of war, as well as occurrences of specific wars. Embedded in these explanations is another aspect of *accountability*: who is to be held responsible for war and where in our current arrangements does impunity tend to lie? War, as Ferguson so wisely notes, is not just something to be explained; war *accounts for* what we see on the ground, in any aspect of social life. These facets—accounting for war and what war accounts for—are inseparable. That war both explains and needs explaining reflects the dialectic of war. Then there is the responsibility of the discipline and ourselves as anthropologists with regard to the great issues of our times. I close the introduction to this volume with a reflection on *anthropological accountability*.

Accounts: Stories from the Frontlines of War

In her "different kind of war story," Nordstrom (1997: 16–17) makes the sharp observation that "most writing about violence in western theory never deals with actual violence … in most of these cases people are writing from the safety of a nonviolent situation." Except maybe anthropologists who, like Nordstrom, can theorize the violence of war while keeping hold of the "'wild cr[ies]' of terror, passion, mystery, rage … despair" (ibid.: 17–18) that real people in real wars experience. The ethnographic project brings anthropologists to the places where bullets are fired, where flesh is torn, where blood, brutality, and death are intertwined.

We need to go to that place and sit with it, learn from it. It is raw and tangible, the content that must be absorbed before we can go to the abstract. "Dead bodies and ruined houses," Woolf tells us, "are not an argument … [but] a crude statement of fact" ([1938] 1966: 11). Dead bodies and ruined houses are war for ordinary folk, the civilian and combat soldier. We do need to understand the ways in which war is the clash of classes, armies, and empires played out on structurally uneven killing fields. We must also see that war is hell, a truth made cliché by fatigue, indifference, misrepresentation, and abstraction.

Poetry and fiction can bring us there, from *Johnny Got His Gun* (Trumbo [1939] 1989) to *Slaughterhouse-Five* (Vonnegut [1969] 1991) and *All Quiet on the Western Front* (Remarque [1929] 1982), the novel that first awakened me to war. "But all limped on, blood-shod. All went lame; all blind," wrote Wilfred Owen, the prolific poet-soldier killed in World War I at age 25 (Fussell [1975] 2000: 288). From Siegfried Sassoon, Owen's friend and fellow poet, came "The Hero" (ibid.: 7):

> Blown to small bits. And no one seemed to care
> Except that lonely woman with white hair

At the level of journalism, ripped bodies so often hide the truth. Ethnography offers a bridge from journalism to theory to reveal that which has been hidden. It is a method that helps us see our own cultural assumptions and definitions, and that forces us to test our abstractions against the experiential. From it we get stories that we then link to other stories, a people's history of war. "[T]he bomb," Nordstrom explains in "Global Fractures" in this volume, "is a locatable event and a personal experience. But it is not singular. It is (quite literally) simultaneously embedded in the person hit, the larger networks of interplay among people and events, the war itself, and the global values and structures that sustain these realities." This linking of context and content is the great promise of anthropology.

The accounts in this volume aim to fulfill that promise. In "Military Occupation as Carceral Society," Avram Bornstein shocks us with the slap in the face he got from an Israeli soldier at the military checkpoint marking the Green Line between the West Bank and Israel. Bornstein brings us the sorrow, confusion, and rage of a Palestinian family battered by the rituals of occupation: surprise home-invasion night raids, violent interrogation, imprisonment, mothers facing choice-less choices. These stories draw us into the systems and structures that are built into occupation, not least of which is the architecture of control: prisons, checkpoints, walls. These systems and structures are implicated in the violence (see Bornstein 2002). The human toll and social consequences are felt by all parties involved. The violence escalates, no one is left unscathed, and nobody is secure.

Jose Vasquez brings us to war from several vantage points. An anthropologist, Vasquez's experience in war zones comes from his duties as a member of the United States Armed Forces, which led to his becoming an activist in Iraq Veterans Against the War.[1] In "Seeing Green," Vasquez focuses on perspective. We view the war through the lens of the latest high-tech equipment, devices that distort our perception of what is actually on the ground. Is it the enemy? An innocent? A human being? The theater of war has been transformed into a personal media center where war is always on, day or night, and *distance* becomes an enabling factor. Players, now armed with night vision goggles, laser range finders, and thermal sights, engage in video game–like competition in which 'targets' are dehumanized entities. In the lens with a view, objects that come into focus are cast in an eerie green glow, more monster-like than human. Thus, distant in space and removed from humanity, the objects get blown up by weapons unleashed by soldier-players on the ground and in the air. What is left, Vasquez says, are "little green men (or children or women) exploding on their screens." Modern warfare makes the Rashomon effect more likely to occur, and less likely that anybody will be held accountable for mistakes. No one feels remorse, a haunting thought considering that 90 percent of all war casualties these days are civilians (Nordstrom 1997: 5; Tickner 2001: 49).

Lesley Gill, Beatriz Manz, and Carolyn Nordstrom are dedicated chroniclers of war-torn societies. Working in the field for several decades, Gill has brought us to a struggling immigrant community in Bolivia (Gill 2000) and the chilling classrooms of the School of the Americas (Gill 2004), and now brings us to Colombia, the focus of her chapter in this collection. Colombia is not merely a sovereign nation-state entrenched in a 40-year civil war, but also a good case study of a US-shaped Cold War/post–Cold War counterinsurgency war in which "a range of new militaries—the decaying remnants of state armies, paramilitary groups (often financed by governments), self-defence units, mercenaries and international troops—engage in new forms of violence [including] … systematic murder" (Shaw 2000: 172). In "War and Peace in Colombia," Gill tells the story of Barrancabermeja, a city located in a hot region of the state's counterinsurgency war and an important oil refinery center fueled by corporate neo-liberalism. Do not be fooled by any appearance of calm in Barrancabermeja, Gill and her informants warn. This place, like many others across the globe, exists at the "ragged edges of war and peace." Statistics come alive in Barrancabermeja. In times past, 80–90 percent of casualties in all wars were military, *not* civilian (Shaw 2000: 172). This was when war had clear-cut frontlines and clear distinctions between warriors and civilians, as Gill points out. Over the years, Barranqueños have disappeared, have been massacred, kidnapped, and assassinated—civilian casualties in a war *of terror* funded by a vast amount of US military aid.

There is no peace with justice in Barrancabermeja. A criminal shadow state has emerged, monopolizing all sectors of material and social life and pressing more Barranqueños into poverty. Feeling vulnerable and nervous, they have become silent. Beatriz Manz is quite familiar with this scenario. She knows of what Gill speaks in describing Barrancabermeja's "tattered social fabric." Manz has been studying the aftereffects of counterinsurgency war for about 35 years, focusing on the rural Mayan communities of Guatemala and their refugees, who have been displaced by a war aided and abetted by the United States (Manz 1988, 2004). "The fabric of society … was shredded during the ferocious internal armed conflict. The legacy of state terror is everywhere," Manz informs us in "The Continuum of Violence in Post-War Guatemala," her chapter in this collection. Over 10 years ago, peace was 'achieved' in Guatemala. But there is no peace, Manz tells us, and she explains why. In Guatemala, poverty is rampant, militarization of daily life is the standard, power gets away with murder, vigilante justice is customary, and people are traumatized, afraid, intimidated, frustrated, and in despair. Murder is on the rise, as is violence against women, and all of this is the aftermath of counterinsurgency war. Although we can root contemporary social dysfunctions in war, this explanation of the present situation in Guatemala is downplayed or ignored. Instead, today's atrocities are described as acts of common criminality perpetrated by individuals and gangs, the latter often fomented in Guatemalan prisons. To stem the violence and counter the legacies of terror would require both a redistribution of resources and an embrace of inclusiveness, fairness principles that are absent from the policies and practices of neo-liberal capitalism and cosmopolitan politics—the key obstacles to peace with justice.

Nordstrom does not report directly from Guatemala or Colombia, but her analysis in "Global Fractures" fits with those places. Nordstrom bases her understanding of the contemporary world on decades of research she has conducted in war zones from Sri Lanka to Mozambique. Her research has led to some of the most important writing on our war-torn world available, including the brilliant *A Different Kind of War Story* (1997) and the illuminating *Global Outlaws*, an ethnography of "invisible (illegal) realities and placeless hyper-placed global flows" (2007: xi). Nordstrom is the consummate storyteller who, with grace and integrity, introduces us to the brave, the resourceful, the resilient, the opportunistic, the creative, the mercenary, the peace-loving, and the violent. "'We are glad you finally came to ask us our story; up until now, everyone has come to tell us what our story is,'" Nordstrom (1997: 79) quotes her Mozambican informants. There is a yearning to emerge from the forced silence no matter the danger. Nordstrom reports in "Global Fractures" that her informant was "so outraged that he was willing to risk telling his stories to an anthropologist." The anthropological account *is* his story, told so that the rest of us can begin to understand, to see. Too many of us *can* see, but do *not* see (Saramago 1998: 292). Silencing and blinding are political projects, weapons of the dominant. Speaking and writing are tools of resistance. *Seeing* is a power that might help us off our current, destructive course.

Nordstrom makes us see. Politically sophisticated and ethnographically rooted, "Global Fractures" is a theoretical and philosophical commentary that inspires and stirs. The world is in crisis, which is understood as more than a singular event situated in one place or at one moment in time. Instead, it encompasses "Badiou's multiple multiplicities"—many events and situations bumping into each other, crashing, pushing others out of the way, others crashing into still others, going backwards, sideways, forwards—"extend[ing] across the borders of sovereignty and temporality to flow into the personal lives, economic markets, and political systems … across war and peace."

This world of crisis within which we are all living is very fragile. The fracture lines can break very easily. It does not take much. We cannot make them out very easily and need a special lens to discern margins, boundaries, and breaks, and how they are inter-connected, inter-twined, inter-dependent. Nordstrom provides that lens, allowing us to trace the fracture lines, to find and follow the trails. The trails are hard to see until we get the focus. Then we notice their footprint and find that they are rather well-established and becoming institutionalized. We see *how* they work (the togetherness of legal/extra-legal, state institutions/extra-legal) and *why* (profiteering for profiteers), and *where* they may be taking us (the human fallout, more crises, more ironies and specific downfalls). With these concepts and descriptors, in "Global Fractures" Nordstrom provides a broad framework within which we can better understand the state of the world, its fragility, its unsustainability. Since no one is invulnerable to the quakes along the fracture lines, the future looks at once grim and hopeful.

In "Global Warring Today," war scholar Stephen Reyna also takes up the idea of crisis, offering the "global warring hypothesis" to propose analytic distinctions between local, global, and world warring. He situates US military violence in the context of capitalist and imperial politics, an explanatory framework that illuminates each of the cases that follow in this collection. Reyna's global warring hypothesis is also prognostic and prophetic. It allows us to anticipate future actions by a dominion thus defined: "For an empire, the conjunction of severe systemic crisis co-occurring with severe competition means that there is little that can be done in its economic sphere to resolve this predicament, prompting recourse to the political sphere and violence. If the scale of this crisis is worldwide, then intense global warring is predicted." The United States, on an imperial mission while at the same time struggling to stay on top in fierce global economic competition, is losing power. This thesis, which has been proposed by scholars and the CIA, more recently has become a topic of discussion in the popular media (see, e.g., Khanna 2008). Operating on the fracture lines, the US reveals its vulnerability by stoking the violence in Afghanistan, Iraq, Lebanon, Chad, Sudan, and Colombia, sites of global warring examined by Reyna. Yet the empire rests on enormous military real estate. According to the latest government records, the Department of Defense is "one of the world's largest 'landlords' … located on more than 5,300 sites [823 overseas, 4,488 in the US and territories], on over 32 million acres" (DOD 2007: 2). Do these figures reflect enormous strength, or is the escalating violence a sign of weakness, as Hannah Arendt might suggest? "Rule by sheer violence comes into play where power is being lost," Arendt wrote nearly 40 years ago. "To substitute violence for power can bring victory, but its price is very high; for it is not only paid by the vanquished, it is paid by the victor in his own power" (Arendt 1969). Reyna makes us wonder if today's "imperial global warriors" will take us all down with them.

In his chapter for this volume, physician-anthropologist Paul Farmer notes the "gruesome symmetry" in two US imperial disasters: Iraq and Haiti, each of which is a "proverb for brutality." An anthropologist by perspective and a healer by practice, Farmer not only analyzes the real costs of war but also fixes the bodies that get torn apart by it. In "Mother Courage and the Future of War," Farmer lays bare for us the structural conditions that lead poor youth of color to enlist in the US 'Army of One', such as Joe, Farmer's young Haitian friend and son to Yolande, a courageous mother who stood up to her US captors and won, although her son still battles in Fallujah. Farmer draws for us the contradictions and the intimate links between the US and the countries it wounds, the people who endure suffering, and the shame and grief of it all—the terrible price of war and empire.

R. Brian Ferguson is a war scholar and anthropologist with an extensive portfolio of writings on the topic. Ferguson's work, which takes the long view, is interdisciplinary in method and comprehensive in scope. He examines archaeological records; reads newspapers; looks to history; probes political science, economics, and philosophy; examines biology and psychology; and, of course, reads almost everything on the anthropology of war. For this volume,

Ferguson gives us "Ten Points on War," a refreshingly clear and direct summary of what is important to know if we want to understand war. In what follows, I use aspects of Ferguson's paradigm to explain war, a discussion to which each of the authors in this volume contributes.

Accounting for War

"Why fight?" Virginia Woolf asks ([1938] 1966: 6). Almost ritualistically, at least in Western thought and conversation, the first response usually goes something like this: "We fight because it is in our nature, human and social. War is inevitable, an inherent part of mankind's instinctual being. It is pre-programmed, coded in our genes. It is just there, always there, ready to explode, anytime and anywhere." This explanation for war got a boost from Thomas Hobbes (1964), whose seventeenth-century treatise on the horrors of human nature fit the prevailing political economy of his time (the English Civil War, British empire building), serving then as it does now to justify the coercive power of the state. Whether we are conscious of it or not, we have been taught to believe that what is needed is a strong, governing authority without which the worst of our instincts will emerge, rendering our lives, as the slogan says, "solitary, poore, nasty, brutish, and short" (ibid.: 85). It is worth repeating Hobbes's view, written in 1651 (ibid: 84):

> So that in the nature of man, we find three principall causes of quarrel. First, competition; Secondly, Diffidence; Thirdly, Glory. The first, maketh men invade for Gain; the second, for Safety; and the third, for Reputation. The first use Violence, to make themselves Masters of other mens persons, wives, children, and cattell; the second, to defend them; the third, for trifles, as a word, a smile, a different opinion, and any other signe of undervalue, either direct in their Persons, or by reflexion in their Kindred, their Friends, their Nation, their Profession, or their Name. Hereby it is manifest, that during the time men live without a common Power to keep them all in awe, they are in that condition which is called Warre.

Although it has been refuted time and again, the 'war in nature' argument is deeply embedded in popular thinking, revived and kept alive by deeply flawed and less than meticulous scholarship, as Ferguson makes clear in the first point of his "Ten Points on War." The argument is still sexy and gets attention in popular and academic publications because 'the horrors of human nature' theory fits the prevailing political economy of *our* times (war, empire).

The 'war in nature' argument has awful consequences. If we buy into the Hobbesian logic, there is no other choice but to have blind faith in sovereign authority, although some forms of authority are superior to others. By this logic, we are better off with fascism than no authority at all. The argument ends discussion of alternative solutions to the waging of war. We are powerless in the face of our destiny and must, for the sake of humankind, submit in humble obedience to a supreme state.

Also, the 'war in nature' argument inhibits us from considering alternative explanations for war. It is the discussion stopper I have all too often experienced in conversations about war with family and acquaintances. However, given the chance to consider alternatives, most people, I venture, would welcome them, yearning as they likely are for truth and hope. "Had you not believed that human nature, the reasons, the emotions of the ordinary man and woman, lead to war, you would not have [asked]," Virginia Woolf remarks to her imaginary interlocutor in answer to his question about "how to prevent war" ([1938] 1966: 6). Woolf reveals here humankind's desire for explanation, a longing for answers despite all *illogic*: why would the interlocutor, a man of means and power, pose this profound question to a woman with neither means nor power (ibid.: 12)?

The great thinkers and moralists are not satisfied with tired, wrong-headed myths. Myths are easy: they provide a pat narrative; they are easy to remember, uncomplicated, and mutually recognizable; they demand nothing of us but obedience or repetition. Reality is just the opposite: the narrative is not linear but interweaving and complex; it is difficult to keep track of all the variables involved; it is complicated and entails disagreements and contradictions; it requires us to think deeply and critically. Reality demands from us passion, action, and partiality. The contributors to this volume are among the great thinkers and moralists of our time. Each offers part of the answer, a piece of the explanation, and aspects of theory that bring us to a fuller, deeper understanding of why we fight. They put forth arguments that collectively account for dead bodies and shattered homes.

In accounting for war, there are two interdependent orders of explanation. One has to do with description, the other with causality. Descriptive explanation reveals general characteristics of war. Intrinsic to those characteristics are the complex of reasons for particular occurrences of war. The descriptions offered in our collection reveal that modern warfare involves extraordinarily sophisticated tools and weaponry that let loose occasions for war across ever-widening spaces, crossing sovereign states and geo-political borders, blurring the boundaries between war and peace (see also Kapferer 2004). The technology may be flawed and not yet entirely perfected, but its capability is there, bringing with it the logic of ever more war. The weapons of the powerful include the built environment: prisons, walls, and checkpoints comprise the machinery of oppression wherever there is war and uneasy peace. The weapons of the vulnerable are in motion as well, in a loop system with high-tech war tools. Nothing stands alone. Weapons, information, and provisions are all cosmopolitan products, circulating in a massive network of global proportions. In Ferguson's paradigm (1999: 389–390), these aspects constitute the infrastructure of war, "the broad conjuncture of variables involving interaction with the physical environment, population characteristics and trends, technology, and the labor techniques of applying technology, which affect a people's physical existence and relation to nature." Infrastructure both constrains and enables the possibility of war.

War cannot happen without the participation of those who enact it and the compliance of the masses who stand on one side or the other of the battle line. Participants need to be pressed into service, and consent and complicity need to be roused. There is a mobilization process where lines are drawn, potent language is utilized, groups are demonized and dehumanized, justification is put on spectacular display, duty is summoned, virtue invoked, trophies bestowed, and the satisfaction of real or perceived needs is tied to outcomes. There is a repertoire of propaganda upon which to draw—war in the name of God, country, democracy, freedom, security. It is calculating, but, as Ferguson (1999: 390) notes, "the values are true to local culture," values that are inculcated, harnessed, and exploited. This aspect of war Ferguson considers superstructural, "the mental constructs of culture, its belief systems, and patterned emotional dispositions" (ibid.).

All this mobilizing and manipulating, harnessing and exploitation are not executed by disembodied entities. While they may be difficult to pin down and identify, *people* make war-related decisions, even though the spheres of influence are not evenly proportioned among all decision makers (nor uniform in effect or in operation), and even though war-related decisions are shaped by the logic of impersonal, socio-political, and economic structures. Imperial capitalism, for example, does not decide to go to war, but the logics that flow from its organizing principles lead decision makers down that path. Scarcity (of resources, even basic ones) is not necessarily an actual condition, but one that needs to be created and maintained to fulfill a functional requirement for capital accumulation. In each war we read about in these pages, manufactured scarcity (the lack of access to resources or protecting access to them) is fundamentally accountable for the violence, leading to further contradictions. As Reyna explains, capitalism's hyper-dependency on oil, a non-renewable, scarce resource, creates the kind of systemic crisis that brings us to global warring.

Although the ultimate logic may rest in impersonal forces, people with the power to make decisions are the ones who make war. "To understand war," Ferguson explains in this volume, "it is essential to understand the structure of decision making and to identify the total interests—internal and external—of those involved in it." In their chapters, Bornstein, Manz, Gill, Reyna, and Nordstrom identify and thread together the set of internal (local) and external (global) interests that in complex interplay result in war, uneasy peace, and the violence they observe on the ground. In Ferguson's paradigm, the structure of war is constituted in the totality of social relationships—how these are organized, patterned, and institutionalized. Since structure comprises "organized social life, patterns of interpersonal connections and divisions sorted into social organization, economics, and politics" (Ferguson 1999: 390), it is at this level that the social dynamics of inequality—the dialectic of social life—can be analyzed. Layered as they are "in a nested hierarchy of progressively more limiting constraints" (Ferguson, this volume), each of the three levels in Ferguson's framework sets the possibilities and limitations for the other levels, forming altogether an accounting for war.

Hobbes was not entirely off the mark. Competition, diffidence, and glory may be identifiable attributes of war, but they are rooted in the logic of particular social dynamics, not in nature. That we can find some general characteristics common to any war does not constitute evidence that war is natural or inevitable—only that it is a patterned social phenomenon that under certain social conditions might even be foreseen.

Impunity and Accountability

Our authors make clear who wins and who loses in war. "Leaders favor war because war favors leaders," Ferguson informs us in "Ten Points on War." Leaders are those representing the interests of the elite who, as Manz explains "enjoy privilege, access to the resources of the society, and the protection of the state apparatus." The killing elite use violence to protect those structures that privilege the few rather than the many. They make violence with weapons of war and of policy, including trade agreements, arms deals, loan contracts, and international finance arrangements. Bombs kill, and so does the denial of the most basic of resources such as water (privatized or dammed up) and food (produced for the market, not use, and the destruction of eco-zones), resources ever more difficult to access in today's global political economy. The death and destruction toll—lives lost, houses ruined, social infrastructures destroyed, bodies maimed, souls lost—are beyond computing.

To come to terms with accountability—who is to be held responsible for all the death and destruction—is terribly difficult. Whose hands are bloody when the logic of a system draws participants into the vortex of violence and war? In his meditation, *On War*, Howard Zinn (2001: 119) writes of the "infinite chain of causes, that infinite dispersion of responsibility, which can give infinite work to historical scholarship or sociological speculation, and bring an infinitely pleasurable paralysis of the will. What a complex of motives!"

Who is to be held responsible? Is it, for instance, weapons-of-mass-destruction engineer Anh Duong, a Vietnam War refugee employed by the Pentagon, featured in the illuminating documentary *Why We Fight*, dubbed by colleagues as "the bomb lady," and regarded by them as "one of the most important weapons-developers of the modern era" (Blumenfeld 2007: A3)? Is it the bombardier who, by virtue of video-game-like high technology, can dispel any qualms about the multitudes of human lives he eradicates? Is it the commander who orders bombardiers to drop which bombs where? Is it he who presides over the most powerful military in the world, under whose command tens of thousands have been annihilated? Today that would be George W. Bush, whose regime of violence sacrifices innocents, "killed to achieve the US killing elite's vision of being blackmailer to the world" (Reyna). Or is it those of us who, like Virginia Woolf's British ladies, however unconsciously "desired 'our splendid Empire' … desired our splendid war" ([1938] 1966: 39) for the benefits we get from these?

In *Eichmann in Jerusalem: A Report on the Banality of Evil*, Hannah Arendt ([1963] 1992: 247) provides an outline for a method of accountability: "[T]he degree of responsibility increases as we draw further away from the man who uses the fatal instrument with his own hands." Put another way, Farmer suggests that we trace "the social life of dangerous things" (Rylko-Bauer 2007: 3; see also Farmer n.d.) to reveal the nested hierarchy of progressively more essential (and thus responsible) cogs in the wheel. Farmer starts with the ethnographically visible, in this case, a little boy who landed on Farmer's surgery table in Rwanda after handling a war weapon that had been placed 12 years earlier during the genocide of 1994. Farmer "pick[ed] out pieces of plastic" from the child's torn body and then sought to identify the fragments. It was a land mine, as Farmer suspected, "manufactured I'm quite sure, not in Rwanda [but] in Europe, the United States, or perhaps Russia," a war weapon that by "sinister design" looks like an innocent plaything (Farmer 2006; see also Farmer n.d.).

In this next account, like all her reports from the field, Nordstrom (1997: 5) follows the footprints, exposing massive inter-linkages across the globe:

> I have seen the same weapons vendors, mercenaries, military advisors, supplies, and military training manuals—both illicit and formal—circle the globe, moving from one war to the next. Politicians, military and paramilitary troops and diplomats meet and talk across virtually all boundaries of nation and state. Business salespeople and blackmarketeers sell the items necessary to outfit troops and launch a battle. Media specialists create a cultural diaspora of every war-related ethos from the Rambo figure to BBC broadcasts reaching the farthest regions of the globe. Propagandists the world over exchange information on how to make casualties palatable to noncombatants and human rights organizations. Everything from development dollars to human rights organizations, from covert operations specialists to illegal industries that gain from conflict, builds on the linkages of these networks that shape war and peace as we know it today.

Identifying those who are responsible does not mean that they will be held accountable for their role in the consequences. Impunity is built into the system, "an aspect of power ... embedded in the process of social differentiation [that] reinforces a highly unequal social order" (Gill 2004: 13). Formal state and international institutions of law have no chance against the mask of impunity. Unaccountability is strategic.

The Accountability of War: What War Explains

"Unaccountability was strategic," Nordstrom concludes as she looks back to the present time from 100 years in the future, a gripping reflection that opens this volume. With the benefit of hindsight, Nordstrom sees how profoundly modern war feeds—and feeds on—lethal inequalities, accelerates local and global economic crises, stimulates the institutionalization of extra-legal activities and organizations, and figures in the decline of the sovereign state with a concomitant rise of the 'para-state' and the 'extra-state'.

Nordstrom's look back is not speculation but evidence-based, unfolding each day, and documented in the daily newspaper—"history in the raw," Woolf ([1938] 1966: 7) calls it—and by others, including some anthropologists. In the presently developing situation, Nordstrom asserts, the state, a collection of linked institutions that provide people with core necessities, is a participant in its own undoing, withdrawing slowly but surely from its purportedly fundamental role. Gill explains the process for Colombia, tired mistress to the United States, where, to extend the metaphor, the domestic state is buttressed by the paramour whose interests are at odds with the greater part of the household. There are uprisings, but the official state apparatus cannot cope—its own rules are obstacles, its enforcers need a hand. Focused on containment and control, the state nurtures paramilitaries and sanctions the violation of law. There is no accountability, and organized crime has become institutionalized. The paramilitaries, Gill explains, "erected a mafia-like 'shadow-state'" and have "in effect become the state itself."

Variations of that domestic scene are patterned across the globe. As significant as the culturally specific differences may be at the level of the local, the fact is that each domestic war scene is tied to global systems that are themselves operating outside of law, regulation, and formal governments, even if colluding with them. In the global and political economy of war, the extraction of resources, the production of war-related and other goods, and the process of distribution are parasitic and opportunistic. Law is observed and state sovereignty respected only when they serve interests. Impunity and invisibility are strategic.

War has its own logic and creates its own outcomes. That war pays is an old saw. These days the profits are enormous, greater than anything war profiteers of old could have imagined. There are, of course, the huge defense contractors who proudly tout their strategic role in local or global warring, display their war weapons,[2] or unabashedly showcase their products in international trade shows.[3] As much as they display, they also hide the autocracy of corporate power (Kapferer 2005: 20), the multiple broken laws, the corruption, the bedfellows, the unsustainability, the destruction.

War drives decisions about the built environment and shapes the relationships of the people living and interacting within these spaces. In complex ways, war produces social identities (learn thy enemy), directs human activity (the work of war, subsistence in the context of war), and shapes social dynamics (more conflictual than cooperative), resulting in a greater likelihood of even more war. Ferguson notes, "Once a given society is internally adapted for war, making war becomes much easier—a necessity, even, for the reproduction of existing social relations." In a world internally adapted for it, war becomes ubiquitous.

It is in the context of this "unsure world" (Nordstrom) that ordinary people struggle for survival. In the face of dead bodies and ruined houses, they invent and scrounge, they construct and they take, they solve, persist, and endure. The violence of war, Nordstrom teaches us, becomes "institutionalized habit," encroaching on all the domains of social life and cutting across boundaries of the formal and informal, the legal and illegal, the global and local, the political and cultural.

When war ends and peace accords are signed, people who are its victims continue to suffer in the aftermath. There are predictable psychological effects of the trauma of war, including extreme anxiety, paralyzing flashbacks, and unbridled anger. The psychological wounds suffered by combatants and civilians often lead to more violence, as Bornstein and Manz point out in their poignant portraits of traumatized peoples. It is not uncommon that the victim becomes the victimizer, with brutality often being directed at those most near and dear. We know that war rips people apart, leaving the social fabric in shreds. Traditional activities of family and community life, work, and shared understandings are amputated, making it ever more difficult to escape the habitus of violence. War creates a "perverse transformation" (Manz) in which social life becomes marked by hostility and estrangement (rather than cooperation and collectivity), violence becomes normative, and weariness and resignation pervade daily life.

In places where overcoming the aftermath of war seems particularly difficult, where the violence is deeply entrenched and the social malaise especially potent, the obstacle is not cultural or social-psychological but rather structural. In these places, where the large-scale structures of domination and oppression remain firmly in place, the conditions that contribute to disaster, violence, and war have not been removed. The material inequalities and social inequities that explain war are still present despite the fact that there is no war—with battle lines drawn—to account for the violence. In these places, it is not just that 'peace' is uneasy and palpably fragile; it is that violence gets turned inward, resulting in domestic assaults, murder, lynching, and rape. These are symptoms of structural violence, although they appear as ordinary criminality, an illusion that places failure on individual or cultural weakness. Thus safely masked, the structures of power, domination, oppression, and inequality are not held accountable. Structural impunity renders it ever more difficult for 'damaged' people to rebuild a more peaceful society.

Anthropology and Accountability

I close this introduction by opening up for further discussion the responsibility of anthropology and individual anthropologists in facing up to the most significant crises of our times. In the prelude to this collection, Nordstrom leaves us no choice but to confront our discipline in its American manifestation and ourselves as professional anthropologists in the United States, considering the role of US imperial structures in warfare and global economic exploitation. Nordstrom grants us more power than we believe we have by alleging that what we do today does indeed configure our "emergent tomorrows."

It is safe to say that anthropologists in the United States do not see themselves as being influential enough to shape the course of future social conditions and events. Others see a kinship between US dominance in the world and American anthropology as a dominant power in the field of anthropology (Evens and Handelman 2005: 7)—*they* can imagine the possibility of such an influence. It is worthwhile for us to consider the possibilities. Perhaps it is pure self-aggrandizement to imagine that we have the power to shape the future. But if it is true, even to some degree, it would suggest that our rather constant claim to marginality is a myth. Buying into the myth of our own marginality is a safe retreat, serves to mask our privilege, and gets us off the hook. Our myths make us vulnerable to that which we refuse to recognize, and, in Nordstrom's words, make us complicit "with dangerous forms of hegemonic power."

Manz does not let us off the hook. She sees our privilege and our responsibility. In this world without borders, she claims, we must become global participants, not mere bystanders. "We have a far broader moral burden of accountability," declares Manz, who asserts that those in the United States "carry greater responsibility." Embedded as we are in the institutions of the state, our privilege is rooted in the current structures of power. For this reason, as Farmer demonstrates in word and deed, we need not question our moral duty as global participants. "Why that should be an embarrassment to academics is beyond me," Farmer (2006) remarked to an audience of anthropologists.

Not just any kind of global participation is appropriate. No matter the motivation, misguided actions that have lethal consequences are not forgivable. "I just can't stand to sit back and watch these mistakes happen over and over as people get killed, and do nothing," an anonymous anthropologist tells a reporter (Packer 2006: 66), thus defining her 'good' intentions in joining the Pentagon's Human Terrain System (HTS), a project established in 2006 at a purported cost of $60 million (González 2008: 21). HTS, allegedly the brainchild of cultural anthropologist Montgomery McFate and social scientist David Kilcullen, is designed to apply anthropological methods to identify local cultural understandings, norms, motivations, and networks in the US counter-insurgency war effort in Afghanistan and Iraq. It is a wretched irony that we may look to endorsement by the US military to assure us that anthropology, in its methods and descriptive data, is not as marginal as we have come to believe.

Although the architects of HTS and its participants claim that their efforts are designed to "save lives" (González 2008: 21; Packer 2006: 66; Rohde 2007), activist anthropologists are systematically exposing the distortions behind those claims, revealing their role in "enabling the kill chain" (Vine 2007: B9; see also Wilcox 2007). While we might concede that understanding local dynamics could result in fewer deadly 'mistakes' on the killing ground (Vasquez), and even that it could bring resolution to disputes (Ferguson), to focus on this narrow truth blinds us to the larger story. As Reyna explains, the war violence in Afghanistan and Iraq perpetrated by the US reflects the political aspect of imperialism. "Empires are especially gory structures," Reyna reminds us. The kill chain is there, and anthropologists who participate in HTS are useful insofar as they are able to better identify the empire's opponents (see also González 2007: 16; Vogel 2007).

Anthropology, it seems, is not so much marginal as subject to selective attention by those outside the academy with power and influence. The history of the discipline is replete with examples of anthropology being central, not marginal, to social policy and action. As the HTS program illustrates, our data and our methods are viewed as precise, valid, authoritative, even useful, and certainly not threatening. It is these aspects of our discipline that are selected for attention.

This leaves theory as the aspect of our discipline selected for dismissal. Theory is nothing more that our explanation of what we *see*. It comprises that which we make visible by analysis. Theory is our interpretation of the data we collect on the ground, and our translation of the stories we hear in the field. It is what constitutes the greatest threat to those who would ignore us. Instead of leaving us discouraged or leading us to believe in our own marginality, we might draw strength from this knowledge. Seeing *is* power.

I do not think Riall Nolan (2006) is correct: anthropology is *not* increasingly irrelevant to the big questions of the day, and *not* content to snipe from the sidelines as soon as it seems safe. There is an emerging movement of US anthropologists, affiliated with activist organizations and new groups[4] as well as long-established organizations,[5] who seem willing to hold our discipline accountable for our emergent tomorrows and are not afraid to report what they see. The contributors to this volume are among the growing number of anthropologists who are confronting war, leading the discussion on the most critical issues of contemporary society, and engaging actively in anti-imperial, anti-war efforts. In these pages, they analyze the arrogance of power; expose the defining attributes and logic of war, with its causes and consequences; and suggest what we might do to undermine the conditions that sustain and perpetuate it.

Alisse Waterston is Professor of Anthropology, John Jay College of Criminal Justice, City University of New York. Her work focuses on the human consequences of structural and systemic violence and inequality. Publications include *Love, Sorrow and Rage: Destitute Women in a Manhattan Residence* (1999), "The Story of My Story: An Anthropology of Violence, Dispossession and Diaspora" (2005), and, with Antigona Kukaj, "Teaching Genocide in an Age of Genocides" (2007). She is the editor, with Maria D. Vesperi, of the forthcoming volume, *Anthropology Off the Shelf: Anthropologists on Writing* (Blackwell).

Notes

1. Vasquez serves as president of the New York Chapter of Iraq Veterans Against the War and was a main organizer of "Winter Soldier Iraq and Afghanistan: Eye Witness Accounts of the Occupations" (http://www.ivaw.org/wintersoldier).
2. See, for example, the image gallery on Boeing's Web site (http://www.boeing.com/companyoffices/ gallery/ids.html).
3. See, for example, IDEAS Pakistan. The tagline for the November 2008 show is "Weapons for Peace" (http://www.ideaspakistan.gov.pk/).
4. See, for example, http://concerned.anthropologists.googlepages.com/home.
5. An example is the AAA's Commission on the Engagement of Anthropology with the US Security and Intelligence Communities (http://dev.aaanet.org/cmtes/commissions/CEAUSSIC/index.cfm).

References

AAA (American Anthropological Association). 2006. "Anthropologists Weigh in on Iraq, Torture at Annual Meeting." Press release. http://www.aaanet.org/pdf/iraqtorture.pdf (accessed 12 May 2008).

_____. 2007. "Anthropologists Oppose US Military Action Against Iran." Press release. http://www.aaanet.org/issues/press/upload/Advisory-Anthropologists-Oppose-US-Military-Action-in-Iran.pdf (accessed 12 May 2008).

Accardo, Gian Paulo. 2005. "Empire of Shame: A Conversation with Jean Ziegler." *Counterpunch*, 19 December. http://www.counterpunch.org/accardo12202005.html (accessed 14 November 2006).

Arendt, Hannah. [1963] 1992. *Eichmann in Jerusalem: A Report on the Banality of Evil*. New York: Penguin Classics.

_____. 1969. "A Special Supplement: Reflections on Violence." *New York Review of Books*. http://www.nybooks.com/articles/11395 (accessed 29 January 2008).

Berreman, Gerald D. 1968. "Is Anthropology Alive? Social Responsibility in Social Anthropology." *Current Anthropology* 9, no. 5: 391–396.

Blumenfeld, Laura. 2007. "Spurred by Gratitude, 'Bomb Lady' Develops Better Weapons for U.S." *Washington Post*, 1 December.

Bornstein, Avram. 2002. *Crossing the Green Line between the West Bank and Israel*. Philadelphia: University of Pennsylvania Press.

Dewey, John. 1927. "Imperialism is Easy." *The New Republic* 50, 23 March.

DOD (Department of Defense). 2007. *Base Structure Report (Listing of Facilities) Fiscal Year 2007*. Washington, DC: Office of the Deputy Under Secretary of Defense. http://www.defenselink.mil/pubs/BSR_2007_Baseline.pdf (accessed 28 January 2008).

Evens, T. M. S., and Don Handelman. 2005. "The Ethnographic Praxis of the Theory of Practice." *Social Analysis* 49, no. 3: 1–11.

Farmer, Paul. 2006. "A Physician Anthropologist Reflects on War and Public Health." Paper presented at presidential panel, War. One hundred and fifth annual meeting of the American Anthropological Association.

_____. n.d. "'Landmine Boy' and the Tomorrow of Violence." In *Global Health in the Time of Violence*, ed. Barbara Rylko-Bauer, Linda Whiteford, and Paul Farmer. Santa Fe, NM: School of Advance Research.

Ferguson, R. Brian. 1999. "A Paradigm for the Study of War and Society." Pp. 389–437 in *War and Society in the Ancient and Medieval Worlds: Asia, the Mediterranean, Europe, and Mesoamerica*, ed. Kurt Raaflaub and Nathan Rosenstein. Cambridge, MA: Harvard University Press.

Fried, Morton, Marvin Harris, and Robert Murphy, eds. 1967. *War: The Anthropology of Armed Conflict and Aggression*. New York: Doubleday & Company.

Fussell, Paul. [1975] 2000. *The Great War and Modern Memory*. Oxford: Oxford University Press.

Gill, Lesley. 2000. *Teetering on the Rim: Global Restructuring, Daily Life, and the Armed Retreat of the Bolivian State*. New York: Columbia University Press.

_____. 2004. *School of the Americas: Military Training and Political Violence in the Americas*. Durham, NC: Duke University Press.

_____. 2007. "Anthropology Goes to War, Again." *Focaal—European Journal of Anthropology* 50: 139–145.

Gjessing, Gutorm. 1968. "The Social Responsibility of the Social Scientist." *Current Anthropology* 9, no. 5: 397–402.

González, Roberto J. 2007. "Towards Mercenary Anthropology? The New US Army Counterinsurgency Manual FM 3-24 and the Military-Anthropology Complex." *Anthropology Today* 23, no. 3: 14–19.

_____. 2008. "Human Terrain: Past, Present and Future Applications." *Anthropology Today* 24, no. 1: 21–26.

Gough, Kathleen. 1968. "New Proposal for Anthropologists." *Current Anthropology* 9, no. 5: 403–435.

Hastrup, Kirsten, Peter Elsass, Ralph Grillo, Per Mathiesen, and Robert Paine. 1990. "Anthropological Advocacy: A Contradiction in Terms?" *Current Anthropology* 31, no. 3: 301–311.

Hobbes, Thomas. 1964. *Leviathan*. New York: Washington Square Press.

Holland, Dorothy, Donald M. Nonini, Catherine Lutz, Lesley Bartlett, Marla Frederick-McGlathery, Thaddeus C. Guldbrandsen, and Enrique G. Murillo, Jr. 2007. *Local Democracy Under Siege: Activism, Public Interests and Private Politics*. New York: NYU Press.

Jones, Delmos J. 1971. "Social Responsibility and the Belief in Basic Research: An Example from Thailand." *Current Anthropology* 12, no. 3: 347–350.

Kapferer, Bruce, ed. 2004. *State, Sovereignty, War: Civil Violence in Emerging Global Realities*. New York: Berghahn Books.

_____, ed. 2005. *Oligarchs and Oligopolies: New Formations of Global Power*. New York: Berghahn Books.

Khanna, Parag. 2008. "Waving Goodbye to Hegemony." *New York Times Magazine*, 27 January.

Manz, Beatriz. 1988. *Refugees of a Hidden War: The Aftermath of Counterinsurgency in Guatemala*. Albany: SUNY Press.

_____. 2004. *Paradise in Ashes: A Guatemalan Journey of Courage, Terror and Hope*. Berkeley: University of California Press.

Nolan, Riall W. 2006. "Torture and Social Scientists." Posted comment, 22 November. http://www.insidehighered.com/news/2006/11/22/anthro (accessed 20 December 2006).

Nordstrom, Carolyn. 1997. *A Different Kind of War Story*. Philadelphia: University of Pennsylvania Press.

_____. 2007. *Global Outlaws: Crime, Money, and Power in the Contemporary World*. Berkeley: University of California Press.

Ortega, Ramona. 2006. "Co-Defenders: How Human Rights Activists and Anthropologists Can Work Together." *North American Dialogue* 9, no. 2: 5–8.

Packer, George. 2006. "Knowing the Enemy: The Anthropology of Insurgency." *New Yorker*, 18 December, 60–69.

Price, David H. 2004. *Threatening Anthropology: McCarthyism and the FBI's Surveillance of Activist Anthropologists*. Durham, NC: Duke University Press.

Remarque, Erich Maria. [1929] 1982. *All Quiet on the Western Front*. New York: Random House.

Rohde, David. 2007. "Army Enlists Anthropology in War Zones." *New York Times*, 5 October.

Rylko-Bauer, Barbara. 2007. "Introductory Remarks: Global Health in the Time of Violence." Paper presented at plenary session on Global Health in the Time of Violence. Sixty-seventh annual meeting of the Society for Applied Anthropology.

_____. 2008. "Applied Anthropology and Counterinsurgency." *Newsletter: Society for Applied Anthropology* 19, no. 1: 1–5.

Rylko-Bauer, Barbara, Merrill Singer, and John Van Willigen. 2006. "Reclaiming Applied Anthropology: Its Past, Present, and Future." *American Anthropologist* 108, no. 1: 178–190.

Sanford, Victoria, and Asale Angel-Ajani, eds. 2006. *Engaged Observer: Anthropology, Advocacy, and Activism*. Rutgers, NJ: Rutgers University Press.

Saramago, José. 1998. *Blindness*. New York: Harcourt Brace & Company.

Shaw, Martin. 2000. "The Contemporary Mode of Warfare? Mary Kaldor's Theory of New Wars." *Review of International Political Economy* 7, no. 1: 171–180.

Singer, Merrill. 1990. "Another Perspective on Advocacy." *Current Anthropology* 31, no. 5: 548–550.

Tickner, J. Ann. 2001. *Gendering World Politics: Issues and Approaches in the Post-Cold War*. New York: Columbia University Press.

Trumbo, Dalton. [1939] 1989. *Johnny Got His Gun*. New York: Bantam Books.

Vine, David. 2007. "Enabling the Kill Chain." *Chronicle of Higher Education*, 30 November.

Vogel, Richard D. 2007. "Mapping the Human Terrain and Developing Kill Chains: Social Science in Service to Capitalism." *Monthly Review Webzine*, 11 June. http://www.monthlyreview.org/mrzine/vogel061107.html (accessed 12 February 2008).

Vonnegut, Kurt. [1969] 1991. *Slaughterhouse-Five*. New York: Dell Publishing.

Wilcox, John. 2007. "Precision Engagement—Strategic Context for the Long War: Weapons Technology Blueprint for the Future." 1 February. http://concerned.anthropologists.googlepages.com/WilcoxKillChain.pdf (accessed 12 February 2008).

Wolf, Eric R., and Joseph G. Jorgensen. 1970. "Anthropology on the Warpath in Thailand." *New York Review of Books*, 19 November.

Woolf, Virginia. [1938] 1966. *Three Guineas*. New York: Harcourt Brace & Company.

Zinn, Howard. 2001. *On War*. New York: Seven Stories Press.

Chapter 1

TEN POINTS ON WAR

R. Brian Ferguson

Over the past 40 years, the anthropology of war has grown from a few scattered works to an enormous field with many areas of investigation and contention. While it used to be possible to read practically everything that came out on the subject, this is no longer the case, and the field is in danger of falling apart into several self-contained realms. I began studying war as a graduate student in 1974, and this chapter is a synthesis of my own subsequent work, boiled down to 10 major, interrelated points.[1] I will not discuss case examples from around the world, elaborate arguments, or provide citations here. To do that over so many topics would require a very lengthy chapter. My goal in this essay is to synthesize one coherent perspective out of many previous publications, in which details and documentation are provided.[2] The first two points are primarily refutations of currently popular ideas about the antiquity of war, but most points involve some contradiction of implicit assumptions on the subject. Going beyond refutations to new perspectives, the 10 points taken together argue for a different conceptualization of what war is about, pointing to a new

Notes for this chapter are located on page 47.

understanding that has direct implications for how we explain the occurrence of wars. To highlight that relevance, each of the points will be applied to the current war in Iraq and related conflicts.

Point #1: Our Species Is Not Biologically Destined for War

For a very long time, there have been theories that war is the outgrowth of some predetermined aspect of the human brain/mind, that we make war because we are born to seek it out. Pre-eminent psychologist William McDougal said that fights arose out of an instinct for pugnacity. Sigmund Freud attributed collective destruction to an outward redirection of the inner death wish. Playwright Robert Ardrey argued that our inborn propensity to kill was what separated us from other apes, while primatologist Richard Wrangham claims that it is not our difference from but rather our similarity to chimpanzees that makes men incline toward war (Ferguson 1984a, 2000). Proponents of innatist theories of war often complain that their science is being opposed out of political correctness. But when specific assertions are compared to available evidence, they do very poorly.

The Yanomami of Brazil and Venezuela are the favorite example of those favoring inborn predispositions to violence. Made famous as fierce warriors by American anthropologist Napoleon Chagnon, they have been used to bolster a wide range of hypotheses attributing human warfare to some inherent aspect of human nature, designed by evolution to maximize reproductive success. But all these claims are made with scant regard for empirical evidence. To demonstrate this, a range of innatist claims were considered against the Yanomami, using exclusively reports by Chagnon himself.

Comparing published claims to Chagnon's data, we find that the Yanomami do not begin wars to capture women. Only some wars are preceded by a conflict over women, and those conflicts are just one of many issues, with other factors being much more predictive of actual fighting. (In my own explanation [Ferguson 1995a], Yanomami wars are seen as the outgrowth of antagonisms related to unequal and exploitative access to Western trade goods, combined with several other destabilizing factors.) An examination of Chagnon's data invalidates his claim that becoming a killer is associated with higher lifetime reproductive success. Wars do not represent a reproductive strategy of young males, as they are initiated and fought primarily by middle-aged married men. A claim that Yanomami men who take wives kill their offspring from other men is without foundation. A claim that Yanomami wars parallel the pattern found between Gombe chimpanzees is contradicted by the fact that, contrary to chimpanzees, most Yanomami are village endogamous (marrying within the village) and that Yanomami raids regularly pose great dangers to raiders (rather than occurring only when they can act with impunity). Contrary to an assertion that Yanomami wars exemplify a human pattern of territorial conquest, Chagnon himself emphasizes they are not fought with territorial gain as an objective or consequence. A 'Darwinian algorithm', said to make war evolutionarily logical, is contradicted at each of its four points by Yanomami data. Some Yanomami conflicts are between groups that are more genetically related within than to their enemies, but in many others, blood kin opportunistically side against other blood kin. 'Cultural pseudospeciation' plays no role in any reports of Yanomami wars (Ferguson 2001).

In the past decade, biological explanations have turned away from specific, predictive theories to broad life science findings on aggression. Different neural structures, neurotransmitters, hormones, and genes have been implicated in different measures of aggression. Some studies stress biological factors associated with maleness. But no work has demonstrated that non-pathological humans have an inborn propensity to violence, and comparisons of males and females are uniformly complicated, qualified, and debatable. The growing appreciation that genetic expression occurs within a system of biological systems, all with environmental inputs, greatly complicates key issues. We are far from being able to clarify how and the extent to which inborn biological variables affect human or male aggressive behavior. But even if we could, it is not clear that doing so would tell us much about the essentially social process that is war. Maleness is one part of biology, biology is one part of aggressiveness, aggressiveness is one part of combat, and combat is one part of war. The explanatory potential of biology thus seems fundamentally limited (Ferguson 2006a).

Reflection on the war in Iraq highlights this limitation. In all the complicated political processes leading up to and opposing the invasion, just how does a supposed biological propensity for war contribute to our understanding? What would such a propensity explain better than its long-standing anthropological alternative—that people have the *capacity* to learn, even to enjoy, war and build it into their social lives and institutions, without any inborn inclination in that direction? It must be kept in mind that any innate tendencies would have to apply equally to everyone involved in the process, both those in favor and those against.

Point #2: War Is Not an Inescapable Part of Social Existence

If humans had an inborn predisposition for violent conflict, then they should have been war makers since, or even before, they became human. Proponents of biological theories regularly invoke a few archaeological studies, claiming that war appears throughout the archaeological record. But those studies are marked by three methodological flaws. First, they list cases where evidence of war is found and extrapolate conclusions to situations where war is not in evidence. Second, they confound the later archaeological record, where war often is ubiquitous, with the earlier archaeological record, where war seems rare or non-existent. Third, they make assumptions from historical situations or recent ethnography, where war is indisputably very common, and unjustifiably project those suppositions onto peoples of the distant past.

Empirical findings from earlier archaeological sequences reveal something quite different. War regularly leaves traces in recoverable remains. Skeletal and settlement materials can clearly show war, as can specialized weapons such as maces, although people can kill with ordinary tools. Artistic renditions of battle also disclose evidence of war, even though most extinct peoples did not leave recoverable art. True, evidence for war, even if it was practiced, could be absent in any particular case, for any number of reasons. But globally, with few exceptions, a clear pattern emerges: signs of war are absent in the earliest remains and then appear later and rarely go away. The standard objection, 'absence of evidence is not evidence of absence', would be valid if the earlier skeletal and settlement remains were so limited that they would not reliably reveal war. That is not the case. In many regions around the world—the Middle East, parts of Europe, the Yellow River Valley—there is good data for centuries, even millennia, with no indications of war. Then evidence of war appears without any qualitative jump in the archaeological data recovered. The situation is not unlike other recognized beginnings—such as plant or animal domestication—that are pinned on the earliest recovered evidence. As a global pattern, the evidence suggests a transition from societies that did not make war to ones that did.

Why did war develop, at different times, in many parts of the world? There appear to be six preconditions, themselves interrelated in various ways, which in combination made the inception and/or intensification of war more likely: (1) sedentary existence, often following agriculture (although war existed in some places before plant domestication); (2) increasing population density; (3) social hierarchy; (4) trade, especially of prestige goods; (5) bounded social groups; and (6) serious ecological reversals. The reason why war went from rare to commonplace around the world involves four long-term processes: (1) as those preconditions became more common, war began in more places; (2) war spread, often quite gradually, into surrounding areas; (3) the rise of ancient states projected militarism deep into their peripheries and along trade routes; and (4) Western expansion since the late fifteenth century often generated or intensified war in contact zones (Ferguson 2003a, 2006b).

One might say that the entire issue of biology makes little difference in conceptualizing war. Whether by culture or by genes, war has been programmed into us. Once initiated and built into cultural systems, war has rarely gone away in the past, so there is no reason to expect its demise in the future. This is a limited, and limiting, perspective. We tend to think in terms of the *foreseeable* future, the next few decades. But in all probability, humankind's future stretches on for countless millennia. Since Boas, and later Malinowski and Carneiro, anthropologists have called attention to the long-term consolidation of political units, where peace reigns within. There is good reason to believe that this trend can continue. Sixty years ago, who could have foreseen the current integration of Europe? In 1988, who foresaw the impending demilitarization of the communist-capitalist divide? On the other hand, who in 1988 foresaw the proliferation of new flags in front of the UN (Ferguson 1988a, 2003b)?

The foreseeable future of war looks pretty robust. The current war between elements of radical Islam and Western nations is not likely to end soon. Nor are the brutal civil wars that still rage through much of the underdeveloped world, although they clearly have been declining in number and casualties. New divisions may arise. Future military confrontations between China or Russia and the US seem like reasonable possibilities. But it is misguided to think of these as permanent conditions. Without doubt, new, unforeseen global communities will emerge over time. People pushing for peace can shape what is to become. The future is beyond our mortal ken, but it is not impervious to hope. Anthropology can effect a positive contribution by making it clear that there is no scientific basis for believing that a future without war is impossible.

Point #3: Understanding War Involves a Nested Hierarchy of Constraints

My approach to war is based on a modified version of cultural materialism. This involves two distinct but complementary research strategies, both founded on the principle that social life is essentially practical (Ferguson 1995b).

The first strategy divides socio-cultural phenomena into infrastructure, structure, and superstructure. Infrastructure includes basic population profiles, technology, labor techniques, and interaction with the natural environment. Structure comprises all patterned behavioral interactions and institutions, including kinship, economics, and politics. Superstructure encompasses the belief systems of a society, its norms and values in general and specific areas such as religion, aesthetics, and ideology. These three dimensions of cultural life are internally complex, interacting systems of subsystems, layered in a nested hierarchy of progressively more limiting constraints. Infrastructure sets possibilities for structure, and structure constrains superstructure, but each level and subsystem also has substantial autonomy (Ferguson 1990a, 1999).

Regarding war, this scheme is intended to explain the general characteristics of war in a given society. To give just a few illustrations, infrastructure defines how war is fought and what it is fought over: the scale of war-making units and parties, the kind of weaponry used, the scheduling of war parties in relation to subsistence activities, and the availability and costs of essential resources. Structure specifies the social patterning of war: the familial ties for mobilizing men within and between war groups, the circulation and distribution of necessities and valuables, decision structures, and patterns of alliance and enmity. Superstructure provides the moral framework for waging war and motivating warriors: the value systems pertaining to violence, religious and/or magical ideas employed in conflicts, and political ideologies invoked to justify war or peace.

Looking at war in this way is useful for unifying diverse theoretical positions that focus on different aspects of war and that might otherwise seem contradictory. It is relatively easy, for instance, to see social structural features such as patrilocal post-marital residence interlocked with competition over local resources and an ideology of male military prowess. But many more aspects of war than that can be fit together using this paradigm (Ferguson 1999). Or it can be applied to one particular case. That has been done for the Yanomami of the Orinoco-Mavaca area of Venezuela. Going from infrastructure through structure to superstructure, and considering how all of them have been shaped by the changing circumstances of Western contact, explains why these particular Yanomami seemed so 'fierce'—not only why they made a lot of war, but also why allies fought bloody, pounding matches and men commonly assaulted women (ibid.: 1992).

Structural and superstructural aspects of the Iraq war, including political arrangements and processes, constructions of social identities, and value systems, will be discussed in later points. Here the topic will be limited to infrastructure. The population scale of the US allows it to put over 150,000 troops in the field, with US casualties directly affecting only a tiny fraction of the populace. Iraqi fighters are drawn from local neighborhoods or tribal groups but also include outsiders from a global Islamic population. Technology shapes military interactions, with drones, laser-guided air strikes, and night vision on our side, and on theirs, plentiful munitions, improvised explosive devices (IEDs), and the Internet. The distribution of oil certainly affected US interests in Iraq and continues to play a critical role in shaping Iraqi politics today. Change any one of those variables, and it would be a very different conflict.

Point #4: War Expresses Both Pan-human Practicalities and Culturally Specific Values

My second strategy regarding war is intended to explain not a general cultural pattern of war, but rather the occurrence of real wars. The basic premise is that variations in actual fighting—periods of war and periods of peace, who attacks and who is attacked—are understandable as the result of those who make decisions on war pursuing their own practical self-interests, within historically changing material circumstances. It is an etic behavioral approach, based on an analysis of what people do in war, rather than what they say about it.

I used this method in studies of all reported wars among Native peoples of the Pacific Northwest Coast and among the Yanomami. Analysis of archaeological records and early explorers' accounts of the Northwest Coast indicate a pre-contact pattern, in which people in areas of limited resources raided those with better supplies of fish and other food. These subsistence conflicts largely ended when diseases, introduced by outsiders, lowered populations and marginal areas were abandoned. In the post-contact period, war was structured by competition in the Western trade. In various ways, groups in different positions tried to control or improve their access to Western outposts or trade ports. In both pre- and post-contact periods, war was waged to capture slaves, although this greatly increased in post-contact circumstances (Ferguson 1984b).

The effects of Western contact preceded even the earliest reports about the Yanomami, so their pre-contact warfare, if any, is unknown. Early-contact warfare was related to defensive measures directed at indigenous slave raiders who traded to the Europeans. In Yanomami wars described by later explorers and ethnographers, which group attacks which, and when, is explained by antagonism based on unequal and exploitative relations regarding access to sources of Western trade goods, beginning with steel tools. This fundamental antagonism is then channeled by structural and superstructural patterns. In contrast, two other hypotheses about Yanomami warfare—that it is explained by scarcity of game or conflicts over women—are not at all predictive of the actual occurrence of war (Ferguson 1995a).

War makers do not talk, and may not think, about war in this materialistic way. In the long discussions that usually precede war, people advocating any course of action convert practical self-interests into the highest applicable moral values—ideas of personhood, accusations of witchcraft, notions of religious duty, invocations of bravery or cowardice, demands of revenge. Such deeply held common values are used to justify plans and persuade others. In an already strained situation, even a seemingly trivial slight, exemplifying a total relation, may provide the trigger for violence, superficially seeming to be its cause. This is manipulation, but not *just* manipulation. The values are true to local culture. Cognitive dissonance theory long ago taught us that contradictory evaluations within individuals are brought into alignment, and this is true in war. Wants and needs are converted into moral rights and duties. This is a fundamental and necessary process of war, as struggles over things must be transformed into imperatives to kill other human beings. In many cases, perhaps the great majority, advocates of war come to believe their rationale themselves. What is good for them becomes the 'right' thing to do. Each side sees the other as responsible for bringing on war (Ferguson 1995a, 2006a).

But systems of thought have their own logic and power, not reducible to practicalities. As the anthropology of violence has taught us, acts of war are expressive as well as instrumental. Slaughters, tortures, exemplary killings—all are performances, laden with deep meaning for the actors, victims, and audiences. They become critical social facts, defining relationships and playing a major role in shaping future actions. The seamless integration of pan-human considerations of practicality and culturally particular values is highlighted by reactions to Western contact. Among very different peoples, political and military responses to powerful intruders—for example, when and why alliances with them are made or broken—display remarkable similarity. Take away identifying characteristics, and the response to a given situation could be transferred anywhere across the world. Yet ethnographic detail on each case makes clear that culturally specific understandings and norms are motivating indigenous actors. Reconciling the two areas of material practicality and symbolic logic remains a great challenge in the anthropology of war and violence, and the devil is in the analytic details (Ferguson 2001, 2003b; Ferguson and Whitehead 1999).

How we got into Iraq illustrates the need for a combination of practical and symbolic considerations. The Republican electoral strategy for victory in 2002 and 2004 was openly and explicitly built on war. A victorious cakewalk through the Middle East could have cemented Republican political power for a decade. Of course, that backfired in 2006, because this war, like most, did not go as planned. In retrospect, too, Saddam Hussein's posture before the war seems self-destructive. But the CIA tells us that Hussein was actually pursuing his own survival against what he saw as the two main threats—his own officers and Iran. Because of Iran, he wanted the world to think he might really have weapons of mass destruction. He believed, until it was too late, that a US invasion would be blocked by the UN. So the stance of both the US and Iraqi regimes was based on self-interest. But the leaders on both sides saw themselves as moral paragons. Hussein was the restorer of Mesopotamian glory and Arab dignity. Bush and Company were the protectors of American values and democracy. Both acted on erroneous information that was tailored by subordinates to suit their bosses' preconceptions: Bush on the presence of weapons of mass destruction, Hussein on the ability of his army to inflict enormous casualties on invaders. Both made miscalculations about things that seemed self-evident to many on the outside: Hussein about the UN's ability to block an invasion, Bush about the stable multi-ethnic society that was supposed to bloom after conquest. Both sides saw the other as morally corrupt. Both sides saw the other as the aggressor. On both sides, self-interests, understandings, and values all fit neatly together. They usually do in war (Ferguson 2006a).

Point #5: War Shapes Society to Its Own Ends

The standard anthropological approach to war is to relate some aspect of war to some other aspect of social life—to ecological stresses, to features of social structure, to belief systems, and so on. This is consistent with twentieth-century social science, which generally sees war as a thing to be explained, not an explanation in itself. What is less obvious is that war is a major causal force strongly affecting all areas of social life. War is a threat to physical and social existence. As such, people must cope with it, sometimes on pain of death.

War leads to the creation and destruction of institutions in many ways. In the archaeological record, war, or more intense war, often led to larger, nucleated settlements, which presumably required new forms of political organization and conflict resolution. War made necessary the redistribution of food and property that became elaborated into the Northwest Coast potlatch. In Amazonia and elsewhere, war generally affects gender relations, usually negatively for women. In non-state societies, the influence of war can be pervasive, accounting for the difference between 'warlike' and 'peaceable' peoples (Ferguson 1983, 1988b, 1994).

War's social causality is strikingly apparent in a comparative examination of ancient and medieval states. War can bring land into cultivation, while at other times it destroys a subsistence base. War increases the emphasis on boundaries and territory. It brings new people into regulated production, including draft labor for major projects. War can reduce population numbers and encourage higher birth rates. It structures the education and training of boys to be warriors. It can transform a landscape with defensive structures and foster the transfer of technologies across regions. It leads to the mixture of peoples and cultures. It can break down kinship relations. Participation in war can be a central aspect of stratification systems. Success in war is often a prerequisite for higher social status and provides avenues for elite competition. War leads to armies and other formal institutions that become weighty actors within societies, including scribes and systems of taxation. It molds religion to provide justification for conquest. It can restructure societal systems of production and intensify internal political control. War can convert balanced into unbalanced trade and tribute, alliances into confederacies and empires, and otherwise extend systems of domination (Ferguson 1999).

There may be militaristic and non-militaristic trajectories of social development. Once a given society is internally adapted for war, making war becomes much easier—a necessity, even, for the reproduction of existing social relations. Commentators have often compared war to a disease, but a more apt analogy is an addiction (Ferguson 1994). We should ask how far the United States has gone in this direction. As Catherine Lutz (2002) and others have documented, over the past several decades, US economics, politics, and popular culture have been restructured to serve war. For anthropologists, the impact of war hits uncomfortably close to home. Ongoing research by David Price (2004) on World War II and the Cold War is revealing extensive connections between the demands of our national security apparatus and the development of US anthropology.

Point #6: War Exists in Multiple Contexts

We are accustomed to conceptualizing war as a contest between two or more groups. But war is also a property of a larger system of groups. The space between polities is highly structured, from the physical distribution of populations and resources, the terrain and its cover, and factors affecting travel; through all the social, economic, and political ties unifying or dividing groups; to the shared understandings, conventions, and expectations of war among adversaries. All of these intergroup circumstances exert strong determinative effects on the decisions and actions of any single group (Ferguson 1999).

Contexts come in layers, starting with local neighborhoods and moving on to regional and inter-regional interactions. Among comparatively egalitarian peoples, such as in highland New Guinea or Amazonia, the effective social universe is made up of neighboring communities of similar scale. But with the development of social hierarchy, more extensive and often unequal intergroup relations prevail. With broadening interactions, there can be systems within systems. For example, the many local war-making chiefdoms of Bronze Age Europe were part of a vast network linked by technology, trade, marriage, and ideology, and this system was itself part of a larger interaction sphere centering on the Middle East and stretching from Egypt to South Asia and beyond (Ferguson 2006b).

Ancient states were surrounded by tribal zones, defined as areas not under a state's control but manifestly affected by its proximity. One consequence of states seeking clear polities to deal with is the creation or reinforcement of more cohesive tribal units and a state-oriented system of militarism. The older war patterns of tribal zones are transformed by new technologies and military organization, and by resistance to or cooperation with state policies and interests. Militarized ethnies (recognized cultural groupings) are commonly used by states and empires to project military force farther than the reach of their own armies, and to protect state interests along trade routes. They are subordinates, and their actions in turn modify the interactions of peoples deeper in the peripheries. These local groups still have their own interests, politics, and understandings, but these are played out in an overarching tribal zone context and would be unintelligible without bringing that context into focus (Ferguson 1993, 1999; Ferguson and Whitehead 1992a).

From the sixteenth century on, tribal zones have been more disruptive than those of ancient states. Previously separated from indigenous populations by vast distances, Europeans brought new diseases, plants, animals, technologies, and trade goods that radically transformed local societies. At the same time, they continued older state policies that encouraged war, such as dividing to conquer and recruiting ethnic soldiers. But European powers also encouraged local wars in a way not typical of ancient states, a fact that merits emphasis because it has so often been neglected in anthropological theorizing on war. The sudden introduction of new trade items, from cloth to steel to guns, provided a whole new set of incentives to fight, and Europe's insatiable demand for captive labor and for land emptied of indigenous populations generated a bow wave of local warfare, as displaced peoples sought a place to live and as slave raiders penetrated deeper and deeper. All these native wars in turn shaped the great games of colonial rivals and empires (Ferguson 1990a, 1990b, 1993; Ferguson and Whitehead 1992a). As Keith Otterbein (1964) pointed out long ago, if the Huron had defeated the Iroquois in 1649, we might be speaking French today.

Skipping several millennia, the 1980s were a time of so-called proxy wars, localized struggles backed by one or more sides in the Cold War. As Eric Wolf (1973) noted, these conflicts were always much more local than realpolitik strategists imagined. The protracted struggle in Guatemala, for instance, had far deeper roots than the ongoing East-West confrontation. In the 1990s, it was the opposite problem, as fierce civil wars erupted in sub-Saharan Africa, the former Yugoslavia and USSR, and elsewhere, which were caricatured as explosions of ancient, local hatreds. It is true that these wars were launched and prosecuted by local actors, but they were heavily conditioned by supra-local changes, which show up repeatedly in comparisons across cases. The end of the Cold War destabilized many situations when formerly well-funded militaries were suddenly cut off as irrelevant to the great powers. Global economic processes led to crashing commodity prices and widespread immiseration in many areas. The illegal trade of drugs, 'blood diamonds', guns, and even oil encouraged criminals, warlords, and corrupt officials, who were often indistinguishable, as Nordstrom (2007) shows. Well-meant humanitarian aid was subject to military control and diversion. The regulation of local governments by international agencies curtailed patrimonial beneficence and the governments' ability to respond to both humanitarian and military challenges. The needs, aspirations, and fears of local players were tied to strings pulled from above (Ferguson 2003b).

In the current 'global war against terror', the levels of context are almost too obvious to mention. Ambitious leaders from one neighborhood make moves to vanquish local rivals, within the larger playing field of a city or region, relating to parallel and connected struggles across international borders, all intertwined with a Cold War-esque global military confrontation. Policies on all sides reflect not just current realities on the ground, but the larger political arenas from which support can be drawn.

Point #7: Opponents Are Constructed in Conflict

In war, a line must be clear between 'us' and 'them', otherwise one would not know whom to kill. Many biologically oriented theories postulate that war is, in some way, an expression of an innate tendency to in-group amity and out-group enmity. In these views, the existence of the group generates the conflict. But it is unusual, if not rare, for war to involve two pre-existing groups, and only them. In actual practice, it is the conflict that firms up the opposed groups.

War groupings vary in duration. Among the Yanomami, they are very ad hoc. Allies can quickly turn into enemies, and vice versa, depending on the situation. Members of one village community may take different sides in group violence (Ferguson 1995a). Elsewhere, where enmities stretch over years or even generations, alignments may be more fixed, although still subject to change. Segmentary systems provide structured fault lines guiding groups in alliance and opposition ("I fight my brother, but with my brother against my cousin, and with my cousin against a stranger"), although these oppositions are less mechanical and more opportunistic than once thought (ibid.: 1984a; 1990a). In ancient states and empires, military solidarity among component parts waxes and wanes over more or less long periods (ibid.: 1999). Since the seventeenth-century Treaty of Westphalia, the basic of unit of war has been fixed on the state. But states rarely go to war without allies, and those depend on the conflict. This is so in the two current US wars: 'us' in Iraq is different from 'us' in Afghanistan.

Considering the identity-linked wars that have torn apart many countries over the past several decades, scholars are long past the idea of timeless entities acting out timeless grudges. We understand that oppositions in war are very contemporary constructions, fixed in recently spilt blood, however much ancient history is invoked by its leaders (or interested outsiders). These struggles are often called 'ethnic', even though most are not about cultural differences at all. The actual basis of the organization of groups going to war differs greatly by situation. Common variables include the groups' position in the hierarchical chain from urban metropole to country village, occupation and other indices of social class, religion, language, caste, race, tribe, clan, lineage, and the corresponding access of all categories to seats of power. These variables mix and morph into endless combinations. Within any grouping, so defined, attitudes toward war are also structured by individual factors of age, generation, and gender.

We have no general term for such conflicts. Understanding their violence is impeded without first understanding their specific social character, or, worse, by misleadingly tagging them as 'ethnic' or 'religious'. Sometimes science needs to invent a new term, and I do so in coining the label 'identerest' (from 'identity' and 'interest'). Although I recognize the natural reluctance to adopt neologisms, I believe this term is justified because of the work it does. First, against some current explanatory divides that stress either self-interest or identity issues (sometimes framed as 'greed vs. grievance'), 'identerism' highlights the point that practical interests and self-identities are very commonly fused into one. Who you are—what kind of person you are—largely determines how you are doing and whether you have gained or lost in recent history. Second, it makes a necessity of clearly specifying the social bases of contending groups, rather than avoiding this critical issue by slapping on an inappropriate label. Calling a conflict 'identerest' creates a question of identities and interests that must be answered (Ferguson 2003b).

This is what we now face in Iraq. There is no insurrection but rather a kaleidoscope of identerest struggles. There are not just two, as in many other violent situations, but countless identerest groups fighting us and each other. News reports of violence regularly show groupings, both large and small, that are defined by geographic region, urban neighborhood, income, ethnicity, language, tribe, lineage, and religious differences. Anti-Americanism is the banner, because it conforms to recent life experiences, just as Islam invokes broad and powerful values. These beliefs bring in recruits and facilitate alliances, but the steam that powers these groupings is generated by local interests and struggles for wealth, power, and prestige (Ferguson 2006a).

Point #8: War Is a Continuation of Domestic Politics by Other Means

War involves people of one side trying to kill those of the other. That is how people typically think of war—as a relation between groups. This is most clear in international relations theory, where war-making states are seen as interacting like billiard balls colliding on the green felt of anarchy, each with clear, unified interests. The domestic politics behind decisions on war are relegated to history, if old, or journalism, if recent. War is seen as essentially international. In one sense this is obviously true. In another, it is profoundly misleading. It is in the nature of war that its politics are internal as well as external (Ferguson 1995a, 1999; Ferguson and Whitehead 1992a).

Some wars are characterized by overwhelming unity within one or both sides. Responses to external attacks tend to be so, at least at first. But these are unusual. In most wars, within the basic political units there are differences of interests, disagreements over actions, and unequal abilities to influence the course of events. Even in the simplest of societies, war is not the result of someone beating on a drum, with everyone rushing off, but of long discussions and debates, frequently combined with internal alliances and log-rolling. Often there are identifiable factions that favor war or not, or one course over another. This is a result not just of different perceptions and interests relating to external affairs, but of those in relation to internal struggles as well. War itself, being a causal factor in social life, commonly has a major impact on the future position of individuals and sub-groups and their rise or fall.

Moving from single polities to larger alliances and beyond, these internal politics are even more critical. Variations in ties of descent or marriage, residential proximity, or prior alliances all play important roles in decisions. War affects future alliances, requiring compensation for losses and pledges of future support. Where intergroup connections involve hierarchies of power, these too shape decisions and are reshaped by war. The realpolitik view of war is fundamentally flawed. Understanding why wars happen requires bringing into theory the internal politics of each side in a conflict.

Internal politics are clearly on display in the current war in Iraq (Ferguson 2006a). That US policy regarding Iraq is closely tied to domestic politics has been up front and clear since 9/11. As I write this, in the pre-primaries period of the 2008 national election, the key issues in all debates are Iraq and terrorism. The candidates of both parties are trying to formulate positions that generate support and help them defeat rivals. It could be no other way. An Iraq plan that did not pay heed to US domestic politics would be a fantasy. Eventually, one candidate, one position, will win, and that victory will be a very important factor (along with many others) in determining the future of the war.

Internal politics are equally well-documented within Iraq. In 2004, al-Zarqawi wrote to bin Laden with his plan for Iraq, premised on the reality of complex and divided political allegiances, clearly stating a strategy of compelling the fractious Sunni to unite behind al Qaeda by provoking indiscriminate retaliation by Shiites (Coalition Provisional Authority 2004). His strategy was remarkably successful, not only in polarizing Iraq, but in convincing many US politicians that this is fundamentally a civil war between those two faiths. Yet Shiite militias fight other Shiites, Sunni militants cooperate with the Mahdi army, and tribal groups pursue tribal interests. Grand Ayatollah al-Sistani may be the most important political player in Iraq, and if he dies any time soon, we can expect a whole new configuration of struggle. In the meantime, the United States demands that Iraqi Prime Minister al-Maliki develop a representative government and prosecute the war in a manner that is practically precluded by internal political alignments (Ferguson 2006a).

We criticize the Iraqi government as if it could be and do otherwise, without acknowledging that our Congress has been equally unable to reach basic agreements. These situations are not aberrations. The real politics of war is an ongoing dialectic of the internal and the external. Failure to appreciate that—to treat domestic politics as any less fundamental than the military violence between adversaries—will lead to severe misunderstandings and unrealistic expectations. It is not a good thing when one's adversaries make plans based on political realities, while one's own strategy is an exercise in wishful thinking.

Point #9: Leaders Favor War Because War Favors Leaders

This is true most of the time, at least at the beginning. This is a subpoint of war as an expression of domestic politics, but it merits special attention. One of the greatest differences between wars by states and wars by tribal peoples is that in states, war decisions are made at the top, with those below being compelled to follow. In comparatively egalitarian societies, that command power is generally absent. But even in politically egalitarian groups, there are leaders who have their own interests and exert substantial influence over decisions. Their actions can shape military behavior. Among the Yanomami, one leader (Fusiwe) fomented an attack on visitors who were favoring another leader in his village. Later, when he seemed bent on starting another war, those closest to him speculated on his motives, concluding that he wanted to force his scattered group to coalesce so that he could be "chieftain of them all" (Ferguson 1995a: 238). In New Guinea, big men assess military possibilities in terms of likely effects on their own political position. Farther up the societal scale, 'chiefly ambitions' has often seemed a necessary, even sufficient explanation for war. The distinctive interests of kings and emperors are obvious. Not only do these leaders experience vastly different costs, benefits, and powers in war, they may also require successful wars in order to establish and maintain rule (ibid.: 1990a, 1994, 1995a, 1999, 2006b).

Certainly, leaders do not always advocate war. It is often in their interests to avoid it. But war has several general consequences that can be used to enhance a leader's position. War often forces a coalescence of groups in a way that makes the management of people more possible. It leads to the acceptance of certain situations—heightened aggression in war leaders and acquiescence to their directives—that would not be tolerated if there were no lethal enemy. Leading and prevailing in wartime can decidedly raise a person's status. Referring back to point #4, leaders' pursuit of self-interest in war may be accompanied by a deep sense of moral correctness. However, wars commonly do not work out as planned, and those who start wars may suffer defeat or death (as Fusiwe did). But such an outcome is not anticipated when the decision to fight is made.

To understand war, it is essential to understand the structure of decision making and to identify the total interests—internal and external—of those involved in it. This is clear in identerest violence and war. Leaders seek wealth, power, and prestige. To build a following, they construct narratives and histories to define 'us' and demonize 'them'. They speak to local cultural understandings and fears, invoke potent symbols, and offer plausible—even if false—explanations of recent miseries (al-Zarqawi's letter to bin Laden is a textbook illustration of such a militarized construction of history, invocation of sacred values, and demonization of the other). Many leap to the cause, providing a hard core of followers to command. Thus empowered, the leaders foster polarization and fear, and start the killing. With the die cast, it becomes a situation of 'follow the leader'. That is what happened in Rwanda (Ferguson 1999, 2003b).

In modern societies, decisions for war involve a complex array of class, corporate, institutional, media, and political positions. It is often difficult to understand even the surface maneuverings, much less get below them. For the war in Iraq, the distinctive interests and values of Bush and Hussein have already been noted. Bookshelves are filling up with investigative journalism on the immediate decisions leading up to the US invasion. But social science should move beyond that to illuminate all of the institutional imperatives and connections that were used to bamboozle the public and get their acceptance of an invasion.

What about terrorist leaders? I define them as non-state actors who deliberately target civilians, although states can wage terror, too. Everything we are told about these organizations indicates clear hierarchical structures with centralized decision making. The leaders are not blowing themselves up, but many *are* gaining power and the benefits that power brings. Late in 2006, news reports described Muqtada al-Sadr as having been partially 'tamed' by his new power, wealth, and prestige—which he does not want to give up. But he was losing control over elements of his loosely constructed militia. One breakaway faction, responsible for many of the torture deaths in Baghdad, was led by a former fishmonger, who some hailed as the Zarqawi of the Sunni (Tavernise 2006). You can be sure he was doing better than a fishmonger.

Point #10: Peace Is More Than the Absence of War

As war needs to be reconceptualized, so does peace. People often think of peace as the absence of war, and given the human costs of war, perhaps that is good enough. But research by Leslie Sponsel (1994), William Ury (1999), Douglas Fry (2006), and others has made it very clear that factors leading to peaceful conflict resolution are quite distinct from those that lead to war. Peace has its own dynamic, including behavior patterns, social and political institutions, and value systems that foster equitable treatment and the rejection of violence as acceptable means to an end. This is a necessary insight for the world today.

We have seen some terrible examples of peacekeeping. Oftentimes, peacekeeping is no more than putting a neutral line of guns between two hostile lines of guns without addressing the more difficult issue of the underlying culture of violence. So war awaits its comeback. Anthropologists who wish to work against war directly face daunting problems. Few are equipped to participate actively in efforts to avoid or resolve civil wars. The effort itself is protracted and extremely difficult. Readers should consult de Waal's (2006) account of Darfur negotiations for an example of the nitty-gritty issues, obstacles, personalities, and frustrations that get in the way of settlement. No effort will work that does not have sustained political and financial support, which is often lacking until the situation has gone well beyond critical. If one approach fails, another must be tried. In making peace, it is truly necessary to 'stay the course'.

In Iraq, with its multiple identerest conflicts already going at full blast, peacemaking seems a fantasy. Anthropological knowledge clearly is being sought by the military, but for the purpose of waging war (Packer 2006).[3] These developments are part of a larger debate about whether or how anthropology should articulate with national security institutions—a discussion that has profound implications for our discipline. Based on past experience, most anthropologists would probably reject such direct cooperation. But what if, under a different regime in Washington, we were asked to use our knowledge to help reduce the incidence of wars and reinforce peaceful cooperation? Our discipline needs to discuss this issue fully and openly.

There is another way that anthropologists can help promote peace outside the halls of power. In the Reagan years I called this the protest route rather than the policy route (Ferguson 1988a, 1989). It involves calling attention to the interests of the powerful, dissecting militaristic propaganda, and dispelling the pervasive myth that war is to be assumed because humans are inherently warlike and thus war will always be with us. This brings us back to point #1 and a good place to stop.

Conclusion

As Carolyn Nordstrom (1998: 148) observes: "War is one of those curious phenomena that is inherently defined. People quite simply *know* what war is. This is not to say that this knowledge is correct, but to point out that people believe it is. Part of the cultural phenomenon of war is that both war and its definition are taken as 'given' in human society." Her point, and mine, is that many aspects of this implicit definition are not only wrong but positively misleading. They prevent us from grappling with the reality of war. Anthropology can offer a different vision, one with real implications for a critical response to the next call to arms.

R. Brian Ferguson is a Professor of Anthropology at Rutgers University. He has written extensively on many aspects of war. He is the co-editor, with Neil Whitehead, of *War in the Tribal Zone: Expanding States and Indigenous Warfare* (1992), the author of *Yanomami Warfare: A Political History* (1995), the editor of *The State, Identity, and Violence: Political Disintegration in the Post–Cold War Era* (2003), and is currently writing *Chimpanzees and War*. He also is engaged in research on the development of organized crime in New York City in the early twentieth century.

Notes

1. This chapter is an expansion of a presentation at the 2006 meetings of the American Anthropological Association. Organizer Alisse Waterston asked me to prepare an overview of my conclusions, and I condensed them down to eight interrelated points (Ferguson 2007). With more room, these have been expanded, and previous points #1 and #2 are each divided into two separate points, making 10 points altogether.
2. My previous publications are at http://www.newark.rutgers.edu/socant/brian.htm.
3. The Army's new counterinsurgency manual includes detailed discussion of social structure and culture as necessary elements in designing military campaigns (DOA 2006: chap. 3).

References

Coalition Provisional Authority. 2004. "Text from Abu Mus'ab al-Zarqawi Letter." http://www.globalsecurity.org/wmd/library/news/iraq/2004/02/040212-al-zarqawi.htm (accessed 2 August 2005).

de Waal, Alex. 2006. "I Will Not Sign." *London Review of Books* 28, no. 23 (30 November). http://www.lrb.co.uk/v28/n23/waal01_.html (accessed 21 June 2007).

DOA (Department of the Army). 2006. *Counterinsurgency.* Field Manual 3-24. Washington, DC: Government Printing Office.

Ferguson, R. Brian. 1983. "Warfare and Redistributive Exchange on the Northwest Coast." Pp. 133–137 in *The Development of Political Organization in Native North America: 1979 Proceedings of the American Ethnological Society*, ed. Elisabeth Tooker. Washington, DC: American Ethnological Society.

_____. 1984a. "Introduction: Studying War." Pp. 1–81 in Ferguson 1984c.

_____. 1984b. "A Re-examination of the Causes of Northwest Coast Warfare." Pp. 267–328 in Ferguson 1984c.

_____, ed. 1984c. *Warfare, Culture, and Environment.* Orlando, FL: Academic Press.

_____. 1988a. "How Can Anthropologists Promote Peace?" *Anthropology Today* 4, no. 3: 1–3.

_____. 1988b. "War and the Sexes in Amazonia." Pp. 136–154 in *Dialectics and Gender: Anthropological Approaches*, ed. R. Randolph, D. Schneider, and M. Diaz. Boulder, CO: Westview.

_____. 1989. "Anthropology and War: Theory, Politics, Ethics." Pp. 141–159 in *The Anthropology of War and Peace: Perspectives on the Nuclear Age*, ed. D. Pitt and P. Turner. Granby, MA: Bergin and Garvey.

_____. 1990a. "Explaining War." Pp. 22–50 in *The Anthropology of War*, ed. J. Haas. New York: Cambridge University Press.

_____. 1990b. "Blood of the Leviathan: Western Contact and Warfare in Amazonia." *American Ethnologist* 17: 237–257.

_____. 1992. "A Savage Encounter: Western Contact and the Yanomami Warfare Complex." Pp. 199–227 in Ferguson and Whitehead 1992b.

_____. 1993. "When Worlds Collide: The Columbian Encounter in Global Perspective." *Human Peace* 10, no. 1: 199–227.

_____. 1994. "The General Consequences of War: An Amazonian Perspective." Pp. 85–111 in *Studying War*, ed. S. Reyna and R. E. Downs. Langhorne, PA: Gordon and Breach.

_____. 1995a. *Yanomami Warfare: A Political History.* Santa Fe, NM: School of American Research.

_____. 1995b. "Infrastructural Determinism." Pp. 21–38 in *Science, Materialism and the Study of Culture*, ed. M. Murphy and M. Margolis. Gainesville: University of Florida Press.

_____. 1999. "A Paradigm for the Study of War and Society." Pp. 409–458 in *War and Society in the Ancient and Medieval Worlds: Asia, the Mediterranean, Europe, and Mesoamerica*, ed. K. Raaflaub and N. Rosenstein. Cambridge, MA: Center for Hellenic Studies, Harvard University Press.

_____. 2000. "On Evolved Motivations for War." *Anthropological Quarterly* 73: 159–164.

_____. 2001. "Materialist, Cultural, and Biological Theories on Why Yanomami Make War." *Anthropological Theory* 1, no. 1: 99–116.

_____. 2003a. "The Birth of War." *Natural History* (July/August): 28–35.

_____. 2003b. "Violent Conflict and the Control of the State." Pp. 1–58 in *The State, Identity, and Violence: Political Disintegration in the Post–Cold War Era*, ed. R. B. Ferguson. New York: Routledge.

_____. 2006a. "Tribal, 'Ethnic,' and Global Wars." Pp. 41–69 in *The Psychology of Resolving Global Conflicts: From War to Peace.* Vol. 1: *Nature vs. Nurture*, ed. M. Fitzduff and C. Stout. Westport, CT: Praeger Security International.

_____. 2006b. "Archaeology, Cultural Anthropology, and the Origins and Intensifications of War." Pp. 469–523 in *The Archaeology of Warfare: Prehistories of Raiding and Conquest*, ed. E. Arkush and M. Allen. Gainesville: University of Florida Press.

_____. 2007. "Eight Points on War." *Anthropology Newsletter* (February): 5–6.

Ferguson, R. Brian, and Neil L. Whitehead. 1992a. "The Violent Edge of Empire." Pp. 1–30 in Ferguson and Whitehead 1992b.

_____, eds. 1992b. *War in the Tribal Zone: Expanding States and Indigenous Warfare*. Santa Fe, NM: School of American Research Press.

_____. 1999. "Preface to the Second Printing." Pp. xi–xxxv, in *War in the Tribal Zone: Expanding States and Indigenous Warfare*, ed. R. B. Ferguson and N. L. Whitehead. Santa Fe, NM: School of American Research Press/James Currey.

Fry, Douglas. 2006. *The Human Potential for Peace: An Anthropological Challenge to Assumptions about War and Violence*. New York: Oxford University Press.

Lutz, Catherine. 2002. "Making War at Home in the United States: Militarization and the Current Crisis." *American Anthropologist* 104: 723–735.

Nordstrom, Carolyn. 1998. "Deadly Myths of Aggression." *Aggressive Behavior* 24: 147–159.

_____. 2007. *Global Outlaws: Crime, Money, and Power in the Contemporary World*. Berkeley: University of California Press.

Otterbein, Keith. 1964. "Why the Iroquois Won: An Analysis of Iroquois Military Tactics." *Ethnohistory* 11, no. 1: 56–63.

Packer, George. 2006. "Knowing the Enemy: Can Social Scientists Redefine the 'War on Terror'?" *New Yorker*, 18 December, 60–69.

Price, David H. 2004. *Threatening Anthropology: McCarthyism and the FBI's Surveillance of Activist Anthropologists*. Durham, NC: Duke University Press.

Sponsel, Leslie. 1994. "The Mutual Relevance of Anthropology and Peace Studies." Pp. 1–36 in *The Anthropology of Peace and Nonviolence*, ed. L. Sponsel and T. Gregor. Boulder, CO: Lynne Reiner.

Tavernise, Sabrina. 2006. "Influence Rises but Base Frays for Iraqi Cleric." *New York Times*, 13 November, A1.

Ury, William. 1999. *Getting to Peace: Transforming Conflict at Home, at Work, and in the World*. New York: Viking.

Wolf, Eric R. 1973. *Peasant Wars of the Twentieth Century*. New York: Harper Torchbooks.

Chapter 2

GLOBAL WARRING TODAY
"Maybe Somebody Needs to Explain"

Stephen Reyna

I'm the Commander—see, I don't need to explain—I do not need to explain why I say things. That's the interesting thing about being the President. Maybe somebody needs to explain to me why they say something, but I don't feel like I owe anybody an explanation. (George W. Bush, August 2002, in Hightower 2006: 3)

Extremely visionary. (Rush Limbaugh's 2006 interview with President Bush on the Iraq conflict, in *RawStory* 2006)

It should be clear—spectacularly so—that since 9/11 the US government has brought 'shock and awe' through direct or indirect military operations in an arc from Afghanistan to Iraq to Lebanon. Indeed, some go further and assert that the US is engaged in World War IV (the Cold War being World War III) (Cohen 2001; Podhoretz 2002; Woolsey in Feldman and Wilson 2003). Why? Perhaps

Notes for this chapter begin on page 66.

an answer to this question could be had from President Bush, the person directing this violence. But unfortunately, the president is "the Commander—see," so he does not need to explain, although he acknowledges, "Maybe somebody needs to explain." This chapter offers such an explanation, proposing a 'global warring hypothesis' that helps us understand current US military violence. First, the concept of 'global warring' is introduced in order to make clear that this type of warfare is significant and, hence, worthy of explanation. Second, a global warring hypothesis is formulated to account for the Bush regime's violence. Third, evidence is provided bearing on it. Finally, Rush Limbaugh's judgment that President Bush's understanding of the current violence is "extremely visionary" is discussed. In order to grasp the significance of global warring, it is necessary to distinguish such violence from local and world warring.

Local, Global, and World War

Since the demise of the Soviet Union, a suspicion has arisen among scholars that there is something novel about current warring. There are a number of terms for this kind of combat: asymmetrical conflict, low intensity conflict, limited wars, insurgencies, guerrilla war, national liberation movements, terrorism. Essentially, what this literature asserts is that 'new wars'—the term is political scientist Mary Kaldor's (Kaldor and Vashee 1997)—are small wars. They are small in the sense that the exercise of violence does not involve two nation-states fighting formal battles involving armies in campaigns to achieve battlefield dominance. Rather, they are, on at least one side, the operations of guerrilla units involving small combat teams that hit and disappear in order to strike again some other day, at some other place. The small war literature has emphasized that these wars are local or at best regional; that is, their origin and conduct are to be explained largely as a result of the local context in which the conflict occurs.[1] Investigators explain such quarrels in terms of local leaders, often tied to particular ethnicities, informed by local cultures, economies, and politics. Some of this literature is offensive, offering pejoratives as explanation. For example, the neo-conservative journalist Robert Kaplan (1994) believes that strife in West Africa during the 1980s and 1990s is a "new barbarism" to be accounted for by the return of "juju warriors."[2] The social science community began to emphasize small wars only in the 1990s.

Earlier, the US military recognized the importance of small wars, after fighting and losing a rather large small war in Vietnam (1959–1975). In the 1970s, senior members of the US military recognized a form of violence they referred to as 'low intensity conflict' (LIC). By the 1980s, they would characterize this violence, as did General Wallace H. Nutting, commander-in-chief of the US Readiness Command, as "the central strategic task" facing the US (in Klare 1986). William Olsen (1985) of the US War College argued that winning LICs was "crucial to national survival." George Schultz (1986), Ronald Reagan's secretary of state, insisted that "the future of peace and liberty" might depend up how well the US did in LICs. The US Marines revived their *Small Wars Manual* (USMC

[1940] 1996). Additionally, they set up a Small Wars Center of Excellence to serve as an "information resource and management tool for the understanding of the history, nature, and relevance of small wars in the 21st century." Make no mistake about it: the military's LIC is what scholars refer to as small wars.[3]

One difference between the scholarly and military small wars literature is that the former does not emphasize US intervention in such violence, while the latter does. For example, Colonel Richard Szafranski (1990: 1), in an article entitled "Thinking About Small Wars," written for *Parameters*, the journal of the US Army War College, argued that in the near future, US "armed interventions" would "increase," and that many of these would involve "small wars." The military elite openly acknowledges US participation in small wars. As Szafranski put it (ibid.: 1–2): "Small wars, whatever their genesis, are likely to be wars fought against the forces of a lesser power, or against the proxies or surrogates of a lesser power. They are fought, and will be fought, in those areas where we perceive our security of interests are imperiled. These interests are political, but within that broad domain may reside considerations of trade, resources, access and basing, protection of our citizens, elimination of criminal elements, maintenance of a regional balance of power, or sustaining a government favorable to our country or the governments of our allies or friends." Indeed, there is considerable evidence—both from progressive (Blum 2002) and neo-conservative (Boot 2003) perspectives—that the US has frequently participated in small wars. Given the importance of such violence, some distinction should be made between the different forms that exist and how small wars can become bigger ones.

Two general types of local and global small wars can be identified. These are distinguished in terms of whether capitalist states, pursuing either formal or informal imperialism, are involved in a small war. Capitalist imperialism is ultimately about the creation, maintenance, or enlargement of the capital accumulation of an imperial state's enterprises (Reyna 2005a). 'Globalization' is the current economic aspect of this imperialism. Violence of different sorts is part of the political aspect of this imperialism. Empires are especially gory structures. Warring in the name of 'pretty' hypocrisies, which presently include 'freedom', 'democracy', 'civilization', is a humdrum part of imperial politics because imperialism is about organizing people so that there are hugely unequal distributions of value. Violence is useful to create such systems, keep them going, or make them bigger. Those involved in strategizing and commanding the implementation of this killing are aptly termed the "killing elite" (Reyna 2005b).

There is general agreement—from the left, center, and right—that the US is an informal imperialist state.[4] Formal imperialism involves making colonies. Informal imperialism is about making, maintaining, or increasing the number of client states. The US killing elite has conceived and implemented a large amount of violence. John Tures (2003), in a study of US military operations based on the United States Military Operations (USMO) data set derived from an earlier Federation of American Scientists data set, finds that the US has engaged in 263 inter-state military operations since 1945, on the order of 4.6 operations per year. Certainly these operations contributed to the subordinating of clients. Let us return to small wars in a world dominated by this imperialism.

If no imperial capitalist state intervenes in a small war, then I consider the conflict to be 'local warring'; if an imperial capitalist state does participate, then the conflict is what I term 'global warring'. Two sorts of local warring presently occur. The first might be called 'purely' local warring. Such wars are between non-state opponents, such as ethnic or kin groups, over goals that are unrelated to the affairs of imperial states in a globalizing world. For example, I conducted fieldwork (1973–1974) in Chad among an Arab group called the Abu Krider—a semi-sedentary pastoral group settled in a relatively well-watered region of the generally poorly watered zone of the *sahel*, the arid savanna just south of the Sahara. This is because their territory is directly east of the Chari River and south of Lake Chad, which means that it is a sort of Garden of Eden since at all times of the year these water sources are available for animals. Perhaps a decade before my fieldwork, the Abu Krider had fought a short, sharp conflict with a group they called the Fellati (Fulfulde speakers). Engagements were recalled by informants as brutal, with Abu Krider recounting the evisceration of their pregnant women and the burial of at least one of their village chiefs up to his neck, the piling of brush around his head, and then the burning of the brush. The Fellati were remembered as being on the move from Nigeria. They were now in new territory in which they had no established rights. Fighting was over access to dry season water, which the Fellati got and then used during transhumance. This conflict was purely local because it involved local actors (kin groups of Abu Krider and Fellati) in conflict over a resource (water) that was necessary to their pastoral versions of the domestic mode of production.

There is a second form of local warring that, as previously noted, Kaldor has termed 'new wars'. Three attributes characterize this new 'mode' of wars. First, they "involve a blurring of the distinctions between war … organized crime … and large-scale violations of human rights" (Kaldor 2007: 2). Second, new wars are set in the context of a double erosion of the autonomy of the state. From above, there has been a "transnationalization of military forces," which has enmeshed governments in transnational institutions and alliances. This "increasing interconnectedness of states" has lessened a state's ability "to use force unilaterally against other states" (ibid.: 4, 5). At the same time, the "monopoly of organized violence is eroded from below by privatization" (ibid.: 6). Private militaries are financed through remittances, diaspora fund-raising, and the diversion of international humanitarian and development assistance. The third attribute of new wars concerns *why* they are fought, and Kaldor (ibid.: 7) says that the battles involve the goals of "identity politics" rather than those of universalist ideologies.

Kaldor's standpoint has been critiqued (Henderson and Singer 2002; Marchal and Messiant 2003; Shaw 2000). Her critics suggest that she has not discovered a new mode of warring but appears instead to have recognized new expressions of old forms of war that happen when a state loses, or never had, a monopoly on force. Let us call such a state Weberian, after the person who defined the state in terms of its monopolistic control over violence (Weber in Swedberg 2005: 265). By the 1980s, a diminution of the Weberian state was identifiable (Kaldor and Vashee 1997) in some places in the developing world and in the former Soviet sphere of influence. Loss of a monopoly on violence certainly facilitates the rise of private militaries. However, this was precisely the sort of warring that characterized medieval and early modern Europe, although the wars with private militaries in earlier times transpired because the Weberian state had not yet developed, while those of current times take place because in some places it has receded.

Kaldor's new wars are local wars in our terms if no imperial state's military has intervened in them. Further, because they occur in situations of attenuation of the nation-state, they might be termed 'weak state' local wars. While such conflicts are of interest, they are of greater significance if they rise to the level of global warring. The conflicts in the disintegrating parts of the old Yugoslavia, which took place from 1991 to 1995, were those of Kaldor's new wars that evolved from a weakened state into a global war when the US and NATO intervened. It is time to discuss this latter form of violence.

Global warring might be metaphorically imagined as a sort of cat and mouse game, with a bunch of mice under the claws of a giant cat. The mice in question are military organizations capable of guerrilla operations in a colony or client state. The tabby is a capitalist state involved in the game of imperialism. A global war involves overt or covert exercises of violence between an imperialist state and military organizations in its own or another empire's colony or client state to create, maintain, or enlarge the imperialist state's capital accumulating powers. Global warring, the situation in which an imperial state is conducting a number of global wars simultaneously or nearly simultaneously, is not a particularly new phenomenon. Modern global warring goes back to the establishment of the Western European empires on a worldwide basis. At that time, in any one year, English or French imperialists might be fighting colonial global wars concurrently in Africa, Asia, and North America. As a result of US and NATO intervention, the fighting in the former Yugoslavia in the 1990s escalated a local war to a global war. At that time, the US was still involved in a global war to drive out the Soviets in Afghanistan, as well as sometimes overt and other times covert operations in the Sudan, Iraq, Guatemala, and Colombia. So it might be said that at this time the US was thoroughly involved in cat and mouse games of the global warring variety.

To recapitulate, I am arguing that there are three forms of small wars currently prevalent: the two forms of 'purely' and 'weak state' local warring as well as global warring. Global warring can, and does, on occasion intensify. Intensification can take three forms: (1) particular small global wars become large wars, as was the case with the US in Vietnam; (2) an empire with few global wars comes to have more of them; or (3) an empire fighting fewer global wars becomes engaged in more and larger global wars, as appears to be the case with current US warring.

Lastly, some global warring can become 'world warring'. World warring refers to those exercises of violence between imperial capitalist states fought on a worldwide basis. World wars are associated with sharp transformations of the capital accumulating capacities of the empires involved in the conflict. In the final years of the seventeenth century and the opening years of the eighteenth century, England and France participated in a series of global wars in which they allied with Native American populations to attack other Native American populations. The French, allied with the Hurons and Abenaki, attacked southward into English colonies in New York and New England. Conversely, the British, united with the Iroquois, attacked northward into French Canada. The fighting was importantly over the fur trade, a major capitalist enterprise in the American Northeast at that time. The British were concerned that their Indians would dominate the beaver hunting grounds, while the French were equally vexed that their Indians would do the same. This global warring contributed to the Seven Years' War (1752–1759) fought in Europe, the Caribbean, India, and North America—a world war that decisively enhanced Britain's capital accumulating prowess when France was stripped of its colonies in North America and India.[5] Jumping from the eighteenth century to the twentieth, historians have emphasized that the governing elite of the German Reich at the turn of the twentieth century believed that global warrings of the older European empires had been so successful as to preclude further German expansion.[6] Consequently, these elite understood that Germany was in dire need of 'breathing room' (*lebensraum*), which they sought in the greatest conflicts of the twentieth century: World War I and World War II. Finally, as indicated at the start of the text, the US—a behemoth of informal imperialism—is involved in substantial global warring. This poses the question: when is global warring likely to intensify? A generalization, the global warring hypothesis, is offered in the following section to provide one answer to this question.

Global Warring Hypothesis

The global warring hypothesis involves four concepts. The first is the *explanandum*, what is to be explained, which is the intensity of global warring. 'Global warring intensity' is a function of the number of global wars waged plus the magnitude of those wars, as measured in terms of their economic costs. 'Intensive' global warring is a situation in which a capitalist empire is waging five or more global wars at very considerable costs.

The remaining three concepts in the hypothesis are its *explanans*, which explain such violence. The three *explanans* are such that if they are present in certain states, then intensive global warring is to be expected. The first of the three concepts is the 'scale of capitalist competition', which indicates *how much* of the globe capitalists are in competition over. The larger the area of competition, the larger the geography an empire might be obliged to contest in order to secure the interests of its economic firms. The other two concepts explicate whether the competition is likely to turn violent.

The second concept in the *explanans* is the 'degree of functionality'. This is the ability of the economic system itself to function and, especially under capitalism, concerns whether capitalist institutions are able to accumulate capital. When an economy turns toward dysfunction with widespread capital stagnation or disaccumulation, it is heading toward a crisis. Two sorts of crises are imaginable. The first involves strings of events fluctuating between expansion and recession that have characterized capitalism since its inception. Such crises are said to be 'cyclical'. The second crisis is one that threatens to make capital accumulation scarcely possible or even impossible. Such crises are said to be 'systemic' because they threaten the system's ability to function. For example, if some means of production necessary to economic activity should become unavailable, then its absence would be a swan song for that activity. *Ceteris paribus*, the greater the systemic dysfunction, the greater the likelihood of resorting to violence, because elites will be anxious to fix this situation that threatens their position and that, precisely because the economy is crashing, does not appear susceptible to economic fixes.

The third concept in the *explanans* concerns a particular cause of economic dysfunction. This is the 'intensity of capitalist competition', which is about the probability that inter-firm conflict will compromise capital accumulation. The type of competition we are concerned with is that which remains even after firms have implemented competition mitigation strategies. The more that such competition reduces accumulation, the higher the competition intensity and the greater the likelihood of violence.

Given the preceding, the global warring hypothesis can be explained as follows: *For an empire, the conjunction of severe systemic crisis co-occurring with severe competition means that there is little that can be done in its economic sphere to resolve this predicament, prompting recourse to the political sphere and violence.* If the scale of this crisis is worldwide, then intense global warring is predicted. Evidence is provided below bearing upon this hypothesis.

Evidence

First, evidence concerning the three concepts in the *explanans* is offered, then that bearing upon the *explanandum*.

Scale of Capitalist Competition

One indicator of the scale of capitalist competition is the amount of direct foreign investments that countries make in other nations, because the greater such investments, the more likely it is that their enterprises' capital accumulation comes from other places on the globe. In 1980, the sum of all countries' direct investments was $500 billion; in 2005, it had risen to $10 trillion. This is a staggering 2000 percent increase in 25 years (Steingart 2006: 2). Trade to gross domestic product (GDP) ratios are another indicator of the scale of capitalist competition. Such ratios are a nation's exports plus imports as a percentage of its GDP. The higher the percentage of GDP due to foreign trade, the greater the number of states that are being exported to or imported from—that is, the greater the scale of a nation's competition. Table 1 (OECD 2002) depicts trends in trade to GDP ratios since the 1970s for advanced capitalist and developing countries. The table reveals a dramatically rising percentage of GDP arising from trade from all countries, meaning that trade, and with it competition, is increasingly global.

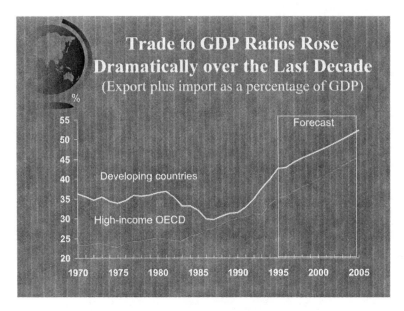

Trade to GDP Ratios Rose Dramatically over the Last Decade
(Export plus import as a percentage of GDP)

TABLE 1 Trends in Trade to GDP Ratios (OECD 2002)

A map picturing the locations in the world that a transnational corporation (TNC) maintains production operations is a useful way of visualizing the scale of capitalist competition. Map 1 offers one example, revealing where Volkswagen (VW) has its production operations—essentially everywhere. The number of TNCs worldwide rose from 7,000 in 1970 to 40,000 in 1995 (Karliner 1997: 2). Readers are now urged to conduct a *Gedankenexperiment* (thought experiment). First, visualize a picture of VW's production operations throughout the world. Next, superimpose 40,000 other pictures of production operations over that of VW—some more extensive and others less so, since not all TNCs are the same size. The final image is the result of the thought experiment, which indicates just how densely the world is interconnected with production operations. Such findings visualize the degree to which capital accumulation, with its attendant competition, overruns the globe. This imposes a policy imperative for capitalist elites throughout the world: when worrying about issues of capitalist competition, the scale of their *angst* had better be global.

Degree of Functionality

There are difficulties with the functioning of the current US and global economies, including a generally reduced level of capital accumulation since the 1970s, especially in the advanced capitalist countries. The world's annual GDP increase averaged 3.6 percent during the 1960s. It fell to 2.1 percent in the 1970s, 1.3 percent in the 1980s, 1.1 percent in the 1990s, and 1 percent in the 2000s

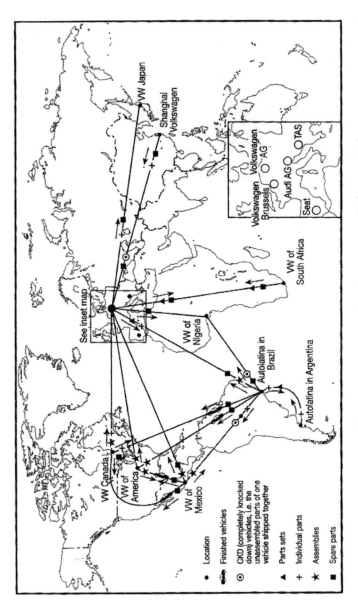

MAP 1 Volkswagen's Transnational Production Network (Steger 2003)

(Bond 2005: 3). Additionally, especially in the US, there has been stagnation or decline in the level of welfare of the lower classes (Bernstein and Allegretto 2005; Yates 2005) and middle classes (Dobbs 2006; Phillips 2006). Economic woes seem to be due to a conjuncture of cyclical and systemic crises.

CYCLICAL CRISIS. Conventional economists see the global slowdown reported above as cycling downward. *Business Week* put it as follows: "But the savings glut is creating new risks for the global economy, which is having a tough time absorbing the unanticipated flood of funds. Instead of going into productive investments, cheap money may be overheating spending and sending asset prices soaring too high, setting the stage for a future bust. 'The odds of a catastrophic scenario have gone up,' says Kenneth S. Rogoff, former chief economist at the IMF and a professor at Harvard University" (in Miller 2005: 2).

Thus, for conventional economists, a global savings glut is cycling the world toward a bust. However, in political economists' terms such a 'glut' is overaccumulation, a situation in which excessive investment has occurred and goods cannot be marketed profitably.[7] A point to grasp is that thinkers of different political tendencies, regardless of whether they are worried about a global savings glut or overaccumulation, believe that the world is in a downward phase of economic cycling. Otherwise put, the current conjuncture exhibits economic cyclical crisis. Consider the possibilities of systemic crisis.

SYSTEMIC CRISIS. Here the big news is the certainty of oil depletion and of global warming. These crises result from capitalism's tendency to extract more natural resources from the environment than is sustainable. Oil is considered first. This key strategic resource, which is needed for almost all capitalist production, is scarce and non-renewable (Klare 2004; Yergin 1993). Geophysicist M. King Hubbert suggested in the 1950s that oil supply might be imagined as a bell curve: it would have an ascending slope as output increased; a highest point before decrease set in; and a descending slope, as output decreased. The high point became known as Hubbert's peak. While there is no consensus on when Hubbert's peak will occur, there *is* a consensus that it will be very soon.[8] The US passed its peak in 1970 (Kunstler 2006: 43). The world rate of discovery of new oil peaked in the 1960s, and "the decreasing rate of discoveries" has "comprised only small fields" (ibid.: 49). Speculation concerning the rate of decline of oil output is vigorous. However, conservative estimates put the end of the oil supply between the twenty-first and twenty-second centuries.

This, then, is a central fact of our times: oil will soon be gone. Replacements are theoretically possible, although not currently feasible, economically or technically, as Kunstler (2006: 100–147) documents. Thus, the energy necessary for capital accumulation will be increasingly scarce, making any such accumulation problematic. This is systemic crisis, and added to it is a second crisis—that of climatic change.

Global warming is a chief cause of climate change. Some argue that the increased temperatures of global warming will affect humans "catastrophically," making "life as we know it impossible"; billions will die, leaving only an estimated thirtieth of the world's current population (McKibben 2006: 2).[9] Such global warming effects would be so great as to severely impair the capitalist system's ability to accumulate capital.

Intensity of Global Competition

Since the latter part of the 1980s, there is acknowledgment of growing international competition (Porter 1986). Further, it is clear that the US has faced, since the early 1970s, "sharpened" economic competition (Harvey 2003: 59). This competition is expected to intensify in part because of a general trend that Wallerstein (2003) has written about in *The Decline of American Power*. The decline that Wallerstein and even the CIA (NIC 2004) are describing is economic, and it is largely relative. No one is saying that the US gross national product has fallen behind that of any other country—at least not yet. Rather, what is asserted is that "the relative economic strength of the US is continuing to weaken" (Foster 2006: 4). Further, "since 1980 manufacturing in the United States has diminished" (Phillips 2006: 306). Whole industries—textiles, electronics, steel, automobiles—are gone or are at risk (Bluestone and Harrison 1982; Cowie and Heathcott 2003; Ullman 1988). This situation is no secret. A recent report by the National Research Council (NRC) of Canada acknowledges it: "The expansion of economies in India and China presents a fundamental challenge ... By 2020, given present trends, China will have an economy that rivals that of the United States in size. India will achieve this mark sometime in the 2040s, and Russia may again emerge as a major player. Some predict a trade war between China and the U.S. ... The traditionally strong trading nations, such as the UK and France, will weaken" (NRC 2005: 1).

There is debate over the cause of the intensified competition. One view links it to the overaccumulation discussed in the previous section (Brenner 2003; Harvey 2003: 124). Regardless of what the determinants of the competition are, the current times are ones of intensifying competition that is part and parcel of a historic shift of wealth and power to the East (Prestowitz 2005). In summary, the three concepts of the global warring hypothesis's *explanans* are in the states that predict global warring, which concentrates attention on the *explanandum*. Is an imperial US currently involved in intense global warring?

Intensity of Global Warring

Two months after the 9/11 attacks, Eliot Cohen (2001: 1), an influential neo-conservative, insisted that the US was involved in "World War IV." Cohen's view was shared by James Woolsey, a Clinton administration CIA director, who opined: "This fourth world war ... will last considerably longer than either World Wars I and II did" (in Feldman and Wilson 2003: 1). I shall argue below that the evidence shows Cohen and Woolsey to be hyperbolic. There is a great deal of warring in the world, but this is intense *global* warring and not yet *world* warring.

Certainly, it is no secret that US military bases are everywhere on the face of the globe.[10] The US military has been involved in overt and covert, direct and proxy combat, shows of force, contingent positioning and/or reconnaissance, evacuation, and peacekeeping throughout the world. Thus, an imperial US is involved in warring globally. However, especially instructive is *where* these operations have occurred in recent years.

Like a laser, the Bush II regime has focused recent global warring in areas where it can secure, maintain, or enlarge its control over oil in ways that either directly or indirectly facilitate US capital accumulation. 'Direct' aid to US capital accumulation occurs when the control over oil enhances profit margins of firms that are part of the American petroleum sector. 'Indirect' stimulation of US capital accumulation comes about when control over oil provides some advantage that the US government or US enterprises can use to establish favorable conditions for American capital accumulation.

A considerable part of global petroleum warring has involved US efforts to control oil in the Persian Gulf and Caspian Sea. These regions possess approximately 70 percent of the world's oil reserves (Klare 2004: 18–19). Since 1980, US government policy in this region has been guided by the Carter Doctrine, which declared that America would fight to defend its "vital interests" in the Middle East (Johnson 2005: 223). The Carter Doctrine became necessary because in the previous year (1979) there had been the double setback of the Iranian Revolution, which swept the US client regime of the Shah out of power, and the Soviet invasion of Afghanistan, which heralded more robust Russian competition in the Middle East. To put teeth into the Carter Doctrine, the Rapid Deployment Forces (RDF) for Middle Eastern operations was organized and headquartered in Florida. The Reagan administration upgraded the RDF to the US Central Command (CENTCOM) in 1983.

CENTCOM has had a busy time of it. Firstly, there was the planning and executing of Gulf War I, then the Afghan War, and now Gulf War II. Gulf War I was not a global war because the US engaged the conventional armies of the Iraqi state. Gulf War II is an exceptionally large global war, with the US losing against a web of guerrilla movements. Estimates vary as to its cost. One approximation suggested that Gulf War II had at the time cost $700 billion (Bennis and Leaver 2005: 1), while another gave a four-year total at $1 trillion (Valenzuela 2007). This is appreciably more in real terms than the cost of the Vietnam War. Staying in Iraq and Afghanistan at current levels over the next decade would nearly double the federal budget deficit (Bennis and Leaver 2005: 1).

At the heart of both Gulf wars is the struggle to control Iraq's oil. Iraq has the world's second largest oil reserves. The policy of the Bush II regime has been to make the country "Empire's gas station" (Valenzuela 2007: 1), because it would be, according to the *Washington Post*, a "bonanza for American oil companies" (in Everest 2004: 267–268), one that would be directly beneficial to their capital accumulation. However, an argument can also be made that these wars provide indirect assistance to American enterprise. It is argued that the US is involved in "petrodollar warfare" in Iraq (Clark 2005) to prevent the loss of the dollar as the monopolistic currency for the international oil market. Such a loss would precipitate a monetary crisis in the US economy, posing dire consequences for capital accumulation.

Additionally, CENTCOM has been fighting in Afghanistan against Taliban and al Qaeda guerrillas. Ostensibly, this fighting is part of the 'war on terror' to destroy Osama bin Laden and preserve the US client regime of Hamid Karzai. However, any US success in this fighting has implications for control over Caspian Sea oil. A dual oil-gas pipeline was proposed (in the 1990s) to be built from Turkmenistan south through Afghanistan to the Arabian Sea coast in Pakistan. Union Oil of California (UNOCAL) was slated to be the major player in this project. According to one source, "Support for this enterprise appears to have been a major consideration in the Bush administration's decision to attack Afghanistan" (Johnson 2005: 176). Today, the US, along with NATO, is fighting a growing resistance that developed as a result of this attack. However, should its Afghan global war go well, then capital accumulation prospects for US industry in the Caspian region will improve because UNOCAL, or some other US oil company, will be able to build a pipeline from the Caspian.

There is a third area of global warring in the Middle East. Tales circulated in 2006 that there were "U.S. covert operations inside Iran aimed at destabilizing the country and toppling the regime—or preparing for an American attack" (*Asia Times* 2006). The most extensive of these reports is that of Seymour Hersh (2006a), which stated that US combat troops were ordered into Iran to establish contact with anti-Iranian government Kurdish, Baloch, and Arab ethnic groups. Additionally, there were charges that the US was using the Muja-hedin el Khalg (MEK) to conduct cross-border operations between Iraq and Iran. This warring has implications for the capital accumulation of American enterprises. Iran has the fifth largest oil reserves of any country. Regime change there might restore Iran to the client state status it had under the Shah. This would provide direct benefits to the US oil sector and indirect benefits to other US companies. Further, it would put an end to Tehran's plans to organize an oil bourse based on euros rather than dollars, which threatens the petrodollar (Clark 2005: 150–157).

There is a fourth place in the Middle East where the US has been involved in recent global warring. The Bush II regime intervened on the side of Israel in 2006 in Israel's war against Hezbollah. This latter institution—part guerrilla movement, part anti-poverty agency—is to a considerable degree supported by the Iranian government. As such, US warring against Hezbollah reinforces its struggle with Iran for influence in the Persian Gulf. US intervention appears to have been twofold. It provided planning for the actual fighting, especially with regard to aerial operations, and it supplied many of the weapons that the Israelis used against their opponents (Hersh 2006b).

There was a final series of military operations in 2006–2007 involving the US that bears upon the Persian Gulf. This is in the Horn of Africa, Somalia, where Ethiopian troops, trained by the US, attacked and defeated the Islamic Courts Union (ICU). The ICU was judged an Islamist regime, opposed to US interests, and the Americans provided Special Forces and CIA operatives, intelligence, and air support to their Ethiopian proxies. The invasion was a success: the ICU was routed, and the US and the Ethiopians stayed on as an occupying force, although resistance to them was heavy in 2008. Why Somalia? The single-word answer is oil. Somalia juts out into the sea lanes that take Persian Gulf oil from producers to markets. A hostile regime in Somalia could expose those sea lanes to threats and play havoc with oil distribution, jeopardizing the realization of oil profits and the many things that Persian Gulf oil does, with nasty consequences for both the US and the global economy. Thus, America wages global war on Somalia in order to maintain sea lanes and thus protect Persian Gulf 'vital interests', which are all about maintaining the stream of oil-related capital accumulation possibilities.

The preceding does not exhaust the scope of US global warring during 2006–2007. The probability is high, although the evidence is covert, that the US has been involved in military operations in Chad and the Sudan. Chad has oil, and a consortium, led by Exxon, accumulates much of the capital generated by this oil's production. The Chinese have indicated an interest in Chadian oil, and the US finds itself in a situation of increasing competition with China over African oil. The current president of Chad, Idriss Déby, faces a situation of violent resistance to his authoritarian regime. During the past two years, the French have openly provided him with military support. The US has provided overt support in the training of his soldiers and probably covert support in areas of intelligence. US military assistance to Déby is necessary to sustain Exxon's capital accumulation.

The Sudan, like Chad, is an oil producer. Unlike Chad, Sudanese oil is controlled largely by Chinese companies, such as the China National Petroleum Corporation (CNPC). Currently, oil is produced in southern Sudan, but there is a possibility of it being produced to the north and west in southern Darfur. Importantly, "Sudan is believed to hold Africa's greatest unexploited oil reserves" (Hennig 2007: 1). Anti-Khartoum guerrilla movements, including the Sudanese Liberation Army (SLA) and the Justice and Equality Movement (JEM), have emerged, motivated in part by the success of the Sudan People's Liberation Army (SPLA) in southern Chad. In 2003, they began attacking government military installations in Darfur. Khartoum, militarily overextended, responded by encouraging a nomadic Arab militia, the Janjaweed, to attack the SLA and JEM (de Waal 2004). The US military's hand in all this is currently hidden. However, behind the well-meaning propaganda of organizations such as the Save Darfur Coalition (partially funded by the Israelis and right-wing US Christian groups), it is "well documented that the U.S., through its closest African allies, helped train the SLA and JEM Darfuri rebels that initiated Khartoum's violent reaction" (Hennig 2007: 1). This fighting and its brutality had led to calls for military intervention from the 'international community', that is, military forces that are proxies for the US. Of course, such intervention might well satisfy US oil interests because it could lead to regime change that would put at risk Chinese investments in Sudanese oil, resulting in the CNPC being replaced by Exxon.

There is a final area where the US is currently involved in global warring. This is in Colombia (see Lesley Gill, this volume). In principle, this involvement is about the US war on drugs, and Plan Colombia was developed to fight this war. Since 2000, this plan, supplemented by other forms of US foreign assistance, has provided $3.3 billion. This makes Colombia the second largest recipient of US aid in the world, after the Middle East (Vaicius and Isacson 2003). Why is there so much American assistance? Colombia is the fifteenth largest supplier of oil to the US in the world, and Occidental Petroleum is the major America oil company in Colombia. Two leftist guerrilla organizations, the Revolutionary Armed Forces of Colombia (FARC) and the National Liberation Army (ELN), threaten Occidental's operations. Three-fourths of US assistance has gone to the Colombian military and police, who are continually engaged in actions against FARC and ELN. At least part of this assistance has gone to the training and equipping of a Colombia army brigade whose sole function is to protect the Arauca/Caribbean pipeline. Arauca itself "hosts the greatest concentration of US military advisors and has Colombia's worst human rights situation" (Weinberg 2004: 1). The US directly assists Occidental Petroleum to maintain its capital accumulation by riding shotgun on its operations.

In sum, during 2006 and 2007, the Bush II regime was involved in at least seven global wars in South America, Africa, the Middle East, and Central Asia. The cost of just one of these, Gulf War II, has been shown to be enormous. This is a record of intense global warring. Let us move to the conclusion, to draw the strings of the argument together and to explore the meaning of the assertion that President Bush is "extremely visionary."

"Extremely Visionary"

The global warring hypothesis predicts such warring when (1) the scale of competition is worldwide, (2) economic systems are tending toward dysfunctionality, and (3) competition is fierce. Such is the situation in which the US currently finds itself. Its companies compete everywhere, and the key resource upon which they, and all other economies depend, is disappearing. Thus, US companies find themselves in extreme competition with all other competitors. What is a struggling empire to do in such a situation? Immediately after World War II, the US would provide capital and services to its allies in its empire "that would benefit both the larger group [of allies] and itself"; now a debtor nation, "it can no longer" do this (Clark 2005: 26). Under such conditions, according to one observer: "If the US controls the sources of energy of its rivals—Europe, Japan, China and other nations aspiring to be more independent—they win" (Dayaneni and Wing 2002: 2). This is precisely the goal to which US global warring is directed. And this global warring is massive.[11] The evidence provided in this chapter is consistent with the global warring hypothesis, which leaves us with our final concern: in what sense is President Bush "extremely visionary"?

This text has formulated a macro-structural approach to the present. Such explanations are never complete until agency has been included in the argument, and there must be some idea of how the actors in the structures make up their minds, which have a vision that informs action. Bush II is said by one former high official in his regime to have a "mind" that looks "for the simple solution, the bumper sticker description of the problem" (Clarke 2005: 243). In

Rush Limbaugh's interview with President Bush, which led Limbaugh to call his president "extremely visionary," Bush had indicated that he knew his Iraq war to be about oil. Specifically, he said "extremists" would win if withdrawal happened, and this would put them "in a position to use oil as a tool to black-mail the West' (in *Rawstory* 2006: 1). The other side of this hermeneutic is that if the US wins in Iraq, and in the other places where there is petroleum, then it 'controls' the oil and gets to be the blackmailer. This is Bush's vision. But it can be conjectured that this vision is not unique to Bush. Rather, some version of it is likely shared by other tough guys in the killing elite at the top of the current US imperial regime. Such a vision might be speculated to be part of the uncon-scious, unreflected upon life-worlds of the Cheneys and Rumsfelds of this world, informing their actions and thereby giving agency to imperial macro-structures. Since Gulf War I it has been the US killing elite's vision to control Iraq's oil, and it is estimated that this conflict plus the ensuing aerial blockade imposed by the Clinton administration led to perhaps 500,000 civilian deaths. It is further estimated that Gulf War II has caused about 655,000 civilian deaths.[12] This is roughly 1,155,000 deaths in a single theater of US global warring, an extremely large number of innocents killed to achieve the US killing elite's vision of being blackmailer to the world. So it is in this sense that Rush Limbaugh had it right when he proclaimed his president to be "extremely visionary."

In August 2002, Bush II did not feel the "need" to explain anything, although he allowed that maybe "somebody" should do so. This chapter has offered a global warring explanation of the foreign policy of his administration. Consider a possible implication of this explanation. Many people know that there is global *warming* and that the fate of the earth hangs upon what is done about it; fewer know that there is intensive global *warring*. Perhaps the fate of the earth will be decided by imperial global warriors with extreme visions well before the devastation of global warming takes effect. Or perhaps the world's fate will be a grim concatenation of global warring and warming.

Stephen Reyna is an associate at the Max Planck Institute of Social Anthropology. His publications include *Wars Without End* (1990), *Studying War: Anthropological Perspectives* (1994, co-edited with R. E. Downs), and *Deadly Developments: War, Capitalism, and the Modern State* (1998, co-edited with R. E. Downs). He authored the theoretical volume *Connections: Brain, Mind and Culture in a Social Anthropology* (2002) and has recently published "Waiting: The Sorcery of Modernity, Transnational Corporations, Oil and Terrorism in Chad" (2007). His research inter-ests include contemporary social and cultural theory, power and conflict, and eco-logical and environmental anthropology. He is currently formulating a domination approach to the political economy of oil.

Notes

1. Much of the small war literature is concerned with ethnic conflict (Fearon and Laitin 2003; Lake and Rothchild 1998).
2. Richards (1996) offers an insightful critique of Kaplan's "new barbarism." Other questionable strands of the small war literature have emphasized primordial ethnic conflict (Enzenberger 1994) and greed (Collier and Hoeffler 2001). Critiques of crude ethnic essentialism and greed theory include Ballentine and Sherman (2003), Marchal and Messiant (2002), and Reno (2004).
3. Hippler (1988: 2), who in the late 1980s had the task of explaining LIC to NATO, explicitly linked LIC to small wars.
4. Since the early days of the Cold War, leftists argued for an imperial America, especially Harry Magdoff (1969), who developed the view, as the title of his book later put it, that there could be *Imperialism Without Colonies* (Magdoff 1978). Center or right social scientists demurred, insisting that America might be hegemonic but certainly not imperial (Keohane 1990). Since the attack on the twin towers, all social scientists, according to Bowden (2002), have been "reinventing imperialism." Harvey (2003) analyzes contemporary US imperialism from the left; Ferguson (2004) from the right; and Bacevich (2002), Johnson (2005), and Mann (2003) from what might be termed a 'progressive center'.
5. Useful texts discussing the global warring that led up to the Seven Years' War include Calloway (1990), Horowitz (1978), and Parkman (1983).
6. There has been a major debate in German historical literature concerning the causes of World War I that pitted the leftist Fritz Fischer against the rightist Gerhard Ritter. Fischer ([1961] 1967) argued that Germany was responsible for the war's occurrence, whereas Ritter (1972) disputed this view. However, both positions share certain commonalities. Both authors understood Germany to be a latecomer to imperialism. In our terms, this means that the global warrings of Britain, France, Spain, and Portugal, among others, had pretty much divided up the world, leaving little for Germany. Both Ritter and Fischer maintained that the German elite chafed at this constraint and attempted to relax it through the instrumentality of war.
7. As David Harvey (2003: 12) puts it: "Global capitalism has experienced a chronic and enduring problem of overaccumulation since the 1970s." This has been the cause of the global slowdown (Duménil and Lévy 2004; Mandel 1989). Brenner (2003) has applied the overaccumulation argument to the post-1970 woes of the US economy.
8. Hirsch, Bezdek, and Wendling (2005: 1–2) survey 12 studies predicting when Hubbert's peak will occur. Seven of them say it will be by or before 2010.
9. There is an enormous literature on the 'environmental crisis' that has existed since the 1980s. This includes Marxist (Foster 2000, 2002; Koven 2002), Christian (King 2002), social work (Hoff and McNutt 1994), and even postmodern (Gare 1995) takes on the crisis. Except for the Marxists, this literature rarely links environmental problems explicitly with capitalism. There is a smaller, and declining, literature that dismisses the suggestion that there is an environmental crisis. These texts are usually supported by conservative think tanks or publishers. For example, Robert Bailey's (2002) book that labels the environmental crisis a "myth" was a product of the right-wing Competitive Enterprise Institute. ExxonMobil, one of the chief environmental crisis deniers, has funded the Competitive Enterprise Institute's work on environmental problems (Mooney 2005).
10. A recent *Base Structure Report* of the Defense Department "gives details on some 725 foreign bases in thirty-eight countries" (Johnson 2005: 154). This excludes numerous bases that are secret and tend to belong to intelligence agencies. Another Defense Department report notes that US military personnel are found in 153 countries (ibid.: 154).
11. There is extensive literature arguing that in some way the US is fighting to control oil in Iraq and beyond. Useful texts making this point include Clark (2005), Everest (2004), Harvey (2003), and Klare (2004). Stokes (2004) discusses US military action in Colombia, while Foster (2006) does so for Africa.

12. There is debate over civilian mortality figures in Iraq due to war. The figures for Gulf War I and the naval blockade of Iraq are from an FAO study (Mahajan 2001), while those during Gulf War II up to 2006 are from a *Lancet* study (Burnham et al. 2006).

References

Asia Times. 2006. "Tehran Insider Tells of US Black Ops." 25 April. http://www.atimes.com/ atimes/Middle_East/HD25Ak02.html.

Bacevich, Andrew. 2002. *American Empire: The Realities and Consequences of U.S. Diplomacy*. Cambridge, MA: Harvard University Press.

Bailey, Robert. 2002. *Global Warming and Other Eco Myths*. Washington, DC: Competitive Enterprise Institute.

Ballentine, Karen, and Jake Sherman. 2003. *The Political Economy of Armed Conflict: Beyond Greed and Grievance*. Boulder, CO: Lynne Rienner.

Bennis, Phyllis, and Erik Leaver. 2005. "The Iraq Quagmire: The Mounting Costs of War and the Case for Bringing Home the Troops." *Foreign Policy in Focus*, 31 August. http://www.fpif.org/fpiftxt/467.

Bernstein, Jared, and Sylvia Allegretto. 2005. *The State of Working America 2004/2005*. Ithaca, NY: Cornell University Press.

Bluestone, Barry, and Bennett Harrison. 1982. *The Deindustrialization of America*. New York: Basic Books.

Blum, William. 2002. *Killing Hope: U.S. Military and CIA Interventions Since World War II*. Monroe, ME: Common Courage Press.

Bond, Patrick. 2005. "Capitalism: Degrading and Destructive." Paper presented at the Capitalism Nature Socialism Conference, Toronto, York University.

Boot, Max. 2003. *The Savage Wars of Peace: Small Wars and the Rise of American Power*. New York: Basic Books.

Bowden, Brett. 2002. "Reinventing Imperialism in the Wake of September 11." *Alternatives: Turkish Journal of International Relations* 1, no. 2. http://www.alternativesjournal.net/ volume1/number2/bowden.htm.

Brenner, Robert. 2003. *The Boom and the Bubble: The United States in the World Economy*. London: Verso

Burnham, Gilbert, Riyadh Lafta, Shannon Doocy, and Les Roberts. 2006. "Mortality after the 2003 Invasion of Iraq: A Cross-Sectional Cluster Sample Survey." *Lancet* 368, no. 9545: 1421–1428.

Calloway, Colin G. 1990. *The Western Abenakis of Vermont 1600–1800: War, Migration and the Survival of an Indian People*. Norman: University of Oklahoma Press.

Clark, William. 2005. *Petrodollar Warfare: Oil, Iraq, and the Future of the Dollar*. Gabriola Island, Canada: New Society Publishers.

Cohen, Elliot A. 2001. "World War IV: Let's Call This Conflict What It Is." *Wall Street Journal*, 20 November. http://www.opinionjournal.com/editorial/feature.html?id = 95001493.

Collier, Paul, and Anke Hoeffler. 2001. *Greed and Grievance in Civil War*. Washington, DC: World Bank.

Cowie, Jefferson, and Joseph Heathcott, eds. 2003. *Beyond the Ruins: The Meaning of Deindustrialization*. Ithaca, NY: Cornell University Press.

Dayaneni, Gopal, and Bob Wing. 2002. "Oil and War." *War Times*, June. http://www.war-times .org/issues/3art1.html.

de Waal, Alex. 2004. "Counter-Insurgency on the Cheap." *London Review of Books* 26, no. 15. http://www.lrb.co.uk/v26/n15/waal01_.html.

Dobbs, Lou. 2006. *War on the Middle Class*. New York: Viking.

Duménil, Gérard, and Dominique Lévy. 2004. *Capital Resurgent: Roots of the Neoliberal Revolution*. Cambridge, MA: Harvard University Press.

Enzenberger, Hans Magnus. 1994. *Civil Wars: From L.A. to Bosnia*. New York: Free Press.

Everest, Larry. 2004. *Oil, Power and Empire: Iraq and the U.S. Global Agenda*. Monroe, ME.: Common Courage Press.

Fearon, James, and David Laitin. 2003. "Ethnicity, Insurgency, and Civil War." *American Political Science Review* 97, no. 1: 75–90.

Feldman, Charles, and Stan Wilson. 2003. "Ex-CIA Director: U.S. Faces World War IV." *CNN.com*, 3 April. http://edition.cnn.com/2003/US/04/03/sprj.irq.woolsey.world.war/.

Ferguson, Niall. 2004. *Colossus: The Price of America's Empire*. New York: Penguin.

Fischer, Fritz. [1961] 1967. *Germany's Aims in the First World War*. New York: Norton.

Foster, John Bellamy. 2000. *Marx's Ecology: Materialism and Nature*. New York: Monthly Review Press.

_____. 2002. *Ecology Against Capitalism*. New York: Monthly Review Press.

_____. 2006. "A Warning to Africa: The New U.S. Imperial Grand Strategy." *Monthly Review* 58, no. 2. http://www.monthlyreview.org/0606jbf.htm.

Gare, Arran. 1995. *Postmodernism and the Environmental Crisis*. London: Routledge.

Harvey, David. 2003. *The New Imperialism*. Oxford: Oxford University Press.

Henderson, Errol, and J. David Singer. 2002. "New Wars and Rumors of 'New Wars.'" *International Interactions* 28, no. 2: 165–190.

Hennig, Rainer. 2007. "UN Darfur Vote Turns Scramble for Sudan's Oil." *Afrol News*, 10 September. http://www.afrol.com/articles/13921.

Hersh, Seymour. 2006a. "The Iran Plans." *New Yorker*, 17 April, 30–31.

_____. 2006b. "The Next Act." *New Yorker*, 27 November, 94–107.

Hightower, Jim. 2006. "A Plan for Victory in Iraq." *Hightower Lowdown*, 13 November. http://www.hightowerlowdown.org/node/978.

Hippler, Jochen. 1988. "Low Intensity Warfare and Its Implications for NATO." http://www.jochen-hippler.de/Aufsatze/low-intensity_conflict/low-intensity_conflict.html.

Hirsch, Robert L., Roger Bezdek, and Robert Wendling. 2005. *Peaking of World Oil Production: Impacts, Mitigation, and Risk Management*. Report commissioned by the US Department of Energy, February. http://www.hilltoplancers.org/stories/hirsch0502.pdf.

Hoff, Marie D., and John G. McNutt, eds. 1994. *The Global Environmental Crisis: Implications for Social Welfare and Social Work*. Brookfield, VT: Ashgate.

Horowitz, David. 1978. *The First Frontier: The Indian Wars and America's Origins, 1607–1776*. New York: Simon and Shuster.

Johnson, Chalmers. 2005. *The Sorrows of Empire: Militarism, Secrecy, and the End of the Republic*. New York: Owl Books.

Kaldor, Mary. 2006. *New Wars and Old Wars: Organized Violence in a Global Era*. 2nd ed. Cambridge: Polity Press.

Kaldor, Mary, and Basker Vashee, eds. 1997. *New Wars*. London: Pinter.

Kaplan, Robert D. 1994. "The Coming Anarchy: How Scarcity, Crime, Overpopulation, Tribalism, and Disease Are Rapidly Destroying the Fabric of our Planet." *Atlantic Monthly*, February, 44–76.

Karliner, John. 1997. *The Corporate Threat*. Berkeley: University of California Press.

Keohane, Robert. 1990. *After Hegemony*. Englewood Cliffs, NJ: Prentice Hall.

King, Carolyn M. 2002. *Habitat of Grace: Biology, Christianity and the Global Environmental Crisis*. Portsmouth, NH: Heinemann.

Klare, Michael. 1986. "Low Intensity Conflicts: The New U.S. Strategic Doctrine." *Nation*, 1 February.

_____. 2004. *Blood and Oil: The Dangers and Consequences of America's Growing Dependency on Imported Petroleum*. New York: Metropolitan Books

Koven, Joel. 2002. *The End of Nature, the End of Capitalism or the End of the World?* London: Zed.

Kunstler, James. 2006. *The Long Emergency: Surviving the End of Oil*. New York: Grove Press.

Lake, David, and Donald Rothchild. 1998. *The International Spread of Ethnic Conflict*. Princeton, NJ: Princeton University Press.

Magdoff, Harry. 1969. *The Age of Imperialism*. New York: Monthly Review Press.
_____. 1978. *Imperialism Without Colonies*. New York: Monthly Review Press.
Mahajan, Rahul. 2001. "We Think the Price Is Worth It." *FAIR Extra*, November/December. http://www.fair.org/index.php?page = 1084.
Mandel, Ernest. 1989. *Late Capitalism*. 2nd ed. London: Verso.
Mann, Michael. 2003. *Incoherent Empire*. London: Verso.
Marchal, Roland, and Christine Messiant. 2002. "De l'avidité des rebelles: L'analyse économique de la guerre civile selon Paul Collier." *Critique Internationale* 16: 58–69.
_____. 2003. "Les guerres civiles à l'ère de la globalisation: Nouvelles réalités et nouveaux paradigmes." *Critique Internationale* 18: 91–112.
McKibben, Bill. 2006. *The End of Nature*. New York: Random House.
Miller, Rich. 2005. "Too Much Money." *Business Week*, 11 July. http://www.businessweek.com/magazine/content/05_28/b3942001_mz001.htm.
Mooney, Chris. 2005. "Some Like it Hot." *Mother Jones*, May/June. http://www.motherjones.com/news/feature/2005/05/some_like_it_hot.html.
NIC (National Intelligence Council). 2004. "Mapping the Global Future: Report of the National Intelligence Council's 2020 Project." http://www.dni.gov/nic/NIC_2020_project.html.
NRC (National Research Council). 2005. "Looking Forward: S&T for the 21st Century." http://www.nrc-cnrc.gc.ca/aboutUs/ren/nrc-foresight-sum_e.html.
OECD (Organisation for Economic Co-operation and Development). 2002. "Intra-industry and Intra-firm Trade and the Internationalisation of Production." Paris: OECD. http://www.oecd.org/dataoecd/6/18/2752923.pdf.
Olsen, William. 1985. "Airpower in Low Intensity Conflict in the Middle East." Ninth Air University Airpower Symposium, 11–13 March, Maxwell Air Force Base, Alabama.
Parkman, Francis. 1983. *France and England in North America*. 2 vols. New York: Viking Press.
_____. 2006. *American Theocracy: The Peril and Politics of Radical Religion, Oil, and Borrowed Money*. New York: Viking Press.
Podhoretz, Norman. 2002. "How to Win World War IV." *Commentary Magazine*, February.
Porter, Michael. 1986. *Competition in Global Industries*. Cambridge, MA: Harvard Business School Press.
Prestowitz, Clyde. 2005. *Three Billion New Capitalists: The Great Shift of Wealth and Power to the East*. New York: Basic Books.
RawStory. 2006. "Bush Tells Rush He's 'Deeply Concerned' about the U.S. Leaving the Middle East." 1 November. http://www.rawstory.com/news/2006/Bush_tells_Rush_hes_deeply_concerned_1101.html.
Reno, William. 2004. "The Empirical Challenge to Economic Analyses of Conflicts." Presented at the SSRC-sponsored conference, "The Economic Analysis of Conflict: Problems and Prospects." Washington, DC, 19–20 April.
Reyna, Stephen. 2005a. "American Imperialism? 'The Current Runs Swiftly.'" *Focaal* 45: 129–161.
_____. 2005b. "'We Exist to Fight': The Killing Elite and Bush II's Iraq War." *Social Analysis* 49, no. 1: 190–197.
Richards, Paul. 1996. *Fighting for the Rain Forest: War, Youth, and Resources in Sierra Leone*. Portsmouth, NH: Heinemann.
Ritter, Gerhard. 1972. *The Sword and the Scepter: The Problems of Militarism in Germany*. Vol. 3: *The Tragedy of Statesmanship: Bethmann Hollweg as War Chancellor, 1914–1917*. Coral Cables, FL: University of Miami Press. Schultz, George. 1986. "Low Intensity Warfare: The Challenge of Ambiguity." US Department of State. *Current Policy*, no. 783 (January).
Shaw, Martin. 2000. "The Contemporary Mode of Warfare: Mary Kaldor's Theory of the New Wars." *Review of International Political Economy* 7, no. 1: 171–180.
Steger, Manfred B. 2003. *Globalization: A Very Short Introduction*. Oxford: Oxford University Press.
Steingart, Gabor. 2006. "How Globalization Drives Down Western Wages." *Spiegel Online International*, 16 October. http://www.spiegel.de/international/0,1518,436976,00.html.

Stokes, Doug. 2004. *America's Other War: Terrorizing Colombia*. London: Zed Press.

Swedberg, Richard. 2005. *Max Weber Dictionary*. Stanford, CA: Stanford University Press.

Szafranski, Richard. 1990. "Thinking About 'Small Wars.'" *Parameters* 20, no. 3: 39–49. http://www.carlisle.army.mil/USAWC/PARAMETERS/1990/szafran.htm.

Tures, John. 2003. "United States Military Operations in the New World Order." *American Diplomacy.org*. http://www.unc.edu/depts/diplomat/archives_roll/2003_01-03/tures_military/tures_military.html

Ullman, John. 1988. *The Anatomy of Industrial Decline: Productivity, Investment and Location in U.S. Manufacturing*. Westport, CT: Quorum.

USMC (United States Marine Corps). [1940] 1996. *Small Wars Manual*. Manhattan, KS: Sunflower University Press.

Vaicius, Ingrid, and Adam Isacson. 2003. "The 'War on Drugs' Meets the 'War on Terror.'" *International Policy Report*, February. http://www.ciponline.org/colombia/0302ipr.htm.

Valenzuela, Manuel. 2007. "Operation Iraq Forever." Information Clearing House, 16 May. http://www.informationclearinghouse.info/article17710.htm.

Wallerstein, Immanuel. 2003. *The Decline of U.S. Power: The U.S. in a Chaotic World*. New York: New Press.

Weinberg, Bill. 2004. "Oil Makes U.S. Raise Military Stakes in Colombia." *CommonDreams.org*, 26 November. http://www.commondreams.org/views04/1126-05.htm.

Yates, Michael D. 2005. "A Statistical Portrait of the U.S. Working Class." *Monthly Review* 56, no. 11: 12–31. http://www.monthlyreview.org/0405yates.htm.

Yergin, Daniel. 1993. *The Prize: The Epic Quest for Oil, Money, and Power*. New York: Free Press.

Chapter 3

GLOBAL FRACTURES

Carolyn Nordstrom

Crisis. This investigation starts with a specific incident of political violence and then follows the complex layers of associations making this event possible that move, quite literally, across the globe. To summarize this point, and this chapter: Does a crisis—say, political violence—extend across the borders of sovereignty and temporality to flow into the personal lives, economic markets, and political systems of the world across war and peace? Does this then represent crises on all these global levels? And to what result?

Fracture Zones

People don't want to look at the big picture, because they are opening Pandora's box. What happens is that they open the box and see all kinds of trails. Who's linked in? What are the linkages? There are always bigger boys out there.

Notes for this chapter begin on page 84.

So it remains an unspoken topic.
It's like there are two levels of knowledge. The first is the face people want out there: "Sure, there's security, sure, we trust the reputable corporations ..."
And then there's what is really going on.

— Sheila Gonzales, LA Port Authority, personal interview, 2004

This chapter introduces the idea of 'fracture zones'—lines of instability that radiate out from specific and discernible crises. Fractures constitute vulnerabilities in trade networks, financial systems, economic enterprises, and socio-political services so great that the very viability of these institutions (as they define the modern state) is undermined. I followed these pathways ethnographically for over three years between 2001 and 2006—from the frontlines of political violence in Southern Africa into global supply chains and the complex relationships of extra/legal and extra/state networks passing through Europe, the US, and parts of Southern Asia.[1] During this fieldwork, I spoke with, and at times traveled with, those working all sides of the law and the state.

The example I focus on here is war, but this is not the only crisis that generates such zones. Fracture zones are often hidden in the shadows of analysis of global power relations, and thus their impact on the economic and political realities of the world often goes unrecognized. There is a logical reason for this. Fracture lines run internationally and follow power abuses, pathological profiteering, institutionalized inequalities, and human rights violations—actions that fill the pockets and secure the dominance of some while damaging the lives of others.

I seek to demonstrate that what are taken to be commonplace international acts of power surrounding political violence are neither logical nor innocent. They set in motion lethal instabilities that can topple political and economic systems in peacetime locales around the globe that are far removed from the site of crisis. Fractures radiating out from a war zone along countries at peace do not appear dangerous. Until a small shock. All that is needed is a slight pressure—an economic downturn, a political conflagration, a natural disaster, an armed attack—and the lines of instability splinter, no longer able to support the society's basic service institutions. Peacetime nations that are instrumental in creating these fractures can crumble along these lines if fractures are sufficiently widespread and institutionalized.

The irony is that people often take these actions as pathways to achieving and maintaining power when the truth is far different.

Crisis

The manifests and all the documents said 'scrap metal', but it sure looked like a MIG fighter when it came out.

— Shipping inspector, personal interview, 2002

War, at its most immediate, personal, and ontological level, is about the experience of violence, the rendering of human flesh. A person walking to the market is hit by a bomb blast. In the unlikely event that this casualty should be recorded in the international media, readers in peacetime locales around the world would tend to find this event tragic but far removed from the political, economic, and personal realities of their lives and countries. Even the manufacturers of the bomb would in all likelihood open their newspapers over coffee and see little association between this war—in terms of casualties and potential casualties—and their own industrial peacetime country.

But what, exactly, constitutes a crisis? What are the boundaries we draw around it? Perhaps more accurately, what boundaries are we taught to see and not see, and what politics defines these? This is situated in Laclau's (2000) fundamental question: "What is inherent in the hegemonic relationship?"

Philosopher Alain Badiou (2003, 2004) suggests that delving into the question of ontology is in fact delving into what he has termed 'multiple multiplicities'. He breaks with modernist-based ideals, which posit that all complex phenomena—all multiplicity—can be broken into constituent parts that can ultimately be traced to singularities. In other words, he does not accept the modernist equation that underneath complexity (many/much) is singularity (isolatable 'ones'). Underneath all multiplicity is multiplicity. Complexity *is*. Reducing any question to a single causal equation, a linear sequence of isolate factors, or a combination of individual generative foci is misleading—the result of knowledge traditions that break the flow of reality into unrealistic divisions.

For example, violence is first and foremost an ontological reality and only secondarily an epistemological investigation. Certainly, the bomb is a locatable event and a personal experience. But it is not singular. It is (quite literally) simultaneously embedded in the person hit, the larger networks of interplay among people and events, the war itself, and the global values and structures that sustain these realities. All of these arenas mutually define one another—a fact critical to understanding the ontology of fractures.

To explain, in Badiou's approach to multiplicity, the bomb blast victim is situated in a larger series of variously embedded, intertwined, overlapping, and expanding concentric layers of contextual crises. With this event, a complicated network of personal survival actions, health care endeavors and providers, preparations for upcoming acts of violence, and so on are set into motion. Cognitive and emotive reactions configure exchanges. These experiences are grounded in, and molded by, larger constellations of considerations: military decisions, rebel retaliations, government programs both altruistic and corrupt, social services, non-governmental organizations, networks of family and friends, profiteers, foreign interventions, natural and human disasters. The bomb is both a 'thing' and a product of global politics and economics, and survival entails understanding the full compendium of this knowledge. Persons, events, structurations, power, places, flows: none can be taken as singularities. All are irreducibly interrelated.

To study just the local, the individual, the cognitive or the emotive, the market, politics, culture, or globalization might be accepted in academia, but such heuristic divisions are a death sentence in the midst of crisis.

Multiple multiplicities.

In order to capture this, Badiou focuses on 'situation'.[2] A situation accommodates what 'is'. What '*is*', then, for this victim of a bomb blast? The personal carnage, clearly. Yet in addition, a number of interrelating fractures radiate out from here. For example:

- People may find themselves unable to gain life-saving necessaries, since the resources of the country have been diverted from social good to military goods.
- Countries may find that their physical resources are garnished to pay for war supplies globally.
- Multi/national companies may find these conditions ripe for forcing tax breaks, providing substandard wages and working conditions, exploiting resources, and profiteering.
- Multiple violences then emerge. As political violence escalates in the world today, so too does criminal and domestic violence. War casualties may survive military violence to face rape, brutality, or death at the hands of those known to them or be targeted by international criminal rings that prey on the war-afflicted for sexual, agricultural, and domestic labor worldwide.

Here we can see both the constellation of factors creating fractures and the fact that no single crisis or embedded system of inequality (in economics, financial systems, profiteering, violence, etc.) can be understood in and of itself. None stand as analytical singularities. Taken as multiplicity, the ways in which these fractures are inculcated into the defining dynamics of the world's econo-political systems, plus the ways in which they cause dangerous vulnerabilities to the very foundations of governing and market systems, can be seen and perhaps changed. But these realities are not transparent: those who benefit from exploiting them work hard to render these processes invisible. Fractures are etched as undetectably as possible into the institutions grounding political and economic relations worldwide. The tendency in research analysis to focus on a single issue (economics, political studies, criminal investigations) helps hide the very realities that it purports to explain.

Mapping Economic Fractures—Invisible Economies

Sitting at the airport in a country at war, watching all the supplies being loaded (both legally and illegally), from weapons to life's simple necessities, I turned to ask the man next to me: What kind of money does this add up to for those who control this flow? He replied:
Money beyond counting.
Almost beyond thinking.
Money like you own a country.

— Field notes, 2002

The bomb striking flesh in rural Sudan, the hills of the Karen region in Myanmar, or the back alleyways of Baghdad is a cosmopolitan product. Like most war-related supplies, it generally comes from peacetime industrial locations. These supplies are not limited to weapons systems. Visualize the global flows that make this 'situation', to use Badiou's terminology, possible: industries that build the transport systems from factory line to blast (ships, trains, airplanes, delivery systems), produce and provide fuel for the transport, train personnel to deliver weapons, provide communications systems to coordinate war, and furnish food, clothing, medicines, lodging, and other necessities to keep the participants alive. Other flows include the values, behaviors, and exchanges that sustain these vast interactive systems. The examples extend throughout the global economic universe.

These commodities and services come at cosmopolitan rates and require payments in cosmopolitan currencies.[3] The national tender of war-afflicted countries is seldom accepted in international markets, but their resources are. Precious minerals, gems, hardwoods, foods, drugs, undocumented labor— these constitute the fodder for industrial dreams. Militaries, political violence, and power struggles are expensive by all economic standards. The complex exchanges of cosmopolitan supplies and raw resources represents a significant percentage of the gross world product.

Every year, trillions of dollars flow along these transaction lines extra-legally (see Nordstrom 2000, 2004, 2007). A great deal is written about the extra-legal trade in arms, illegal narcotics, and trafficking in people—often called the three most lucrative illegal practices. While accurate statistics do not exist by virtue of their illegality, taken together as a whole, these three trade systems generate around a trillion unrecorded (extra-legal) dollars every year (Naím 2005). While authors such as Naylor (2005) take into consideration extra-legal gold transactions and the global impact of illicit banking practices as well as arms transfers, many assessments of the extra-legal do not add in such monies, much less the unrecorded profits on non-weapons military supplies (such as medicines, transport, and communication systems), undocumented labor, white-collar crime, or the illicit trade in everyday goods ranging from information technology to food.[4] For example, my research suggests that as much money can be made on extra-legal sales of pharmaceuticals as on illegal narcotics (Nordstrom 2007). The trillions generated through the extra-legal as a whole thus represents a significant percentage of the approximately $70 trillion making up the legal gross world domestic product.

Virtually all extra-legal activities intersect with state institutions and practices: in laundering profits to legitimacy; in using state systems of transport, communications, and industry; and in wresting political authority in these processes. Thus, fracture zones following the extra-legal do not run apart from state institutions but rather through the very heart of them.

Value and Values—Linking Profiteering to the Failures of Social/National Services

> Some cocaine smugglers just aren't bad people. When I've arrested some of them, they say, "Hey, I work 18 hours a day, and this is the only way I can feed my family." And I say, "Hey, it's illegal and I have to bust you."

But at the end of the day, the whole system doesn't hold together totally. Who makes the rules? The dominant class. How does this compare with some poor family with three kids who gets chucked out of their flat? What are the morals? Where is the good and the bad? How do we balance the values of money with caring societies?

> — David Hesketh, International Assistance Branch of Her Majesty's
> Customs and Excise, UK, personal interview, 2002

Something else is sold along with the commodities that follow the war zone/ industrial center circuit: value systems. In the journey from production to practice, the idea emerges that the predictable destruction that comes with warring is acceptable—commendable, even. This idea becomes professionalized and, simultaneously, rendered invisible to formal accounting.

This one fact results in a number of fractures: if casualties are recognized, medicines and health services must be made available to treat them, social services are needed to support them, and laws must be implemented to protect them.

There is a subtle but powerful interconnection between profiteering and the failure of social and national services: profiteering does not produce taxes/ social services. As an example, the harbormaster in Cape Town, South Africa, pointed out to me: "Consider the true impact: under-declaration of goods [a form of smuggling] creates a huge tax gap in South Africa. We figure we lose $1 billion a year."

Profiteering that conjoins the legal and extra-legal is an offshore loop,[5] ensuring that value is restricted to a few. This is the institutionalization of inequality. Of not seeing. It rests on what Paul Farmer (2004) calls "pathologies of power."[6] The 'something' sold along with the weapon is the (erroneous) belief that the economic dominion based on these profits can shield against social collapse.

Fractures in Finance and Sovereignty—Using Invisible Profits to Manipulate Nations

> I guess we know it. But we don't. Because this all works by not asking. We don't ask the site manager how he got a system up and running. He does, or he doesn't. We ask for the formal reports. We know not to ask for the, ah, details.
>
> This is how the vast non-formal works—how it is both possible and undisclosed at the same time. It is a fact of all business.
>
> — CFO of a well-known multinational corporation, personal interview, 2002

Crime rises in contexts of political violence. Crises are embedded in crises; profits are layered in profits; beliefs are hidden in values. These are Badiou's multiple multiplicities—intertwined, overlapping, interpenetrating contexts. Contexts that, in this case, ripple across all of the world's continents. Castells (1998) and Strange (1996) were among the first to point out that as we moved toward the twenty-first century, criminal systems were becoming dynamic transnational networks, with the constituent trade policies, business agreements, mediation specialists, financial frameworks, and social codes that accompany all multinationals. Authors such as Naím (2005), Naylor (2005), van Schendel and Abraham (2005), Lilley (2006), MacGaffey and Bazanguissa-Ganga (2000), and Perkins (2004) have provided more recent in-depth explorations of these processes, showing the complex linkages of crime and state.

In following these linkages it becomes clear that little corruption is solely national. The vast majority involves international associations, often legitimate businesses. In the cosmopolitan commodities-for-raw-resources circuit (colloquially referred to, e.g., as the blood-diamond or arms-for-oil circuit), national elites may bank considerable profit. But it is the multinational corporations that gain the resources ensuring industrial hegemony and transnational political power.

All extra-legal proceeds must be laundered into legality to have value. Trillions of dollars are laundered into the legal economy in uncharted ways. They enter through businesses, stock markets, financial centers, loans, and multinational transfers. The elite in this extra-legal world can move monies in such a way as to shape the economies of smaller countries, as well as parts of markets in larger ones. As John McDowell and Gary Novis (2001) write:

> Unchecked, money laundering can erode the integrity of a nation's financial institutions. Due to the high integration of capital markets, money laundering can also adversely affect currencies and interest rates. Ultimately, laundered money flows into global financial systems, where it can undermine national economies and currencies.
>
> In some emerging market countries, these illicit proceeds may dwarf government budgets, resulting in a loss of control of economic policy by governments. Indeed, in some cases, the sheer magnitude of the accumulated asset base of laundered proceeds can be used to corner markets—or even small economies.

McDowell and Novis base their conclusions on such considerations as the Asian stock market collapse in the 1990s, which was in part related to extra-legal financial transactions, and on instances of the manipulation of emergent economies across the globe. Other authors (e.g., Lilley 2006) have added examples of successful extra-legal moguls such as drug lords, who control more money than the gross domestic products of their home countries and, in the sheer act of manipulating their laundered investments, are able to influence national markets. Volkov (2002) demonstrates how the collapse of the Soviet Union and the emergence of the economy of contemporary Russia have been shaped by extra-legal networks ranging from mafias to business leaders. My own work documents the ways in which highly successful businesspeople working both sides of the law can hold political offices and control national markets to their own benefit (Nordstrom 2007).

Splintering across Daily Life—Embedding Fractures within General Societies

> In truth, society deserves the type of crime it gets. Looking at crime honestly raises uncomfortable questions. About the inequality in society. About who holds power in society.
>
> — Scotland Yard Detective Richard Flynn, personal interview, 2002

Trade routes are not easy to set up: transport is expensive, borders must be breached, security forces enlisted or avoided, markets arranged. Once a system of routes has been established, all kinds of commodities and people can be moved, including arms, drugs, children forced into sexual and agricultural labor, fake pharmaceuticals, substandard industrial components, banned weaponry, endangered species, and body parts. Such routes easily extend worldwide. In 2005, I took a photograph in northern Burma, near the border with China, of a shop (called, curiously, Foot Cure Push the Oil) advertising "Massage: Young Ladies from China, Russia, Vietnam" in three languages. It sits next to stores offering gold bars, counterfeit Gucci fashions, live pangolins, banned pornography, and phony medicines. A strong set of trade routes links this remote village global mart along new silk roads that now travel easily from Europe and Asia to Africa and the Americas. Much of this runs in the shadows.

As Rear Admiral Peter Neffenger of the Coast Guard explained to me in a conversation we had about security at US ports in 2004:

> You can identify lots of problems if you study *all* smuggling. If you figure out smuggling for the more common, less dangerous goods as well as well as the more harmful ones, you can begin to get a much better handle on how the more dangerous stuff is moved. You have to look at the whole picture.
>
> Levi's, Nikes ... there's the biggest threat. You have a smuggling route, and you can put anything into it to move it. You move counterfeit Levi's, you can put weapons into this supply line and move them. A route is a route is a route.

When the pathologically abusive—that which violates human rights and endangers lives, such as forced labor and fake medicines—is institutionalized within social systems, values attaching to it come to have a far broader impact. The lines of il/legality are strongly blurred. Average businesses use undocumented labor; average citizens fuel the sex industry, make and buy goods ranging from counterfeit information technology to medicines, carry a fake Gucci.

These actions involve deeper values: how many people getting a massage at the Foot Cure Push the Oil from an underage person forced into the sex industry, in Burma or the US, will empathize with the child's plight? By extension, how many will be outraged by the bombing that hit the teen in a faraway war? How many will work to uphold the laws that prevent that teen from being trafficked (should he or she have the luck to survive), especially if they in any way profit from these actions?[7] Here, the sheer pervasive institutionalization of fractures is visible, inculcated in the daily practices enacted across a broad swath of society—indeed, across continents.

A World at Risk—Building Sovereignty on Fracture Zones

You want to know who we most commonly catch breaking the law? The big name corporations whose products we all buy everyday. We bust them, and they just call their 'friends' in DC.[8] We then get a call telling us to drop the case. We have no choice, the call comes from people too powerful for us to fight. This is the post-9/11 world we have to work in.

— US Customs official, who asked to remain anonymous, 2004

Sovereignty requires cash—not a weak national currency, but one that trades on international markets. Cash requires resources. Resources require cheap laborers. The greater the labor, the greater the sovereignty/profit. The cheaper the 'bodies', the greater the sovereignty—as long as it is not officially recognized. States find themselves in a position where they gain perceived economic and political strength by breaking state law. The result is the same whether this involves Western corporations providing weapons systems for oil contracts (Cilliers and Dietrich 2000) or state complicity in large-scale resource-exploitation and criminal rings (see Global Witness 2005a, 2005b, 2006). Sovereignty is in part built, quite literally, on the backs of people who cannot escape the losing side of profiteering.[9]

States, like all political organizations, are an experiment: they can fail at what they intend. Indeed, all political forms eventually fail, collapsing under the weight of fractures to be replaced by new and emergent forms of political organization. The Mozambicans have a term for the rise and fall of political systems: *dumba nengi*, which means 'vote with your feet'. If voters believe that the political regime they are living under is abusive or unresponsive, they are encouraged to leave it and find or create another. With astute political irony, they refer to the large, sprawling illicit market in the capital of Maputo, which sells everything from eggs to guns, as *dumba nengi*—a complex comment on the ability of economics to meet citizens' needs.

A nation, and equally a global order, that accepts not only the creation of desperation but the use of that desperation as a means of engaging in both business and pleasure (e.g., 'buying cheap bodies', whether for industry or sex) is weakened at the most fundamental level. This comes from multiple interconnected fronts: unregulated criminal economies; the overwhelming impact of impoverishment (which debilitates a nation's ability to respond at all); the violence necessary to maintain inequality and the resistance that this generates; and the inability to sustain core social services and governing institutions in the face of all this.

A nation is bankrupted of that which makes it a nation. Infrastructure and services are hollowed out at a national level. Institutions are emptied of content amid claims of security, power, and the logic of need. Mozambicans explain that when people vote with their feet, when they deem a political order illegitimate, it collapses.[10]

Consider the following interrelated linkages that 'fracture' across war zones to involve peacetime nations and cosmopolitan locales.

While countries and their financial institutions may well decry extra-legal activities and laundering, they may, more covertly, welcome these transactions. For industry, a gun sold is a sale, regardless of whether it is a legal sale or not. Obtaining cheaper resources results in greater profit, irrespective of whether the resources are obtained legitimately or not. Similarly, money flowing through a financial institution is money that the institution can use and enjoy profit from, regardless of how it was generated. While this may appear to be victimless white-collar crime, financial markets taking part in unrecorded multi-billion dollar flows are unstable at best and ripe for collapse.

My research indicates that the extra-legal is generic to industry. When I asked representatives of Scotland Yard, the Netherlands police, and customs officers in the United Kingdom and the United States—as well as smugglers themselves—what percentage of businesses in the Western world crossed the line of the law in some way, all responded that the figure was virtually 100 percent. Thus, in addition, industry is adverse to official actions that might uncover the extent to which legal businesses engage in extra-legal behaviors, with regard to actual (and not rhetorical) port security, transport inspections, and trade monitoring. Potential collapse, in sum, is not investigated.

The same cycle is in place for what states define as more dangerous illegalities: exploitation of humans and resources, corruption, and trade in hazardous and banned commodities. Many of these practices are covertly but effectively centralized within legal businesses and their intersections with the state (Nordstrom 2004).[11] It is a cycle in which business benefits from avoiding taxes and restrictive laws, the government perceives benefit in the ideals of strong industry, and the elites in both business and government concretize their own personal econo-political hegemony. This represents the ethos of robber barons. Codified into state practice, it becomes foundational to sovereignty.[12]

Unrecorded flows of monies and resources may not seem dangerous until the sheer magnitude of the flows demonstrates the impact that they have on inter/national financial realities. When we consider the unrecorded trillions laundered yearly into the legal economy, it becomes apparent that the checks put in place (e.g., after the economic crash of 1929) cannot control a significant percentage of financial transactions. The manipulation of financial markets and economic crashes both appear inevitable.

These kinds of profiteering seldom generate monies for social and national services. A dearth of social services may not appear catastrophic until countries are ravaged by war, a pandemic, AIDS, or natural disasters. The inability to respond to Hurricane Katrina in the US provides an example of trying to marshal services at the national level that simply are not there. Years after the disaster, crises continue to plague the region. Children suffer from a debilitated school system, with African American students ranking at the bottom of state accountability assessment scores (Delpit and Payne 2007). Cases of post-traumatic stress disorder (PTSD), contrary to all definitions, are rising, and little by way of effective treatment is available. The US might do well to heed the research undertaken by South Africa's Centre for the Study of Violence and Reconciliation, which demonstrated that widespread PTSD affected workers to the point that it impaired industry and hindered national development (personal communication, 1996).

As basic social infrastructure and programs decline, and as a country's resources are increasingly used in the government/industry exchanges outlined above, countries are less able to meet even moderate crises: like earthquakes, they can level towns far from their epicenter that lay along zones of foundational instabilities. An 'economic quake'—a market crisis, a run on financial institutions made with un/recorded monies, a political or natural disaster—can thus bring a country to its knees. For example, the crash of the South African rand in 2001–2001 (affected in part by unrecorded financial manipulations) showed the deleterious impact on the entire country's standard of living. In the one year that the rand's rate halved in exchange to the US dollar, numerous businesses went broke; the cost of all daily necessities increased to the point that the average population could not meet all general food, energy, health, and educational needs; governmental services were curtailed; and health/standard of living indices suffered. A few—those with the financial resources to weather the crash and acquire the businesses of those who went broke—made a veritable killing. This financial crash was limited in time and scope: those who manipulated the markets for their gain during that time sought to maximize economic control, not cripple the country. People as diverse as longshoremen in the US and police and customs officials in the Netherlands have told me that for those seeking to cripple a country, the bombing of key shipping nodes would shut down a significant part of a country's infrastructure (interrupting critical food, energy, medical, and industrial necessities). It would be as serious a blow, and as likely to generate fractures, as a financial crash.

In sum, the results of these 'quakes' are political in the largest sense of the concept. It is important in this analysis to remember the sheer fragility of governing systems. The history of the human race is often charted by the development and collapse of systems of political organization. Although something new always comes along to replace the failed system, the cost in lives and human suffering can be disastrous. This becomes clear in returning to Badiou's point that complexity, precisely, *is* complexity. Fractures take definition within the compendium of fractures. For reducing the irreducible—exploring only economic flows and structurations *or* processes of power *or* interpersonal experiences of violence, etc.—produces not accurate knowledge but instead political fiction.

To summarize these linkages, cosmopolitanism is embedded in industrial culture, which requires cheap and readily accessible raw materials—minerals, food, bodies—and loyalty to the system. Since loyalty within systems of inequality is difficult to achieve, creating circuits of cosmopolitan commodities for resources in contexts of political violence ensures desperate workforces. In order to translate profit into power, the extra-legal is often exploited, and both financial and commodity flows are rendered opaque. They can thus be used to create economic and political power in ways that cannot, by definition, be assessed or controlled.

This goes far beyond a loss of taxes and a failure to promote national development and services. It speaks to an embedded political philosophy-as-worldview that values these cosmopolitan industrial developments over the welfare of the citizenry. Resources are moved into these large-scale (and perhaps extra-legal) corporate domains and away from generalized infrastructure and services (medicine, transport, education, safety) and planning for crises, disasters, and violence. Rear Admiral Neffenger captured this during our 2004 conversation about security at US ports:

> Superiors don't walk the frontlines. And then they say, "We've got it all locked down. All is fine." We just laugh and say: "You *know* that we don't have it all locked down. Why are you saying this?"
>
> So I look for people on my staff who 'get it'. And I make sure to link into the larger community here of people who get it—and these tend to be the people who live and work on the tough life-and-death stuff: fires, earthquakes, riots, security, and so on … These are the people I will work with if a disaster occurs, and we prepare for this. These people say, "If you 'get it', you're welcome to come to the table. If not, we'll take care of it."

I am reminded of the Mozambicans shaking their heads and saying *dumba nengi.*

* * *

Elite political and economic regimes can survive for a while through the combination of diverting national resources to industry, maintaining stark systems of inequality that ensure profits, gutting social services, creating extra-legal financial empires capable of shaping national economies, and using violence to enable these systems.

However, there is a time limit on this. Financial systems that are ostensibly based on legal transactions but are in fact shaped by unregulated extra-legal actions will not stay stable. When banking systems fail, the financial justification for the state falters. When social services are not operating—when core logistics such as food, clean water, safe housing, medicines, critical transport, and security cannot be provided—state institutions lose viability. Externally, this leaves a country vulnerable to foreign aggression. Internally, people vote with their feet. *Dumba nengi.* They will develop systems that meet their needs—extra-state systems. Governing forces often react with violence to people's decisions to develop alternate economic and authority systems. But as Hannah Arendt demonstrated, when states resort to violence to maintain their power, they are on the verge of collapse.

The final irony is that those who create and maintain these networks of profit that splinter out from the explosions of wartime bombs are themselves as vulnerable to quakes along the fracture lines outlined here.

The Tomorrows of Crises

> If uncertainty is found in society, then those who examine society (let us for now call these people sociologists) should view society in the same way as the con man. This is to examine a world shrouded in morality by going back to its origins—a state in which pure cons, pure imagination and pure transformation is possible. (Ogino 2007: 113)

We can read the deeper ontologies of crisis in the networks that extend out from the bomb victim. The very flows of weapons, commodities, services, exploitations, and values *are* crisis patterns. In reading these through the lens of Badiou's 'situations', crises are not bounded by traditional definitions that delineate an individual event from the global market, action from value, here from there. If something exists, if it 'is' in Badiou's framing, then it is worth consideration in the larger context. And in this way we can see how such mobile realities as massive extra-legal flows, human rights abuses of enforced labor, and the pathologies of power that raze social services can in themselves become institutionalized within the scope of global sovereignties and cosmopolitan market practices. These realities rest beneath, or aside from, the official explanations of state and market, their invisibility to formal analysis being actively maintained by those who benefit from them. These layers—formal and extra-state political and economic realms, seen as multiplicities—are all fundamental to defining the world as people live it. The fact that we are trained not to 'see' the extra-legal and the ensuing fractures is part of this definition. When crisis is institutionalized, it is ensured.

Carolyn Nordstrom is Professor of Anthropology, University of Notre Dame. Her principal areas of interest are political violence and peace in the contemporary world, transnational extra-legal economies and power, globalization, and gender. She has conducted extensive in-site fieldwork in war zones worldwide, with long-term interests in Southern Africa and South Asia. She is the author of *A Different Kind of War Story* (1997); *Shadows of War: Violence, Power and International Profiteering in the Twenty-First Century* (2004); *Global Outlaws: Crime, Money, and Power in the Contemporary World* (2007); and the co-editor of *The Paths to Domination, Resistance, and Terror* (1992) and *Fieldwork under Fire: Contemporary Stories of Violence and Survival* (1995). She was recently awarded John D. and Catherine T. MacArthur and John Simon Guggenheim Fellowships.

Notes

1. I use the slash in this fashion—extra/state, extra/legal, il/legal— to refer to both embedded terms together. The term 'extra/state' is something that is both extra-state and state at the same time—such as corruption that depends on holding a formal political office—with the result that both non-state and state systems not only intersect but are each further developed by these actions. The term 'extra-legal' refers to all activities that fall outside legality as it is formally defined and used in law and law enforcement. This includes illegal, illicit, and informal actions, as well as those that are undeclared, unregistered, and unregulated. The term 'extra-state' refers to all activities that take place outside of formal state ruling systems.
2. Badiou thus eschews the Heideggerian and post-Heideggerian division of Being and being, where Being (the ontology and dynamic phenomena of existence) is separated from being (people reduced to singularity, to person). He does not limit what '*is*' to specific realms or merely to what exists as tangible or objective reality—it can include what is manifest, potential, possible, and contingent.
3. Cosmopolitan centers, when referring to hyper-developed industrial-social centers, are vortices of finance, political decision making, market forces, and social production of what is taken to be the elite worldview. These centers are found worldwide, from Shanghai to Nairobi and Rio de Janeiro to New York. The use of the definition is contextual: Baghdad is cosmopolitan compared to the more remote pasts of Iraq (see Breckenridge et al. 2002). In my volume *Shadows of War*, the definition is more directly tailored to global considerations of war, with such a center being described as "the site where weapons are manufactured, resources crafted into global markets, and money banked" (Nordstrom 2004: 128).
4. To give an indication of the universe of the extra-legal, as much as 20 percent of the world's financial deposits are located in unregulated banks and offshore locations. The profit from unregulated sex trafficking, the pornography industry, and the trade in endangered species nearly rivals that of arms and drugs. Moreover, mundane informal economies can generate as much as the dramatically illegal: a person in Miami can make as much money selling freon gas, contrary to environmental laws, as selling narcotics, and gangs on the coast of South Africa have found that they can make more money smuggling protected species, such as the Patagonian toothfish, than narcotics. Half of all cigarettes are sold on the black market. In South Africa, 50 percent of the software that computers depend on is illicit, compared to 98 percent in Vietnam and China. The computer industry would be satisfied if these countries could achieve the 'success rate' of the United States with only 30 percent illicit software. Smuggling food and oil can generate as much income as smuggling people. A brisk and highly profitable illegal trade exists in everything, from nuclear waste to human organs.
5. I refer here to using offshore financial arrangements to avoid taxes and legal monitoring. This drains resources and profits away from the country where they are generated, thus impeding rather than enhancing development. See the chapters on money laundering in *Global Outlaws* (Nordstrom 2007) for a detailed description of how this works.
6. In this chapter I am addressing only abusive forms of extra-state behavior. In other publications (Nordstrom 2002, 2003, 2004, 2007) I have written about the complex nature of the extra-legal and the fact that it can be dangerously exploited, while simultaneously being a means for average people to gain life's essentials in conditions of deprivation or oppression. Profiteering, as I use it here, refers to the exploitative.
7. Many people do not fall into this category, and they express outrage at the pathologies of profiteering. Thus, those engaged in harmful extra-legal activities expend considerable energy to keep their actions, their trade routes, and their abuses invisible to formal accounting. Since the most successful can control more money than the GDP of many countries, creating invisibility is not overly difficult. Laws target low-level criminals, while security forces are directed to bust street-level mules rather than the CEOs of legitimate corporations who do not declare arms sales. The media and the pundits rage

endlessly against illegal narcotics, yet a small fraction of this attention is directed toward pharmaceutical companies producing substandard drugs. Street crime is presented as more threatening than white-collar crime, despite the fact that while a life may be lost to street crime, millions of lives can be lost to substandard medicines. In addition, white-collar crime can empty the coffers that support critical social services to countries.

8. The official explained that the most common ways well-known and respectable businesses break the law includes under-representing and misrepresenting the goods they are transporting to reduce or avoid the taxes. Also common are shipments of goods to locales that break sanctions or trade agreements; and transporting or selling banned materials.

9. The modern state has long sought to justify the inequalities upon which it rests. Rationalizations, in the Weberian sense, are legion, from creating and exploiting racisms that blame the poor to arguing that a state can be strong only if its core industries are wealthy—and that this benefits even the impoverished and exploited. These justifications have become so common that they are often accepted as truths in the public realm. Yet the very actions that states and their industries claim promote sovereign strength may prove their downfall.

10. See Little (2003) for a discussion of Somalia as an example of a collapsed state in which new governing regimes—both beneficial and abusive—quickly emerged.

11. Examples are numerous: businesses that use offshore 'sweatshops'; companies that skirt laws to dump toxic wastes; corporations that employ illegal 'Enron-esque' practices; twenty-first-century versions of the Iran-Contra deals; and government contracts that favor officials' business partners. At its most deadly, this includes corporate reliance on 'economic hit men' like John Perkins (2004) to undermine entire countries, thus making them vulnerable to external control. These practices are not isolated actions. They exist in a larger political universe that allows them to take place. As the US Customs official quoted at the beginning of this section explained to me, "Corporations breaking the law and government officials willing to back them go hand in hand."

12. There are, of course, countervailing forces that seek to diminish hegemonic control, abusive monopolies, human rights abuses, and exploitation. One need only consider the custom official quoted above to recognize the individuals and organizations devoted to justice based on transparency. The official speaking to me was incensed at his office's inability to prosecute well-known companies for breaking the law and at being unable to refuse politicians' demands that such cases be ignored. He was so outraged that he was willing to risk telling his stories to an anthropologist. Entire organizations, from the Scorpions (the South African detectives whose mandate is to reign in corruption and illegal business at the elite level) to Transparency International (which produces global indices of corruption), are dedicated to changing political processes grounded in exploitative practices. At the political level, these countervailing forces can engender peaceful democratic competition or violent rebellion. None of these actions has succeeded in stemming the unequal extra-legal flows that run through states or the value systems that seek to make these flows invisible to accounting and analysis.

References

Badiou, Alain. 2003. *Infinite Thought: Truth and the Return of Philosophy.* Trans. and ed. Oliver Feltham and Justin Clemens. London: Continuum.
_____. 2004. *Theoretical Writings.* Ed. and trans. Ray Brassier and Alberto Toscano. London: Continuum.
Breckenridge, Carol, Sheldon Pollock, Homi Bhabha, and Dipesh Chakrabarty, eds. 2002. *Cosmopolitanism.* Durham, NC: Duke University Press.
Castells, Manuel. 1998. *End of Millennium.* London: Blackwell.

Cilliers, Jakkie, and Christian Dietrich, eds. 2000. *Angola's War Economy.* Pretoria: Institute for Security Studies.

Delpit, Lisa, and Charles Payne. 2007. "Katrina's Last Victims?" *Nation,* 1 January, 20–21.

Farmer, Paul. 2004. *Pathologies of Power.* Berkeley: University of California Press.

Global Witness. 2005a. *Annual Report 2004.* London: Global Witness.

———. 2005b. *An Architecture of Instability.* London: Global Witness.

———. 2006. *Digging in Corruption.* London: Global Witness.

Laclau, Ernesto. 2000. "Identity and Hegemony: The Role of Universality in the Constitution of Political Logics." Pp. 44–89 in *Contingency, Hegemony, Universality: Contemporary Dialogues on the Left,* ed. Judith Butler, Ernesto Laclau, and Slavoj Žižek. London: Verso.

Lilley, Peter. 2006. *Dirty Dealing: The Untold Truth about Global Money Laundering.* London: Kogan Page.

Little, Peter. 2003. *Somalia: Economy Without State.* Oxford: James Currey.

MacGaffey, Janet, and Rémy Bazanguissa-Ganga. 2000. *Congo-Paris: Transnational Traders on the Margins of the Law.* Bloomington: Indiana University Press.

McDowell, John, and Gary Novis. 2001. "The Consequences of Money Laundering and Financial Crime." *Economic Perspectives* 6, no. 2 (May). http://usinfo.state.gov/journals/ites/0501/ijee/state1.htm.

Naím, Moisés. 2005. *Illicit.* New York: Doubleday.

Naylor, R. T. 2005. *Wages of Crime: Black Markets, Illegal Finance, and the Underworld Economy.* Ithaca, NY: Cornell University Press.

Nordstrom, Carolyn. 2000. "Shadows and Sovereigns." *Theory, Culture and Society* 17, no. 4: 35–54.

———. 2002. "Out of the Shadows." Pp. 216–239 in *Intervention and Transnationalism in Africa: Global-Local Networks of Power,* ed. Thomas Callaghy, Ronald Kassimir, and Robert Latham. Cambridge: Cambridge University Press.

———. 2003. "Public Bad, Public Good(s) and Private Realities." Pp. 212–224 in *Political Transition: Political and Cultures,* ed. Paul Gready. London: Pluto Press.

———. 2004. *Shadows of War: Violence, Power, and International Profiteering in the Twenty-first Century.* Berkeley: University of California Press.

———. 2007. *Global Outlaws: Crime, Money and Power in the Contemporary World.* Berkeley: University of California Press.

Ogino, Masahiro. 2006. *Scams and Sweeteners: A Sociology of Fraud.* Trans. Lotte Lawrence. Melbourne: Trans Pacific Press.

Perkins, John. 2004. *Confessions of an Economic Hit Man.* San Francisco, CA: Berrett-Koehler.

Strange, Susan. 1996. *The Retreat of the State: The Diffusions of Power in the World Economy.* Cambridge: Cambridge University Press.

van Schendel, Willem, and Itty Abraham, eds. 2005. *Illicit Flows and Criminal Things: States, Borders, and the Other Side of Globalization.* Bloomington: Indiana University Press.

Volkov, Vadim. 2002. *Violent Entrepreneurs: The Use of Force in the Making of Russian Capitalism.* Ithaca, NY: Cornell University Press.

Chapter 4

SEEING GREEN
Visual Technology, Virtual Reality,
and the Experience of War

Jose N. Vasquez

There was a time in the history of warfare when nightfall meant the end of fighting for the day. During the nineteenth and twentieth centuries, several techniques for overcoming darkness during combat maneuvers were developed, including illumination of the battlefield with flares or searchlights as well as forecasting nighttime visibility provided by ambient light from the moon, stars, or surrounding light sources. These techniques were useful but usually offered equal benefits to both sides of the battle. Recent advances in visual technology are giving modern warriors a competitive edge over less technologically advanced opponents and changing the experience of war in dramatic ways.[1] For example, among the many dangerous tasks that infantry soldiers are asked to perform in Iraq, the night raid is perhaps one of the most difficult. The night raid brings with it the potential for accidental 'friendly fire' incidents, civilian casualties, or both. Under the cover of darkness, charged with adrenaline-induced nervous anticipation, squads of grunts bash their way into the home of an unsuspecting resident to confiscate weapons, gather intelligence, and detain suspected insurgents. When planning operations, commanders know that the key to a successful night raid, along with good human intelligence and the element of surprise, is the ability to see through the darkness. The majority of combat troops currently in Iraq are carrying night vision goggles (NVGs), which allow them to see while maneuvering and fighting at night. Figures 1 and 2 give a sense of the individual soldier's perspective when looking through NVGs and convey how war is experienced on a daily basis. During 24-hour operations, some soldiers may spend several hours per night wearing these goggles, especially when driving or flying.

The ubiquitous use of night vision devices among US military forces raises a number of questions that I will address regarding the experience of combat through the lens of visual technology. The first explores how night vision and other technologies shape the average combat soldier's experience of war. While numerous scholars have written on the history of military technology (Adas 1989; Bacevich 1996; Hacker 1994; Owens 2002; D. Smith 1993), the articulation of science and warfare (Greenwood 1990; Gusterson 1996; MacKenzie 1986; Simons 1999; M. Smith 1985; Virilio 1989, 2002), and the traumatic psychological effects of war (Grossman 1995; Grossman and Christensen 2004; Lifton [1973] 1992; Shay 1994, 2002; Simons 1999; Young 1995), little has been written on the experience of war through high-technology devices. Conceptualized as 'cyber warriors',

FIGURE 1 Members of the Iraqi Civil Defense Corps (ICDC) Search a Home in Baghdad (Public Affairs Office, 1st Armored Division)

FIGURE 2 Soldiers Conduct a Cordon and Search during Operation Iron Hammer in Baghdad (Public Affairs Office, 1st Armored Division)

'cyborgs', and 'digital soldiers', the futuristic war fighters once thought of as purely science fiction are gradually becoming reality (Bevin 1995; Dunnigan 1996; Friedman and Friedman 2004; Levidow and Robins 1989; Shukman 1995; Vest 2002). The military spends billions of dollars annually to develop what it calls its Future Force Warrior (FFW) and Soldier as a System (SaaS) concepts. Equipped with sophisticated helmets supplying an array of digital data, visually enhanced targeting, lightweight lethal weapons, and protective body armor, the soldiers of the future will occupy a virtual reality of battlefield information (Goonatilake 1998). Friedman and Friedman speculate that "the multi-spectral sensors, high-speed computers, and brilliant munitions ... raise the possibility of a superior soldier ... a *supertroop*" (2004: 356; emphasis in original). Viewing the world through the green screens of NVGs is simply the first stage in this radical transformation in the experience of war for combat troops.

Given the increasing availability of military equipment in the civilian market, the second question I will explore is the way in which visual technology has changed war as it is experienced by people whom Virilio (1989) refers to as tele-spectators—those viewing war from a distance. A cursory search for digital cameras and video recorders on the Internet will yield a plethora of devices that have night vision capabilities. In addition, riflescopes are widely used among law enforcement officers and sportsmen for working or hunting at night. The same companies that developed night vision for the military have gone public, so to speak, vending their technology to the broader consumer market. Thus, the notion of 'seeing green' carries a double meaning, the first referring to the color viewed through night vision displays and the second to the money being made by companies involved in developing visual technology for the military. This is not a new trend by any means, since numerous electronic devices commonly used by the general public were first developed within the massively lucrative military-industrial complex (Greenwood 1990; Hacker 1994; M. Smith 1985). An increasing number of journalistic reports feature night vision footage from combat zones around the world, and Hollywood renditions of war use night vision technology to enhance the audience's experience of 'being there'. Nifty sensory-enhancing gadgets are no longer limited to the military or James Bond–type characters but are accessible to the general public. This marks an important development in the experience of war by tele-spectators because now combat can be portrayed in its entirety, day or night.

Lastly, I will examine the way in which virtual reality, the next step in visual technology, is changing combat training for soldiers. The next generation of infantrymen will be trained in basic squad tactics, urban warfare, and enemy recognition using "the Close Combat Tactical Trainer (CCTT). Infantrymen will be placed in a room and outfitted with helmets that will cover their eyes. They will 'see' a combat situation, from terrain to enemies, and they will carry weapons that will have the feel of the real thing. A camera will track the movement of their bodies and adjust the picture accordingly. They will feel as if they were in combat—except they will be perfectly safe, and the simulation can be run over and over again" (Friedman and Friedman 2004: 361). Reminiscent of Goonatilake's (1998) insightful essay on the growing human interface with computer technology, the CCTT brings virtual reality into the military sphere, pulling soldiers deeper into cyberspace than the average citizen. Indeed, the possibility that a soldier could spend extended periods in cyberspace is confirmed by the goals of military research and developers, who are working toward a time when "[a]n infantryman could be fitted with a completely opaque helmet—identical to those used in training—inside of which he would see as real images and icons the data that was being fed into the system by sensors" (Friedman and Friedman 2004: 362). Similarly, military pilots spend dozens of hours in flight simulators, practicing takeoffs, landings, and battle drills, before ever experiencing a 'real' flight.

The experience of virtual reality systems articulates seamlessly with an existing familiarity with the intense and often violent graphics of video games. As James Dunnigan, an analyst of military affairs, notes "taking more than a cue from the creators of computer games, the soldiers now have computer screens full of detailed and easy-to-understand images" (1996: 291). Virtual reality intensifies the experience with three-dimensional visual displays and instant reactions to the users' body movements. Military pilots and gunners are already fitted with helmets that control targeting and weapons systems that they can manipulate by moving their heads. Wherever the gunner looks while wearing his helmet, the weapons system will follow. However, as I demonstrate below, the video game feel of virtual reality opens the door to serious violations of the rules of engagement dictated by the laws of war. While neither visual technology nor virtual reality alone causes soldiers to kill, studies suggest there is a positive correlation between violent games and aggressive behavior in children and adolescents (Ferguson 2007; Konijn, Bijvank, and Bushman 2007; Tamborini et al. 2004; Weber, Ritterfeld, and Mathiak 2006), especially among males (Polman, de Castro, and van Aken 2008). The military is aware of this fact, which is why it developed the video game *America's Army* as a recruitment tool (Lugo 2006). Seeing enemy combatants as merely figures on a screen, identical to how bad guys are depicted in video games, makes it all too easy to kill them without hesitation: "It looks like a game, but the deaths are not simulated" (Dunnigan 1996: 291). The thrill associated with identifying targets and successfully neutralizing them in the virtual world of video games and virtual reality systems provides the training to do the same in the combat environment, sometimes in an indiscriminate fashion.

These are just a few of the issues that emerge when one considers the relationship between the military, visual technology, and the experience of war. Drawing on work in anthropology, philosophy, and science and technology studies, I argue that visual technology makes the experience of war more intimate while creating psychological distance between the human subjects engaged in combat. Following Nandy's (1988) concern with shifts in the purpose of science vis-à-vis the state and human violence, I will explore the significance of visual technology and its relationship to personal and institutionalized experiences of war. Using digital photos and video recorded by soldiers and civilians in Iraq that I collected from the Internet, I demonstrate how visual technology shapes the experience of war for both participants and tele-spectators. I begin with an expanded discussion of night vision technology, followed by an analysis of digital video taken from an AH-64 Apache attack helicopter gun tape, and end with an exploration of the possibilities presented by virtual reality.

Owning the Night

Prototypes of night vision and infrared technology, which amplify light and heat signatures respectively, were developed as early as World War II, but it was not until the 1960s that devices such as the Starlight Scope used in the Vietnam War became available in a portable, mass-produced form widely available to combat troops. This first generation of night vision technology was soon superseded in the following two decades by more compact and powerful devices. The 1991 Persian Gulf War provided the first major test of second-generation night vision technology. The decisive US military victory over Iraqi forces led to claims that advanced visual technology allowed the US military to 'own the night'. Indeed, the ability to see at night, both on the ground and from the air, was a major contributing factor in the brevity of that war. Marking an important shift in modern warfare, commanders were able to plan for nighttime operations with a high degree of success due to advanced visual technology. Although the Air Force and Navy's 'smart bombs' and the Army's Patriot missile systems presented technical problems during their initial fielding in combat, visual technology performed well and is now a central component of US military hegemony. Commanders in Operation Desert Storm relied on "intelligence, surveillance, and reconnaissance systems that could achieve dominant battle space awareness, new communications systems that could transfer that awareness quickly and surely, and precision guidance that could deliver violence over greater distances with speed, accuracy, and devastating effect" (Owens 2002: 207). This is particularly true with regard to the Air Force, Navy, and Special Forces, since most major combat operations in modern war begin with an intense bombing campaign. Generally, Special Forces commandos are clandestinely inserted within enemy territory prior to the bombing in order to locate specific targets and to 'paint' targets with lasers that aircraft can detect from the sky. Air Force stealth bombers carrying heavy payloads conduct high-altitude sorties destroying key infrastructure, while Navy cruise missiles fired from miles offshore pinpoint enemy strongholds and communications. During the Gulf War, there was a sustained bombing campaign prior to the commencement of the ground assault, and all of these events usually occurred at night to give US-led forces a distinct advantage over the Iraqis.

However, the military did not have a monopoly on night vision technology since the American media also had cameras with night vision capabilities. Among the most memorable images of the Gulf War was the Cable News Network (CNN) night vision footage of Iraqi anti-aircraft guns firing blindly into the night sky over Baghdad during the first hours of the air campaign (fig. 3). The now famous live newscast by CNN reporters during that bombing may be the first time night vision footage was broadcast internationally.[2] Aside from boosting the status of the fledgling CNN, the video helped project US military prowess to the world by demonstrating its ability to rain strategic air strikes on targets anywhere, at any time. In the following days and weeks, every major news network carried the CNN footage as well as military briefings that featured either night vision or infrared footage of smart bombs successfully hitting their targets.

The Pentagon ensured that coverage of Operation Desert Storm looked very different from how the Vietnam War was portrayed. Gone were images of bloody grunts trudging through the combat zone, soldiers coming home in body bags, and the human suffering exacted on the local population. Instead, the international audience was captivated by the techno-spectacle of precision-guided bombs made possible through advanced visual technology. With the audience becoming intimately engrossed, the war appeared controlled and, perhaps more importantly, bloodless. Watching bombs splashing on the green (night vision) or gray (infrared) screens as they pulverized bridges, bunkers, and tank berms,[3] tele-spectators were drawn closer to the awesome violence of war while distancing themselves from the reality of the human carnage happening right before their eyes. This, along with numerous Hollywood movies that use night vision video to re-create the warrior's perspective, brings the spectator into a very different relationship with war.[4] What was once hidden in the fog of war is now visible and therefore knowable, intimate. Civilians can vicariously experience war through the darkness and from a distance, in the comfort of their own homes. Because of the way night vision and infrared work, the blood and gore of combat are not so much hidden as obscured. This allows tele-spectators to marvel at the power of technology to bring the experience of war home without having to comprehend fully or process its human cost. The tele-spectators of war are

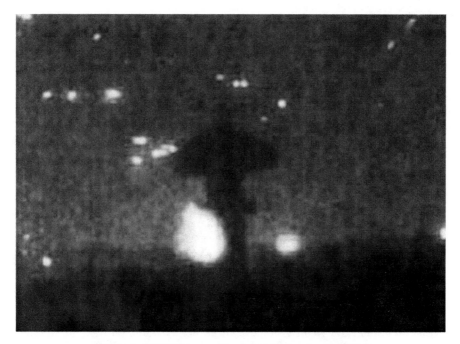

FIGURE 3 CNN Footage of Baghdad during the Gulf War

informed about the execution of combat operations but are rarely brought face to face with the consequences of those operations. This is significant because it makes it easier for politicians and military experts to sell wars to their fellow citizens by focusing on the advantages of superior firepower while ignoring the devastation that those weapons cause to those on the receiving end.

Prior to the 2003 invasion and occupation of Iraq, Secretary of Defense Donald Rumsfeld touted the 'shock and awe' campaign as a strategic use of overwhelming force, mostly through bombing, which was designed to cut off Iraqi lines of communication and diminish the Iraqis' will to fight (Safire 2003; Ullman and Wade 1996). Media coverage and unclassified military footage again highlighted the use of visual technology to portray the war with familiar scenes of bunker-busting bombs splashing across television screens around the world (Stanley 2003). Added to the spectacle were front-line reports by so-called embedded reporters who managed to capture the fighting while censoring the carnage. The overly dramatized rescue of Private Jessica Lynch by Special Forces commandos was also captured using a night vision camera (Kristof 2003). These carefully monitored real-time images brought tele-spectators closer to war than ever before, while at the same time dissociating them from the human side of it. This is particularly true in the US since other international news sources, notably the BBC and Al Jazeera, showed uncensored images of refugees and casualties on both sides of the war. Meanwhile, the Bush administration banned even the photographing of flagged-draped coffins containing the remains of US casualties. Learning from the Vietnam War, the administration realized that "electronic mass media could have a decisive effect on public opinion and political decision making" (Dunnigan 1996: 267). Seeing soldiers coming home in body bags might be good for television ratings, but it would be bad for maintaining public support of the war.

A riveting example of the everyday use of NVGs in the combat zone can be seen in the recent documentary film *Occupation: Dreamland*.[5] Both the documentary crew and the infantry soldiers featured in the film utilized night vision technology as they conducted dangerous missions in Fallujah, Iraq. Some of the most powerful scenes in the film—such as a house raid in which young Iraqi children huddled in a corner stare terrified into the lens as soldiers search their house for weapons and detain all the military-aged men—are captured using night vision cameras. The children appear haunting, with green skin and glowing eyes reflecting the dim light. Another poignant scene occurs during a guard duty shift as an infantryman tries to communicate in broken Arabic with an Iraqi man working in the compound. The encounter highlights the irony of possessing advanced visual technology but not having the ability to communicate properly with the local population. While the US military owns the night, serious deficiencies in language and cultural competencies make the work of occupying Iraq difficult and haphazard. Night vision enhances soldiers' ability to see through the darkness while looking past the human beings right in front of them (fig. 4).

The disconnection between the benefits of visual technology and the inability to communicate with Iraqi civilians raises a number of questions. First, what strategic purpose does it serve to keep soldiers in the dark, so to speak, about the local population? If the military wanted its troops to be well informed about the language and customs of the Iraqis, education could easily be incorporated into units' pre-deployment training. The fact is, however, that few soldiers, outside of civil affairs, military intelligence, or Special Forces units, get any substantial linguistic or cultural training in their area of operations—which raises another question. Why is that? Could it be that the military is concerned about soldiers identifying with the local population, of seeing 'them' as human beings? Would that lead soldiers, particularly those in combat units, to ask questions about why the US is in the war to begin with? Given the difficulties in discerning between so-called insurgents and civilians, how are soldiers expected to know the difference without being able to speak the language or interpret information from locals who may be willing to help find enemy personnel? Lastly, if high-tech war on one side leads to 'guerrilla warfare' and 'irregular tactics' on the other side, where is the enterprise of war headed?

Visual Technology and the Rules of Engagement

In addition to overcoming the darkness, the ability to see enemies at a distance gives the US military a tactical edge over its opponents. Long-range sighting systems, such as high-powered scopes, radars, satellites, and unmanned aerial

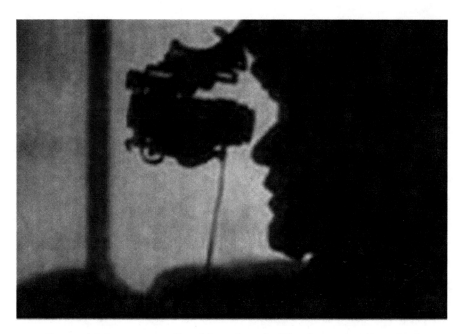

Figure 4 Infantryman on Guard Duty, from the Film *Occupation: Dreamland*
(used with permission)

vehicles (UAV), assist in intelligence gathering, target acquisition, and tracking. One of the most effective devices in use by the military in Iraq is Forward-Looking Infrared Radar (FLIR). Numerous weapons platforms, such as main battle tanks and helicopters, are fitted with these sophisticated thermal-imaging devices. FLIR displays produce a grayscale image in which objects that emit heat appear white. They are particularly useful in locating personnel and equipment at night or in concealed positions (fig. 5).

A powerful example of the FLIR device in action can be viewed in a widely available digital video circulating on the Internet. I first saw this short, disturbing video at an Army leadership school for sergeants, the Basic Non-Commissioned Officer Course, during the summer of 2004.[6] Another sergeant, a member of the Florida National Guard who had recently returned from service in Iraq, volunteered to share the video, stored on his laptop computer, with the rest of the class. That day we were discussing the rules of engagement—the guidelines set in a theater of war that dictate when soldiers can fire upon the enemy. Firing only when fired upon or shooting anything that moves in a specified area are two examples of the rules of engagement. The Florida sergeant thought that the video demonstrated how the rules of engagement are implemented in a combat environment as the helicopter pilot seeks permission to fire from his chain of command. What is ironic about choosing this video to demonstrate the proper procedure for following the rules of engagement is that, in my opinion, the video shows a war crime being committed by US military personnel. I felt that

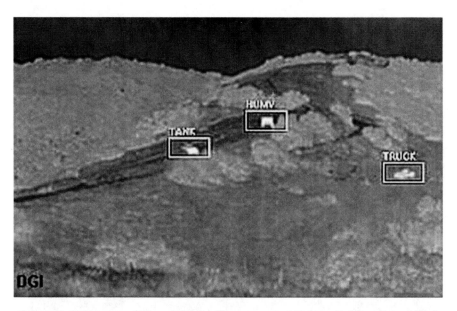

FIGURE 5 FLIR Image of Three Vehicles (Department of Defense Public Affairs Office)

the rules of engagement were violated and failed to save the lives of potentially innocent people. What is more, despite the high-tech advantage that they had over their targets, the helicopter pilots were unable to distinguish between combatants and non-combatants, which made me wonder how many other innocent civilians have been killed by US military personnel. I cannot explore this question in this chapter, but I do address how the military's reliance on visual technology solves tactical problems while ignoring humanitarian problems of dealing with civilians on the battlefield.

What follows is my analysis of three versions of the video that are circulating on the Internet and their significance vis-à-vis the experience of war that is being projected through visual technology. Depending on how the footage is edited and what the accompanying text has to say about the scenario depicted, three very different interpretations of the video have emerged. These interpretations are important in shaping public perceptions of the war and in understanding how the rules of engagement are implemented.

Version 1: 'Insurgents' Emplacing a Weapon

The first version of the Apache helicopter gun tape opens with an image of two Iraqi men, presumed to be insurgents, walking in front of a cargo truck parked in an open field.[7] The voices of the Apache crew—a pilot and gunner—are overheard as they attempt to determine the range of their intended targets, which include the cargo truck, a small pickup truck, and a farm tractor.

The viewer soon learns that their main targets are actually three men, none of whom appear to be armed. According to numerous interpretations on Web sites that provide a link to this video, the three men are suspected of emplacing an improvised explosive device (IED) or some other weapon in an area where American convoys are expected to pass through. The helicopter, however, does not seem to be in any immediate danger. Unbeknownst to the alleged insurgents, the helicopter is hovering several hundred meters away, following their every move with its FLIR sighting system while aiming a 30mm cannon armed with high-explosive rounds. The crew takes an initial shot at one man in the crosshairs, whom I will call Insurgent A, but misses, sending him racing across the field toward Insurgent B, who is sitting in the tractor. As Insurgent A gets near the tractor, Insurgent B steps off, after pausing briefly to say something, and begins walking right across the screen toward the parked trucks. Meanwhile, Insurgent A has walked around the front of the tractor and to the left side of it where he reaches in to pull out a heavy cylindrical object, perhaps an artillery shell. The helicopter's crosshairs pan right following Insurgent B as Insurgent A and the tractor move out of the frame on the left. The pilot and gunner are in constant communication, and as the gunner states, "Range auto ... all right, got auto range on him," the pilot exclaims, "Roger, hit him." Suddenly, the sound of the cannon is heard going through a rapid cycle of ammunition—*rat-tat-tat-tat*—and a burst of rounds explodes around Insurgent B. The gunner makes a direct hit, sending parts of Insurgent B's exploded body careening all over the open field. The FLIR system picks up heat signatures creating a splash of bright white where Insurgent B took his last steps. There is nothing left of him but a pool of blood giving off its heat.

Unfortunately for this doomed trio of would-be insurgents, Insurgent B is not the only one hit by that first successful burst of rounds. Insurgent C, pictured in the far right corner of the screen, doubles over at the same time that Insurgent B meets his demise. The high explosive rounds fired from the 30mm cannon send shrapnel across a wide kill radius, within which Insurgent C was standing. After the gunner confirms that Insurgent B is down by exclaiming, "Got him," the pilot states, "Good," directing the gunner, "Hit the other one." The camera pans left back toward Insurgent A, who seems to be frantically unsheathing the artillery round as he crouches down to the left of the tractor. The crosshairs line up on him, and the cannon opens up with another volley of fire. Insurgent A virtually disappears under the hail of 30mm rounds. The pilot says, "Go to the right. See if anybody is moving by the truck." The camera pans right, surveying the immediate area around the parked vehicles. Insurgent C, after sustaining shrapnel injuries from the attack on Insurgent B, has crawled under the cargo truck. While the helicopter crew is scanning the area, Insurgent C's upper body becomes visible for a brief moment behind the left front tire of the cargo truck. The pilot notices him and states, "Oh, there's another guy moving right there." The gunner responds, "Good ... firing ... hit him." Rounds rain down on the truck hitting the front grill and left front tire, behind which Insurgent C is hiding, sending smoke trailing away from the vehicle. The gunner asks, "Want to take the other truck out?" to which the pilot responds, "Roger

... wait for movement by the truck." Insurgent C has rolled out from under the cargo truck and down a slight embankment. The gunner notes that the third man is wounded, but the pilot says, "Hit him!" The gunner replies, "All right, I'm hitting the truck," but the pilot responds, "Hit the truck and him." The final burst of machine-gun fire shatters the back window of the pickup truck and kicks up dust and debris around the motionless body of Insurgent C.

Watching the video was disturbing on a number of different levels. First, because this version of the video is an excerpt, we can only speculate on what transpired prior to and after the events depicted. Knowing whether the helicopter crew received intelligence reports alerting them to the activities of the alleged insurgents or if they were on station conducting reconnaissance of this area—and thus being the first soldiers to have eyes on the targets—would help us interpret the circumstances of these graphic images. Certainly, from the perspective of a US service member stationed in Iraq, any vehicle movement in the middle of an open field at night would immediately be considered suspicious. However, all three men appeared to be unarmed at the beginning of the video, and the object that I interpreted as a possible artillery shell, a common component in IEDs, was not visible until after Insurgent B was splattered all over the field. The pilot and gunner never mention why these men are being fired upon, and given the fact that the Apache helicopter is nearly undetectable at night from a distance, its crew was never under direct threat from the insurgents.

Another unsettling aspect of this video is that the force used to 'neutralize' these three men far surpassed what was necessary. The caliber of an Apache helicopter's cannon, 30mm high-explosive rounds, is normally reserved for engaging vehicles and equipment (granted these are usually operated by individuals who invariably get destroyed along with their vehicles and equipment). Firing on unarmed individuals with such high-powered ammunition far exceeds the guidelines of Articles 48 and 51 of the 1949 Geneva Conventions.[8] One would be hard pressed to say that the three individuals in the video were definitely combatants or part of some military objective. Visual technology has thus increased not only the sensory abilities of soldiers but also their capacity to commit war crimes, with helicopters targeting individuals on the battlefield and deploying lethal force that exceeds the Geneva Conventions. Even if they were combatants, the fact that the Apache crew continued to engage a wounded man (hiding under the truck) is a clear violation of the Geneva Conventions. While all wars foster dehumanization, the FLIR creates circumstances in which soldiers can see their enemies better than ever before and yet interact with them as if playing a video game.

Version 2: The Original Military Edit

The second version of the video begins approximately two and a half minutes earlier than version 1, providing a broader context for interpreting the pilot's initial identification of the targets and the decision to engage them with machine-gun fire.[9] As the crew is scanning an open field, a pickup truck pulls into the frame and parks just short of the stationary cargo truck. The pilot and the gunner discuss the situation. The conversation regarding whether the gunner had permission to fire is what the Florida sergeant I mentioned earlier wanted us to focus on. From his perspective, the pilots demonstrated how soldiers are supposed to follow the rules of engagement. The problem I have with this interpretation is that the pilot and gunner never positively identify any weapons, are never in imminent danger, and do not witness the alleged insurgents attacking friendly forces. Following the guidelines set forth by the Geneva Conventions, it is not clear that any military advantage was gained by killing these three men. It is also important to note that although this version of the film is longer and provides more context than the previous version, the question remains as to why the pilots were tasked to scan this area in the first place. If the helicopters were simply on a reconnaissance mission, the time between their spotting of the suspected insurgents and their decision to engage them seems exceptionally brief. On the other hand, if the helicopters were sent to respond to specific intelligence reports of insurgent activity in the area, the fact remains that the behavior of these three men could hardly be perceived as imminently hostile to the helicopters or any other US personnel. Thus, the scene serves as a metaphor for the whole war in that the helicopter crew initiated a pre-emptive strike against a perceived enemy that did not pose an imminent threat based on limited intelligence regarding the possession of weapons.

Version 3: An Extended Edit with Commentary

Finally, the third version circulating on the Internet offers a compelling interpretation of the events as they unfold.[10] An unidentified commentator, with a subtle British accent, orients the viewer to key terrain features and details about infrared technology to make his case. He contends that the three men we see in the footage—interpreted as insurgents in version 1—are actually farmers plowing a field. According to this narrator, the objects that the first two men dropped in the open field were not rifles or bombs but markers to help guide the third man who is driving the tractor. Although it is admittedly difficult to make out precisely what these men drop in the field, the most plausible part of this interpretation is the fact that fresh, evenly distributed plowed rows are easily visible in the image. As the tractor pulls into view, it becomes clear that it is pulling a plow that leaves grooves through the soil in its wake. Another important aspect that the editors of this version highlight, by repeating and encircling, is that when the pilot is asked, "Do you see them with the weapons in their hands?" the answer is "Yes." However, it is abundantly evident in the video that none of the men have weapons in their hands when the question is being asked.

My own interpretation is closer to version 3 with some important qualifications. In my view, Iraq is an atrocity-producing situation that forces soldiers to take on a survivor mode of existence. There is an explicit reward system for confirmed kills in combat, and career-minded soldiers understand the value of combat experience. For example, members of the infantry covet the Combat Infantryman's Badge (CIB), which is awarded to personnel who have come under enemy fire and retuned fired. In performing their job successfully, which is to close with and engage (kill) the enemy in a combat environment, infantrymen are rewarded with badges that carry weight in the military's promotion system. If we assume that the pilots were competent individuals who would not intentionally seek out innocent civilians to vaporize, then how could this have happened? After studying this nasty, brutish video, I have concluded that the gunner was more reluctant to kill the three men than the pilot was. This is especially the case with the last man who was wounded. It was the pilot who urged his gunner, "Go forward of the truck and hit him!" Not unlike soldiers in the infantry, pilots form tight bonds of trust but also experience intense peer pressure to kill on command. Even college-educated specialists like the pilots flying the Apache helicopters can buckle under the institutionalized pressure created by the military to ensure unquestioning loyalty and commitment to the mission.

Were the three Iraqi men there to plow a field or emplace improvised explosive devices? We may never know what their true intentions were. What is clear, however, is that the technological advantage offered by the FLIR did not result in capturing any enemy intelligence and did not prevent the undeniable slaughter of potentially innocent people. As Dunnigan (1996: 273) points out: "[T]he American troops closest to the fighting, namely the pilots and ground fighters, are most aware of how thin the high-tech advantage is." Although looking through a FLIR does improve one's ability to detect objects at a distance through the darkness, such a device cannot enhance one's ability to judge the proper course of action under questionable circumstances. While billions are spent in the US on new gadgets for the troops, less emphasis is placed on training soldiers in restraint and cultural competency. What if the pilots were more aware of the way of life of Iraqis rather than operating under essentialized notions of Arabs? If the three Iraqi men killed were actually plowing and not setting booby traps, would it not be useful for soldiers to know that plowing season had begun? These are difficult questions that go to the heart of the psychology of war, civil-military relations, and the dehumanizing aspects of armed conflict. I think we need to acknowledge the futility of war and interrogate the logic that prioritizes investments in technology over the widespread deleterious effects that war has on human beings on both sides of conflicts. Rather than improving our ability to cause human suffering on a mass scale, we should be looking at ways to alleviate it.

Virtual Reality and Beyond

The difficult scenes discussed in the previous section perhaps foreshadow things to come. As more money is invested in lightweight battle suits and sophisticated helmet systems for the average ground-pounding infantryman, we are destined to see war from an even more individualized perspective. Much like the gung-ho space Marines depicted in the movie *Aliens*, helmet-cams will yield intense footage of house-to-house close quarters combat. Fitted with night vision and infrared like the Apache helicopter crew, infantrymen will see war at least partially through some form of visual technology. Will this mean that, like Arnold Schwarzenegger's famous character in *The Terminator*, infantrymen will become killing machines incapable of feeling any remorse for the little green men (or children or women) exploding on their screens? This certainly seems to be the Pentagon's goal, judging by its massive expenditures on research and development. This is a fact not lost on defense contractors, who proudly showcase their latest contributions to the Future Force Warrior at expos like the International Defense Exhibition and Seminar (IDEAS) 2006 that took place in Karachi, Pakistan.

Virtual reality training is gradually working its way into the everyday lives of soldiers. Indeed, the soldier depicted in figure 6 is scheduled to hit the ground running by 2025. Yet this rapid development of military technology leaves a number of important considerations unexamined. For example, because the US and other advanced industrialized nations are so far ahead technologically, it would be futile for other countries to attempt warfare in the conventional sense, with aerial dogfights and open tank battles. Instead, guerrilla warfare and irregular tactics are the only sensible option available to the rest of the world's combatants. Iraq has shown how effective these time-tested strategies can be at stymieing a superpower. Dunnigan (1996: 260) recognizes this situation: "The big problem is that the likely enemies come in two flavors: clones of yourself and primitives. The former are easy to understand, as they are trained,

FIGURE 6 Future Force Warrior Concept Equipped with Helmet Displays and Lightweight Weapon (Department of Defense Public Affairs Office)

equipped, and likely to fight pretty much like you are. The latter are usually guerillas or irregulars of some sort armed with yesterday's weapons, plus some of today's gadgets. The primitives are primitive only in the sense that they don't have all the technology you have. What the primitives do usually have is smarts, knowledge of the area they are fighting in, and a lot of determination."

Aside from his problematic characterization of guerrilla fighters as 'primitives', I think Dunnigan describes perfectly the situation that the US is facing in Iraq today. The Iraqi insurgency is using a mixture of old and new weapons and tactics to foil the US occupation. Would the Future Force Warrior be any better equipped to deal with this situation? Other than improved body armor for protection against explosive blasts, I would say no. Again, Dunnigan is in agreement when he claims (1996: 287): "Technology is not much help in guerilla operations; of more use is good old-fashioned 'getting to know the locals and the lay of the land.' As armed forces place more of their emphasis on technology, they become less able to deal with low-intensity warfare and dealing with guerillas. The next decade will reveal whether or not many, or any, nations have decided to deal with this problem head-on and trained for these 'little wars' ahead of time." I think that as long as the military-industrial complex continues to operate as it does now, with new contracts driving further research and development (and corporations profiting handsomely), token gadgets as opposed to more useful training will be the norm. Without the ability to understand the language and culture of the 'enemy', no amount of technology, visual or otherwise, will make warfare any easier than it was 3,000 years ago. What will become easier is the ability to kill on a massive scale without fully comprehending the devastation happening on the screen. Night vision, infrared, and virtual reality act simultaneously as amplifiers and filters, mitigating the experience of war.

Acknowledgments

I would like to thank Murphy Halliburton and Shirley Lindenbaum for comments they offered on an early version of this chapter. I would also like to thank Alisse Waterston for encouraging me to submit it for publication. A draft of this chapter was presented at the Eighth Annual Conference of Critical Themes in Media Studies at the New School, New York City.

Jose N. Vasquez is an anthropology doctoral student at the City University of New York. His research with military veterans returning from Iraq and Afghanistan focuses on the politics of veteran status in contemporary US society. He is an active member of Iraq Veterans Against the War and was a key organizer of "Winter Soldier: Iraq and Afghanistan, Eyewitness Accounts of the Occupations," a four-day event held in 2008 that brought together veterans from across the US to testify about their experiences in Iraq and Afghanistan

Notes

1. By visual technology I mean high-powered lenses, night vision, and infrared devices such as goggles, scopes, and cameras. The advent of virtual reality, which uses computer-generated images coupled with motion sensors and three-dimensional displays, is the next step in visual technology.
2. For an extended discussion of the impact of CNN's coverage of the Gulf War on popular perceptions of war, see Virilio (2002).
3. Berms are earthen mounds used as fighting positions, like foxholes for tanks.
4. As an example, the opening scene of the popular film *Courage Under Fire*, starring Meg Ryan and Denzel Washington, depicts a nighttime tank battle in which Washington's character orders his gunner to return fire at what he perceives to be an enemy tank. He quickly learns over his radio headset that the tank his crew has destroyed was a 'friendly' tank. In other words, he ordered his gunner to commit fratricide. The audience vicariously experiences the tense tank battle, switching perspectives from the gunner's view through green night vision screens to the inside of the cramped tank.
5. For a trailer of this 2005 film featuring night vision, see http://www.occupationdreamland.com/trailer.html.
6. I served in the US Army as a cavalry scout (reconnaissance specialist) from 1992 to 1996 and in the US Army Reserve as a medical specialist, nurse, and health services instructor from 1997 to 2007. During that time I served in numerous units and earned the rank of staff sergeant, which is what put me in the Basic Non-Commissioned Officer Course where I first viewed the FLIR footage I refer to above. As a cavalry scout, I trained extensively with night vision goggles, laser range finders (binoculars that measure distance), thermal sights, and the sighting systems associated with TOW (tube-launched, optically tracked, wire-guided) missiles and Bradley Fighting Vehicles. In January 2005, after much soul searching, I applied for conscientious objector status and received an honorable discharge after 14 years of service. My opposition to war began with what I view as the unnecessary invasion of Iraq and grew into an opposition to war in any form. I joined Iraq Veterans Against the War in June 2005 and have been an active member since then, serving on the Board of Directors and as the New York City chapter president.
7. Follow this link to view version 1: http://www.youtube.com/watch?v = 4KHKyXYQ6TY.
8. Article 48 states: "[T]he Parties to the conflict shall at all times distinguish between the civilian population and combatants and between civilian objects and military objectives and accordingly shall direct their operations only against military objectives." Article 51 states: "An attack which may be expected to cause incidental loss of civilian life, injury to civilians, damage to civilian objects, or a combination thereof, which would be excessive in relation to the concrete and direct military advantage anticipated." See http://untreaty.un.org/unts/60001_120000/1/24/00001166.pdf.
9. Follow this link to view version 2: http://www.youtube.com/watch?v = q2HdVBuBGwE. A message now appears on this site: "This video or group may contain content that is inappropriate for some users, as flagged by YouTube's user community. To view this video or group, please verify you are 18 or older by signing in or signing up."
10. The link for version 3 (http://www.youtube.com/watch?v = gORLv7bGyls) has since been removed from YouTube "due to terms of use violation."

References

Adas, Michael. 1989. *Machines as the Measure of Man: Science, Technology, and Ideologies of Western Dominance*. Ithaca, NY: Cornell University Press.
Bacevich, Andrew J. 1996. "Morality and High Technology." *National Interest* 45: 37–47.

Bevin, Alexander. 1995. *The Future of Warfare*. New York: Norton.

Dunnigan, James F. 1996. *Digital Soldiers: The Evolution of High-Tech Weaponry and Tomorrow's Brave New Battlefield*. New York: St. Martin's.

Ferguson, Christopher. 2007. "The Good, the Bad, and the Ugly: A Meta-analytic Review of Positive and Negative Effects of Video Games." *Psychiatric Quarterly* 78, no. 4: 309–316.

Friedman, George, and Meredith Friedman. 2004. "The Return of the Poor, Bloody Infantry." Pp. 355–374 in *America's Military Today: The Challenge of Militarism*, ed. Tod Ensign. New York: New Press.

Goonatilake, Susantha. 1998. "Virtual Reality: Philosophy on the Nintendo." Pp. 201–218 in *Toward a Global Science: Mining Civilizational Knowledge*. Bloomington: Indiana University Press.

Greenwood, Ted. 1990. "Why Military Technology Is Difficult to Restrain." *Science, Technology, and Human Values* 15, no. 4: 412–429.

Grossman, David A. 1995. *On Killing: The Psychological Cost of Learning to Kill in War and Society*. New York: Back Bay Books.

Grossman, David A., and Loren W. Christensen. 2004. *On Combat: Psychology and Physiology of Deadly Conflict in War and Peace*. Belville, IL: PPCT Research Publications.

Gusterson, Hugh. 1996. *Nuclear Rites: A Weapons Laboratory at the End of the Cold War*. Berkeley: University of California Press.

Hacker, Barton C. 1994. "Military Institutions, Weapons, and Social Change: Toward a New History of Military Technology." *Technology and Culture* 35, no. 4: 768–834.

Konijn, Elly A., Marije N. Bijvank, and Brad J. Bushman. 2007. "I Wish I Were a Warrior: The Role of Wishful Identification in the Effects of Violent Video Games on Aggression in Adolescent Boys." *Developmental Psychology* 43, no. 4: 1038–1044.

Kristof, Nicholas D. 2003. "Saving Private Jessica." *New York Times*, 20 June, A23.

Levidow, Les, and Kevin Robins, eds. 1989. *Cyborg Worlds: The Military Information Society*. New York: Free Association Books and Columbia University Press.

Lifton, Robert J. [1973] 1992. *Home from the War: Learning from Vietnam Veterans*. Boston: Beacon Press.

Lugo, William. 2006. "Violent Video Games Recruit American Youth." *Reclaiming Children and Youth* 15, no. 1: 11–14.

MacKenzie, Donald. 1986. "Science and Technology Studies and the Question of the Military." *Social Studies of Science* 16, no. 2: 361–371.

Nandy, Ashis. 1988. "Introduction: Science as a Reason of State." Pp. 1–23 in *Science, Hegemony and Violence: A Requiem for Modernity*, ed. Ashis Nandy. Delhi: Oxford University Press.

Owens, William A. 2002. "Creating a U.S. Military Revolution." Pp. 205–220 in *The Sources of Military Change: Culture, Politics, Technology*, ed. Theo Farell and Terry Terriff. Boulder, CO: Lynne Rienner Publishers.

Polman, Hanneke, Bram Orobio de Castro, and Marcel A. G. van Aken. 2008. "Experimental Study of the Differential Effects of Playing versus Watching Violent Video Games on Children's Aggressive Behavior." *Aggressive Behavior* 34, no. 3: 256–264.

Safire, William. 2003. "The Way We Live Now: 3-30-03: On Language; Shock and Awe." *New York Times*, 30 March, sec. 6, 10.

Shay, Jonathan. 1994. *Achilles in Vietnam: Combat Trauma and the Undoing of Character*. New York: Maxwell Macmillan.

_____. 2002. *Odysseus in America: Combat Trauma and the Trials of Homecoming*. New York: Scribner.

Shukman, David. 1995. *Tomorrow's War: The Threat of High-Technology Weapons*. New York: Harcourt Brace.

Simons, Anna. 1999. "War: Back to the Future." *Annual Review of Anthropology* 28: 73–108.

Smith, David A. 1993. "Technology and the Modern World-System: Some Reflections." *Science, Technology, and Human Values* 18, no. 2: 186–195.

Smith, Merritt R., ed. 1985. *Military Enterprise and Technological Change: Perspectives on the American Experience*. Cambridge, MA: MIT Press.

Stanley, Alessandra. 2003. "A Nation at War: The TV Watch; Networks Make the Most of Their Frontline Access." *New York Times*, 21 March, B11.

Tamborini, Ron, Matthew S. Eastin, Paul Skalski, Kenneth Lachlan, Thomas A. Fediuk, and Robert Brady. 2004. "Violent Virtual Video Games and Hostile Thoughts." *Journal of Broadcasting and Electronic Media* 48, no. 3: 335–357.

Ullman, Harlan K., and James P. Wade. 1996. *Shock and Awe: Achieving Rapid Dominance*. Washington, DC: National Defense University.

Vest, Hugh S. 2002. "Employee Warriors and the Future of the American Fighting Force." Report no. A957024. Maxwell Air Force Base, AL: Air University Press.

Virilio, Paul. 1989. *War and Cinema: The Logistics of Perception*. Trans. Patrick Camiller. London: Verso.

———. 2002. *Desert Screen: War at the Speed of Light*. London: Continuum.

Weber, Rene, Ute Ritterfeld, and Klaus Mathiak. 2006. "Does Playing Violent Video Games Induce Aggression? Empirical Evidence of a Functional Magnetic Resonance Imaging Study." *Media Psychology* 8, no. 1: 39–60.

Young, Allan. 1995. *The Harmony of Illusions: Inventing Post-Traumatic Stress Disorder*. Princeton, NJ: Princeton University Press.

Chapter 5

MILITARY OCCUPATION AS CARCERAL SOCIETY
Prisons, Checkpoints, and Walls in the
Israeli-Palestinian Struggle

Avram Bornstein

The Israeli Army has maintained an unwelcome military occupation in the West Bank and Gaza Strip for over 40 years. During this time, an increasing carceralization of society has occurred, most evident in three architectural forms: prisons, checkpoints, and walls. These three forms and their accompanying practices of social control, which have been refined and developed, are purportedly intended to prevent Palestinian violence against Israelis. But carceralization has had more insidious outcomes: dividing Palestinians, confiscating their land, destroying their livelihoods, and, thus, giving rise to some submission (collaboration with occupiers or emigration) but mostly to resistance (ranging from non-cooperation to militancy).

References for this chapter begin on page 128.

Understanding the broad impact and costs of a military's carceral architecture and practices from a comparative perspective is especially important at this point as the US has embarked on long-term, occupation-like involvement in Iraq and Afghanistan. It is now evident that misinformation allowed both the invasion of Iraq and its subsequent debacle to occur. White House officials argued that there were weapons of mass destruction in Iraq. They decided that the war could be fought with a small number of forces because the US would be welcomed as liberators. They contended that getting rid of Saddam Hussein would advance the war against the Islamist terrorists who had struck on 9/11. The tragic folly of these White House arguments and their journalist propagandists is now apparent, but this knowledge has not stemmed the tide of misinformation and misrepresentation propelling the continuing tragedy in Iraq. Foremost among these misrepresentations is referring to the occupation as 'reconstruction'. Examining the overall process of military occupation from a comparative perspective may allow us to see the likely contours of long-term occupation, and may help prevent us from being even more beguiled by the self-serving lies of militarists and war profiteers.

Foucault's (1979) study of a carceral society provides a starting point from which to examine critically and comparatively the architecture of modern control. Foucault's idea of a carceral society explains how the prison extends beyond its walls into other institutions of modern life: the factory, the school, the army, and elsewhere. The Israeli Army does not use the discipline discourse described by Foucault, in which the careful organization of prisoners' space, activity, and time—what he called a 'micro-physics' of power—reforms and corrects the criminal delinquent into a productive person. On the contrary, as Brown (2004) explains, the closures in Israel-Palestine create an immobile mass, resembling the pre-modern, plague-quarantined town described by Foucault. Instead of a discourse of discipline, the Israeli government uses a security discourse, in which Palestinians are framed as irrational terrorists and Palestinian areas need to be quarantined or "encysted" (Bowman 2004, 2007).

As in the penology discourse analyzed by Foucault, in Israel-Palestine there is a disjuncture between the discursive logic of the carceral society and its actual practices and outcomes. Foucault explained that the discourse of discipline failed to reform convicts. In actuality, prisons became recruiting opportunities for criminal organizations and police informers, and recidivism became the norm. In the Israeli Occupation there is also a disjuncture between the discourse of security and the actual practices and consequences of the army's carceral system, which, instead of creating concession and acquiescence, has led to sustained and escalating violence. The main successes of the discipline and security discourses have been legitimizing the status quo and, perhaps Foucault's greatest insight, producing new social facts, such as the 'delinquent' and the 'terrorist', that are used in struggles of hegemony.

A handful of recent studies in Israel-Palestine draw critical attention to the architectural elements of occupation by analyzing both the builders and those who suffer the impact and by providing a broad and deep portrait of the carceralization of Palestinian society under the Israeli Occupation. Weizman (2007) presents a landmark examination from the inside of Israeli military and set-tler building projects, such as the gentrification of Jerusalem's Old City, military fortifications, strategic-summit settlements, border passages, the wall, the Israeli Army's urban warfare tactic of moving through (rather than around) buildings, and the airspace above and subterranean space below Israel and the Occupied Territories. Weizman, an Israeli architect, describes the sophisticated spatial planning of these architectural operations and how they negotiate the intentions of the Israeli military and Israeli settlers to control and colonize the territories, with the political and legal restrictions, both national and international, that govern occupiers.

Several ethnographers write about how this military architecture of occupation shapes Palestinian experiences. Ethnographers of prisons (Bornstein 2001; Peteet 1994; Rosenfeld 2004), checkpoints (Bornstein 2002; Brown 2004; Hammami 2004; Kelly 2006), and the wall (Bowman 2004, 2007; Brown 2004) show that despite the military's explanation that the structures were being built to contain danger, these forms of control are an assault, widely perceived as collective punishment, and an attempt to encourage Palestinian acquiescence or emigration. As Escobar (2004) points out, such "dirty little wars" create conditions favorable for capital accumulation by others—not necessarily by exploiting their labor, but by chasing them away from their rightful claims.

Ethnographers of prisons, checkpoints, and walls in the Israeli Occupation also give evidence demonstrating that these architectural forms are locations of contact that shape and are shaped by the national identity of Israelis and Palestinians. Like Barth's (1969) examples of boundary making, or even Said's (1978) critical studies of Orientalism, this kind of anthropology illustrates how identities are constructed dialectically, within and against an opposing other, and not essentially, or made up of key features, as it is often portrayed. Israelis perform and experience some of the meanings of being Israeli with and against Palestinians, and Palestinians perform and experience some of the meanings of being Palestinians with and against Israelis. Bowman (2003), in a historical analysis of Israel-Palestine and the former Yugoslavia, explains how violence by an enemy rendered diverse people as discursively the same, giving life to a nationalist imaginary and a logic of mobilization aimed at transforming the world through struggle. Confrontations between Israelis and Palestinians in these locations help define conceptual borders and markers of national difference that create and reinforce in-group and out-group dichotomies, thus facilitating and perpetuating cycles of reciprocal violence.

After a review of the growth stages of the carceral society under the Israeli Occupation, the bulk of this chapter examines prisons, checkpoints, and walls over the last 20 years. Based on over three years of direct observation (during a dozen visits spread out over two decades) and a review of existing research, the sections below describe (a) how these architectural forms work, (b) the official reasons given for constructing them, (c) critical assessments of their goals and outcomes, and (d) the resistance they have engendered. On the whole, the Israeli Occupation has created an increasingly prison-like society for Palestinians. The result has included some degree of submission but also new vectors of resistance. The final section offers a comparison of the Israeli carceralization of the Occupied Territories and the US occupation of Iraq, and suggests that similar patterns are evident in these rather different settings. A thoughtful consideration of such tactics and outcomes in comparative perspective is urgent because of the threatened possibility of extended military occupations in Iraq, Afghanistan, and perhaps elsewhere.

From 'Open Bridges' to 'Closures'

The Occupied West Bank and Gaza Strip are zones of land cut out and shaped by a series of military conflicts. Despite political and military opposition in the surrounding Arab world, the State of Israel was established in 1948, largely by European Jewish refugees and émigrés, on about three-fourths of the British Mandate of Palestine (1918–1948), which was formerly part of the Ottoman Empire. The capital was divided into Israeli West Jerusalem and Palestinian East Jerusalem. After the 1948 Arab-Israeli War, the remaining one-fourth of the British Mandate was annexed by Jordan (East Jerusalem and the West Bank) and occupied by Egypt (the Gaza Strip). The Israeli Army, with Britain and France, first attacked Egypt in 1956, capturing the Gaza Strip and Sinai Peninsula, but withdrew in 1957 under international pressure. The Israeli Army attacked Egypt again in June 1967, this time drawing neighboring Arab countries into the war. In six days of fighting, Israeli forces captured the Gaza Strip and Sinai Peninsula from Egypt, the Golan Heights from Syria, and the West Bank (including East Jerusalem) from Jordan. Some members of the Israeli government aspired to exploit their military victory by extending Israel's borders, while others thought the land could be traded for concessionary peace treaties with neighboring enemies. The Sinai was returned to Egypt as part of a treaty signed in 1978. The Golan Heights were annexed in 1981, and its Syrian Druze residents were offered citizenship, although most refused, believing that the act would be treasonous. The Syrian government still demands to have this land returned. East Jerusalem was annexed, and its Palestinian residents were offered citizenship, although many refused there, too. The rest of the West Bank and the Gaza Strip were not annexed because offering citizenship to so many Palestinians was a threat to the Zionist ideal of a Jewish State of Israel. For over 40 years, the West Bank and the Gaza Strip have remained Occupied Territories. The chronology of this 40-year occupation can be divided into four periods, each demonstrating an increasing generalization of the carceral: 1967–1987, 'open bridges' policy; 1987–1993, the First Intifada; 1993–2000, Oslo; and 2000 to the present, the Second or al-Aqsa Intifada.

After the military conquest in 1967, the initial approach to ruling civilians in the Occupied Territories was referred to as 'open bridges' (Gazit 1995). This policy was designed to normalize Arab-Israeli relations through Palestinians, who would be subordinately integrated into Israel, while keeping the West Bank's bridges to Jordan open. The Israeli Ministry of Defense ran the civilian administration of Judea and Samaria (the West Bank), which issued identification cards, commercial licenses, permits, and automobile license plates, and dealt with other civil matters. Workers from the Occupied Territories were soon welcomed into the Israeli labor market in undesirable, laborious jobs, such as those in agriculture and construction. By the mid-1980s, about 120,000 Palestinian workers from the Occupied Territories—approximately 80,000 registered and 40,000 unregistered—went to work in Israel every day (Semyonov and Lewin-Epstein 1987). The infrastructure of the West Bank (roads, electric power, water, telephones) was linked into the Israeli networks (Gazit 1995: 169; Tamari 1980, 1981). Palestinian militants and political activists, largely from secular nationalist groups (e.g., Fatah) or leftist organizations (e.g., the Popular Front), were arrested and exiled, and their houses destroyed. However, large-scale control during the first 20 years of the Occupation was sought through subordinate integration. The systems created by this unequal integration were widely characterized as relations of colonial dependency (Nakhleh and Zureik 1980; Owen 1989; Roy 1991, 1995; Saleh 1990; Samara 1989, 2001; Sayigh 1986; Tamari 1980, 1981, 1990).

For the most part, Palestinian civilians passively endured the dependency of the Occupation and looked to the Palestinian Liberation Organization (PLO) in the diaspora to lead the national struggle against Israel. But in the 1980s, several factors encouraged people to organize what eventually became a grassroots rebellion. Politically and militarily, Palestinians in the Occupied Territories felt abandoned when Egypt signed a peace treaty with Israel in 1978, and when the Israeli Army invaded Lebanon in 1982 and ejected the PLO. Economically, Palestinians in the Occupied Territories were strained because they were receiving fewer remittances from the Gulf (a decline in oil prices had caused a recession in the Arab world), and new Israeli taxes were being collected by the Israeli Army (Tamari 1990: 163). Perhaps most important, a new right-wing government supportive of the settlement movement came to power in Israel in 1977, and the number of settlers in the West Bank grew from 3,176 in 1976, to 57,000 in 1987. Palestinian youths saw little in their future but to live life as suffered by their fathers and mothers—with their lands stolen by settlements and their labors given to hewing wood and drawing water for Israelis.

The First Intifada erupted in December 1987 when a series of clashes in the Jabalya refugee camp in Gaza spread across Gaza and the West Bank. Palestinian children took to the streets, throwing stones and Molotov cocktails at soldiers, burning tires in their paths, and attacking known collaborators. The violence created a spectacle, but more significant was the initiation of non-violent mobilization to disengage from Israel. Villages, town councils, labor unions, women's organizations, and Islamic centers became politicized (Hiltermann 1992; Nasser and Heacock 1990). Merchants boycotted Israeli goods, refused to pay taxes, and shut their stores every day at noon. Competing leaderships from Fatah and the Sunni Islamist organization Hamas called strike days. Civil servants resigned from government jobs. An 'alternative economy', based on cottage industries and a return to peasant subsistence techniques, was promoted (Tamari 1990: 160). Wedding celebrations during the summer, usually loud, public events in the villages and camps, were curtailed and brought indoors. While uplifting for Palestinian dignity, the Intifada caused increased suffering. Strikes called by Palestinians and curfews enforced by the Israeli Army prevented people from going to work (Roy 1991: 61). The Israeli Army responded to these acts of resistance with the arrest of tens of thousands and the beating of many more. Integration, although not eliminated, was turned back, and the prison itself became more widely used as a form of social control.

The Israeli government and the PLO signed a series of agreements (Oslo I, Oslo II, Wye River) in the mid-1990s that allowed the PLO to return to Palestinian towns in the Occupied Territories and establish a Palestinian Authority (PA), with civilian and limited security control, while Israel began a phased withdrawal from those towns. The major issues of contention, such as the right of return for Palestinian refugees, the Israeli settlements in the Occupied Territories, and the status of East Jerusalem, were put on hold in the hope that interim peace would build trust toward future compromise. PLO leader Yasser Arafat entered Palestinian towns with police officers and tens of thousands of armed security personnel to carry out the explicit, mandated task of controlling attacks against Israelis.

The PLO takeover of security and civilian affairs might have led to further steps toward compromise, but the process was quickly undermined. First, checkpoint-enforced closures on the Green Line made it much more difficult for Palestinians to work in Israel. Second, Israeli settlements in the West Bank ballooned as thousands of Israelis, driven by the immigration of about 900,000 Jews from the former Soviet Union, sought cheaper housing east of the Green Line but within commuting distance to places like Jerusalem and Tel Aviv. By 1995 there were 147,000 settlers, and by 1999 close to 180,000, not including an additional 200,000 in areas of the Occupied Territories incorporated into metropolitan Jerusalem. Third, with this growth of settlements came more checkpoints, not only on the Green Line but also between PA zones. With major strips of settlement east of Jerusalem and east of Tel Aviv, these internal checkpoints divided Palestinians into three discontinuous blocks (see fig. 1). It was not long before the Oslo arrangement of PA autonomous zones became fragmented enclaves—like the 'bantustans' of South Africa. Fourth, violence poisoned the Oslo process. Settlers regularly victimized Palestinians, not only by confiscating their lands, but also by vandalizing their property and assaulting them. This degree of settler militancy was dramatically demonstrated on 25 February 1994 by an attack in which settler Baruch Goldstein shot dead 29 men and wounded 150 more in a mosque in Hebron before being killed himself. In retaliation for that massacre, Hamas began its now infamous suicide bus bombings in April 1994. Control during the Oslo years was sought through a proxy Palestinian police department, but checkpoints, settlements, and violence undermined progress toward peace and increased the carceralization of society under the Occupation.

While violence was continuous through the 1990s into the Oslo years, any semblance of détente vanished when the Second or al-Aqsa Intifada ignited in September 2000. Member of Parliament (MP) Ariel Sharon toured the Dome of the Rock, an Islamic holy place, with hundreds of police, setting off Palestinian demonstrations the next day. The Israeli Army retaliated at a higher than normal level of force. Dozens of Palestinians were killed in the first few

FIGURE 1 Three Zones in the West Bank as Designated by
Israeli-Palestinian Agreements in 1994 and 1998

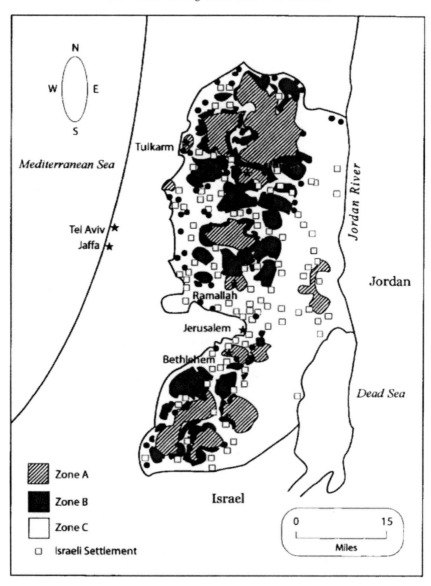

Source: Bornstein (2002).

Note: In Zone A, Israeli forces withdrew from the ground, and the Palestinian Authority had civil and security control. In Zone B, the Palestinian Authority had civil control, but security was shared by Israeli and Palestinian authorities. In the remainder of the West Bank, Zone C, the Israeli government had sole authority. Palestinian zones became isolated from each other by checkpoints, and blocks of settlements east of Jerusalem and east of Tel Aviv divided the West Bank into three discontinuous blocks: north, central, and south.

days, including 13 Palestinian Israelis. The fatal shooting of one small boy, Muhammed al-Durrah, crouching behind his helpless father, was videotaped and became an icon for Palestinian suffering. Now armed, Palestinian militia attacked settlements in the Occupied Territories and inside Israel and sent numerous suicide bombers. Israel responded by using attack helicopters and fighter jets and a surge of troops in 2002 that reoccupied several Palestinian autonomous zones. Given the few settlers in Gaza and the high cost of protecting them, the Israeli Army evacuated the settlers in September 2005 but maintained control of its borders.

The al-Aqsa Intifada has devolved into an internal struggle between Fatah and Hamas over paramilitary operations, with both competing against Israel as well as each other. Despite talk of unilateral Israeli actions such as the 'withdrawal' from Gaza or the building of a wall, the Occupation persists. The use of armed violence by soldiers and settlers, from rubber bullets to fighter jets, continues, and particular architectural forms of social control run by the military, such as prisons, checkpoints, and walls, subject everyone to chronic suffering. These architectural forms have created a carceral society that is less understood than armed violence by those outside the conflict. In this society, destruction and defiant resistance perpetuate cycles of violence.

Prisons

In April 1995, I went to visit my friend Muhammed in the Tulkarem prison. I had met him the previous fall when he first enrolled as a freshman at Birzeit University, my academic home away from home during fieldwork in the early 1990s. Before dawn I drove from Tulkarem to the village of Jayoos, about 20 minutes away, to pick up Um Muhammed (Muhammed's mother) and two of his cousins for the visit. His mother carried a plastic basket of fruit, cooked chicken, a bottle of olive oil, and sweets for her son.

In the car she told me that about six weeks previously soldiers had raided her house in the middle of the night, demanding Muhammed. He was away at the college, so the army took her husband's and younger son's identification cards and said that they should get Muhammed and bring him to the army base in Tulkarem, and then they could have their identification cards back. Otherwise, they would be arrested. These men could not travel to the university without their identity cards, so Um Muhammed left before dawn with her youngest son, Mahmood. With the help of some students, Um Muhammed found her son in class and, sobbing, pulled him out in order to deliver him to the army.

Such an event was already common by 1995. During the first years of the Intifada, 20,000 to 30,000 Palestinians experienced arrest annually, with about 14,000 to 15,000 Palestinians in custody at any given time (B'tselem 1992; Human Rights Watch 1994). Anyone could be detained by police or soldiers for 96 hours, and an officer could authorize another 18 days, after which a military commander or judge could issue a renewable six-month period of 'administrative detention'. "Administrative detention, as defined by law, is meant to prevent the actions of an individual whom the authorities believe is liable to endanger security and public order in the future. Administrative detention was not meant to replace the judicial process" (B'tselem 1992: 81; see also Golan 1992).

Sometimes the police made arrests with soldiers in the middle of the night in order to avoid crowds and resistance, as they tried to do with Muhammed. These surprise raids drew the entire family into the experience. Mothers and sisters would sometimes try to force themselves in between their male relatives and the soldiers. Their homes were violated and their ability to sleep soundly permanently threatened. Arrests also happened at checkpoints on auto and pedestrian thoroughfares, with or without obvious provocation, and identification cards would usually be checked against a list of wanted persons. Some people did not know that they were wanted until they were taken into custody.

After turning himself in, Muhammed was interrogated for about two weeks. Like the thousands of detainees before him, he was hooded, bound, confined, deprived of sleep, threatened, and beaten during these first weeks of custody (Al-Haq 1989, 1990; B'tselem 1991, 1992; Ginbar 1993, 1998; Human Rights Watch 1994). Torture and detention are illegal based on the United Nations Universal Declaration of Human Rights (1948), the Geneva Convention IV relative to the Protection of Civilian Persons in Time of War (1949), the International Covenant on Civil and Political Rights (1966), the UN Declaration on Torture (1975), and the UN Convention against Torture (1984). However, in the 1987 Landau Report on the General Security Services (GSS), Israeli courts decided that it was permissible to use "moderate physical pressure" in security matters (B'tselem 1991). In 1994, Prime Minister Yitzhak Rabin declared that because of the increase in suicide bombings and terrorist activity, the gloves would be taken off, and even the Landau restrictions would be suspended. The Israeli High Court reversed this decision in September 1999, but numerous accounts of severe abuse continued.

The official reason for torture during interrogations was to induce the victim to provide the names of those active in the Intifada so as to intercept a 'ticking time bomb'. But Mahmood (1996: 9) argues: "Even when people do have information to give, they typically lose track of it utterly in the torture situation. The goal of torture therefore must be understood in terms other than mere acquisition of knowledge, despite the common claim of torturers the world over that this is why they torture." The motive for using torture was important from the standpoint of the Israeli courts, some of the Israeli public, an international audience, and maybe even the interrogators themselves, in order to maintain their belief that they were civilized individuals who were being compelled to act against irrational, uncivilized, terrorist enemies.

However, the torture of Palestinian boys and young men was understood by its victims as being intended to teach them fear, to destroy their will to resist, and to discourage participation in the Intifada. Former detainees "reported constant verbal humiliation—abuse, insults, slander, cursing—by the interrogators. Almost all reported that their mothers, sisters, or wives were cursed by their interrogators: 'We will bring your sister and your mother here, and we will fuck them while you watch,' is one of the sayings reported ... 'Your mother is pregnant by a GSS man' and 'Your wife is already pregnant? Good thing for you' are also phrases often attributed to the interrogator" (B'tselem 1991: 56). These tactics seem intended to humiliate. The attention given by interrogators to beating the testicles and threatening to rape female relatives strikes at the masculinity of the victim and also at the collective representations of national identity (Seifert 1996).

After two weeks, the lawyer at Birzeit University was informed via the Red Cross that Muhammed was out of interrogation and could be seen in Tulkarem prison, where he awaited trial. Visiting day was every other Wednesday, and this was the first time that Um Muhammed would see her son since he had been incarcerated. She had gone to visit him two weeks previously but had arrived too late, so on this day we were there early.

In the 1990s, the Israeli Army operated nine of their own detention facilities. These were separate from the 21 prisons operated by the Israeli Prison Service, six of which were in the territories, to hold criminal prisoners. Israeli Army prisons and detention facilities were for political or 'security' prisoners. Most detainees in these facilities lived in crowded tents with poor sanitary conditions. During the Intifada, there were five main detention centers: Far'ah, north of Nablus; Dhahriyyah, south of Hebron; Beach camp (Ansar II), in Gaza; Megiddo, inside Israel; and Ketziot, called Ansar III by Palestinians, also inside Israel in the Negev desert. Ansar III, created in the mid-1980s to cope with the increasing number of arrests, was the largest detention facility, holding close to 6,000 detainees (B'tselem 1992: 103). Prisoners at Ansar III, like those at Beach camp and Far'ah, were kept in tents, with approximately 25 to 30 prisoners per tent (B'tselem 1992; Human Rights Watch 1991). The Tulkarem prison was a smaller indoor facility that was located within the compound of the Israeli Army's civil administration headquarters for the Tulkarem district.

Waiting in the street in front of the Israeli Army compound, I noticed there was very little movement in town for a Wednesday at 7:00 AM. Then I remembered that it was a holiday, Holocaust Memorial Day, in Israel. Around 9:00 AM, a group of soldiers came out of the side gate where we were waiting. The soldiers told the crowd—mostly women, children, and old men, numbering around 40—to back away across the street as they read aloud the names of those who could receive visitors today. Muhammed's name was not on the first list. The initial group of visitors went in, and we were told to wait half an hour for a second list. Indeed, half an hour later, a second list was read, and Muhammed's name was on it.

I accompanied Muhammed's mother and his cousins to the gate. We gave our identification to the soldiers, were searched, and entered the compound. In a crowd of about 20 visitors, we were ushered under close watch—surrounded by soldiers and with stern orders of "quickly, quickly"—into a long, fenced cage that was locked behind us. On one side of the cage there was an adjacent cage where the prisoners were soon brought. An old man and woman and two young girls stood next to us. Hearing my non-native Arabic, the old man asked where I came from. Hearing my answer, the old woman said, "It is good that you should see what they are doing to our children."

The prisoners were brought into the opposite cage, walking single file. Muhammed, only 18 years old, looked like one of the oldest. They had taken all of the prisoners' shoelaces away. We all reached through little holes in the fence for each other's hands. The women were crying. Muhammed looked well. He was trying to grow a beard. He was so excited to see us that he started to bang on the cage. The guards got angry and shouted at him to stop.

We were all asking what we could do for him. Um Muhammed told him about the bag of food that the guards would pass along to him after checking it. He thanked her but surprisingly said that he did not need food. I asked if he wanted me to bring him his textbooks from the university, which were in my car outside. He did not want them. He asked for only one thing. He wanted a specific Koran from his home, the one with interpretations in the margins and a green cover with gold letters.

Muhammed said that he needed the Koran because he was studying and teaching. Palestinian men often spoke of the prison as the 'other university'. They organized into self-segregated groups, each affiliated with outside resistance organizations, primarily Fatah and Hamas. They set up programs of teaching in which students, teachers, professionals, and all kinds of people gave instruction on Islam, 'traditional' Palestinian life, security outside the prison, the history of Palestine and the Zionist movement, literacy in Arabic, and even Hebrew or English as a second language. New inmates were invited to join these organizations if they did not already have affiliations.

We had been there about 10 minutes when a soldier came behind the prisoners and told us all in Hebrew to be silent. The first time he said it, no one listened. Then he yelled it. The prisoners and men shut up at once. Many of the women did not even know what the soldier was saying, so they went on talking. The soldier said to the prisoners, "You better make them shut up." Everyone began to realize that they had to be quiet. The guard said, "Two minutes, quiet." Because it was Holocaust Memorial Day, at 10:00 AM exactly sirens whined for one minute all over Israel as the nation observed a moment of silence. The visiting mothers and sisters, unaware of what was happening, began to whisper to each other. The guard became visibly furious and said, "Tell them to shut up!" In silence we cowered, listening to the memorial siren. When it ended, we resumed talking and soon said good-bye.

Muhammed came before the court in May and was sentenced to six months for participating in Hamas for three months in 1992. He confessed to spray-painting and rock throwing in his village. By the time of his sentencing, he had already served half that time, so we were all relieved that we would see him by the end of the summer.

I took Um Muhammed to visit her son in two other prisons and saw him the day he arrived home that summer. But I returned to the US soon afterward, and it was not until a year later, in the summer of 1996, that I finally had a chance to talk with Muhammed about his experiences. It had been a horrible year. His mother had died. She had been sick with diabetes for years, but he said that her friends insisted that it was Muhammed's troubles that had killed her. He explained that he was rearrested again in the spring of 1996, but this time it was by the Palestinian police. The Palestinian Authority had arrived in their village in the winter, and when bombings occurred in Israel in the spring of 1996, they had arrested hundreds of Hamas sympathizers. Muhammed was beaten, questioned, and then released after 10 days without being charged. He claimed that the Palestinian interrogators, who were largely Fatah loyalists, were much worse than the Israelis. The Israelis, he said, were professionals. When they tortured, they mainly used psychological pressure and isolation to interrogate him, and when they began beating and choking him, they had army doctors checking to make sure that he was not dying. Under Palestinian detention and interrogation, he said, there was no method, no doctor, and no Red Cross. He feared that the Palestinian interrogators would kill him by accident (see Human Rights Watch 1998). The experience had made him more convinced of the righteousness of the Hamas movement.

Well over 100,000 Palestinians, mostly young men, have been security prisoners of the Israelis. Many were violently interrogated. While it was intended to break resistance, the suffering that they endured at the hands of the Israelis became instead a kind of status symbol that further encouraged resistance (Bornstein 2001; Khalil 1988; Peteet 1994). In her extensive study of the Dheisha refugee camp, Rosenfeld (2004) argues that the lengthy imprisonment of Palestinians heightened the politicization not only of the individuals themselves, but also of their families and neighbors. Those who served many years in prison were said to have sacrificed for the nation and were treated as the vanguard of the struggle. By the 1980s, the portrayal of the prison experience as a rite of passage and a metonym for all Palestinians under occupation was evident in conversation and in the arts, including "Prison," the poem by Mahmoud Darwish (1980), the most famous Palestinian poet; *Cell 704*, the prison memoir by Jabril Rajub (1986); and *Ansar*, the play by Fateh Azza (2003), which was first performed in East Jerusalem by the El-Hakawati Theater Company in 1990. Rajub, the writer of the prison memoir, later became chief of the Fatah interrogators of Hamas as head of the Preventive Security Services in the PA. Palestinians have celebrated and reinscribed prison experience as a form of resistance (Peteet 1994); however, it has been deeply damaging and traumatic to the individuals involved and their society (Bornstein 2001). That damage includes the separation of families, lost opportunities for education and employment, post-traumatic stress disorders, and the bitter experience that former prisoners have become the jailers and have learned to oppress their own.

Checkpoints

Permanent checkpoints on the Green Line were created in March 1993, ending almost 25 years of 'open bridges'. The Green Line is the 1949 armistice line between Israel and Jordan, but under the Israeli 'open bridges' policy, it was rarely marked and easily crossed. From the mid-1970s until 1993, work authorization papers were only an issue of payroll taxes and insurance and were not strictly enforced. But in March 1993 they became a security tactic to limit the entry of Palestinians into Israel. The ostensible reason for the checkpoints was a response to Palestinian attacks that had killed 15 Israelis that month. The Israeli government also said that the closures were a step leading toward the separation of Israelis and Palestinians, and a move toward Palestinian autonomy. However, settlers and soldiers remained free to cross, and only Palestinians were denied freedom of movement. This preceded, by only a few months, the announcement of phased withdrawals of Israeli soldiers from Palestinian population centers. Israel had negotiated a more circumscribed form of control, and West Bankers and Gazans felt more imprisoned in their towns.

A soldier at a checkpoint could be polite, or could try to humiliate those who pass. In the 1990s, it was not unusual to hear of beatings. For example, just before the Second or al-Aqsa Intifada began in fall 2000, the *Washington Post* reported the following:

> JERUSALEM, Sept. 18 — After they had finished pummeling their three Palestinian detainees, finished smashing them with their fists, elbows and boots, slamming their heads against a stone wall, forcing them to swallow their own blood and cursing their mothers and sisters, the young Israeli policemen did an unusual thing: Using a disposable camera, they took photographs of themselves with their victims, holding their heads by the hair like hunting trophies ...
>
> In fact, this month's incident, which took place within sight of Jerusalem's Old City walls, may never have come to light but for two things, human rights groups say. One is that the policemen photographed themselves with their victims and failed to destroy the negatives. The other is that the Palestinians' boss, an Israeli rabbi, was so furious that after his employees were released from the hospital he took them to the authorities to complain. (Hockstader 2000: A16)

According to the article, the three Palestinians were heading home after working until 2:30 AM delivering groceries, when police stopped them at a checkpoint near the entrance to Abu Dis, a Palestinian autonomous zone near Jerusalem. The police ordered them out of their car, ordered the men to stand against a wall, and, according to the indictment, proceeded to beat the three men for about 40 minutes, despite the fact that they had work permissions.

In 1994, I was in a shared taxi in thick traffic between Ramallah and Jerusalem, waiting to cross an Israeli military checkpoint marking the Green Line. At the checkpoint, a half-dozen concrete blocks, each about a cubic meter in size, fortified the Israeli soldiers who manned the crossing. The soldiers were checking to see that everyone entering Israel had either a citizen's blue identification card or, if one had an orange West Bank identification card, work authorization. When our taxi arrived at the crossing, we rolled down our windows, and the Israeli soldier asked for our identification cards. I gave him my US passport. He looked at me. It was winter, and I was wearing a Palestinian scarf, a *hatta*. He said in Hebrew, with disgust, "What is this? Get out of the car!" I stepped out, perhaps with too much confidence, and asked in my non-native Hebrew if there was a problem. Without a word he slapped me across the face, put my passport in his pocket, ordered me to sit on the ground, and told the taxi to drive on. He did it as if he had done it many times before.

I was not physically hurt by the slap but rather shocked, emasculated, and humiliated by being treated like an animal. I stopped speaking in Hebrew and said in loud, clear English, "Get the officer." The soldier's face registered surprise, not necessarily with comprehension but perhaps with shock at my arrogance. Another soldier, perhaps an officer, crossed the road and asked calmly what the problem was. My car was slowly advancing through the traffic, so I was in great haste. I said to him in Hebrew, "He has my passport. Take my passport. Can you read English? Read my name." He looked at my name. Then he asked, "Are you Jewish?" I replied, trying to challenge him, "My name is Avram Bornstein. You think I am a terrorist?" Then, as so many soldiers at checkpoints have done before, he asked me, "You're not afraid?"—meaning to be with Palestinians. I gave him the same retort I gave each time I was asked this question at a checkpoint. I said, "I'm afraid of you [the plural form], the army." Such an answer was often met with some confusion, as if I had mixed up who is who. Israeli soldiers would then often warn me not to be in these areas and not to trust the Arabs. I have been told countless times, "You are not from here. We know them because we live with them."

Before I could be given this predictable lecture, I asked for my passport back. The soldiers complied, and I ran after my car. I got back into my seat, and the other passengers cheered me for having gotten past the soldiers. "Bravo to you," said an old woman. I was too embarrassed to tell them that I had used the soldiers' prejudices against Palestinians and for Jews to motivate them into letting me go. Like so many other times during my stay in the West Bank in the 1990s, I was stopped because soldiers thought I was another 20-something-year-old Palestinian and released when they realized I was a Jew.

Since the al-Aqsa Intifada erupted in 2000, checkpoints on the Green Line and also inside the Occupied Territories between Palestinian Authority zones have increased. B'tselem, a leading Israeli human rights organization, reports that there are 58 permanent checkpoints within the West Bank, an additional 15 in Hebron alone, 35 checkpoints between the West Bank and Israel, a weekly average of 200 temporary checkpoints inside the West Bank, and over 400 physical obstructions (concrete blocks, dirt piles, trenches) that make roads impassable.

The explicit reason that Israeli Army spokespersons give for checkpoints inside the West Bank and on the Green Line is security. The Israeli Army Web site puts it clearly: "Almost on a daily basis, the Israel Defense Forces have captured Islamic terrorists at Israeli Army security checkpoints in both the West Bank and Gaza attempting to smuggle both weapons and explosives into Israel" (Israel News Agency 2007). It cites suicide bombings in 2005 and 2006—one on the Green Line, one approaching a West Bank settlement, and two in Tel Aviv. This was also explained to me by a young soldier at a checkpoint near the Green Line in 2002. While traveling with foreign human rights observers, our group noticed three Palestinian teenage boys detained at the side of the road. We inquired why the boys were being detained. "It's not your business. Go back to your cars," the soldier told us. When we persisted in requests to free the boys, the young commander came over and tried to reason with me. He said in English, "Look, because of them, three of my friends are no longer living." "Because of them? These three boys killed them?" I asked. "No, not these three exactly, but three like them," he said.

Hass (2002) argues that in the 1990s, the checkpoints and the phenomenon that became known as 'closure' had the political intention of compelling the PLO to accept Israel's 'final offer'. But the strategy proved a failure when the PLO rejected Israeli demands in the summer of 2000. In the fall of 2000, the closures in the West Bank intensified to stop the al-Aqsa Intifada. However, as Hass reports (ibid: 20), closure, "far from helping to crush the defiance, is now adding fuel to the fire of the frustration and wrath."

By being treated equally with suspicion, all Palestinians experience oppression directly at the hands of armed Israeli soldiers, who go through personal belongings and give orders that must be followed. B'tselem (2007) argues that the checkpoints violate international law because the policy is "based on the assumption that every single Palestinian is a security threat, thereby justifying restrictions on his or her freedom of movement. This assumption is racist and leads to the sweeping violation of the human rights of an entire population on the basis of national origin." It is perceived and experienced as a collective assault.

Many Palestinians chose to resist by going around the checkpoints. This was true for the tens of thousands of workers who depended on jobs—building, picking, cleaning, and manufacturing every day in Israel—but could not get permits, as well as those who had to travel to other parts of the Occupied Territories. During some seasons enforcement was strict, while at other times it was loose. Near Green Line checkpoints, detained workers could be seen sitting in groups on the ground next to the checkpoint, their identification cards held by the Israeli soldiers. In 1994, the police would usually write them a ticket for 450 New Israeli Shekels (NIS) (about $150), which was about a week's wages for most people, and send them home. Outlawing undocumented workers put an entire population in jeopardy of arrest or police violence, and this danger is something employers used to exploit employees by paying them less, or sometimes not at all, and allowing substandard working conditions (Bornstein 2002).

Other Palestinians resisted by attacking the checkpoints. In the late 1980s and 1990s, after school or after Friday prayers at the mosque, usually (but not always) boys and young men would march to within sight of the checkpoints and throw stones at the soldiers from a distance, preferably from a location where they could take quick cover. Sometimes burning tires were rolled toward the checkpoints, creating a wall of fire between the two sides. Israelis responded with a variety of tactics. Sometimes they took out batons, charged on foot, and beat and arrested the young men. Other times they used tear gas, sound grenades, rubber bullets (with metal cores), or even live rounds of ammunition.

After the al-Aqsa Intifada began in 2000, checkpoints became locations for frequent gun battles. In the Tulkarem district it was not unusual to hear in the night the *tac-tac-tac* of a small gun, such as an AK-47, attacking a fixed Israeli position, soon answered by the heavy *doom-doom-doom-doom* of mounted Israeli guns. Sometimes the exchange was over quickly. Sometimes it continued for a few minutes, stopped, and resumed again later. Sometimes I could hear ambulances. During the daylight hours, the evidence of the destruction was clear. The concrete buildings in sight of the checkpoints were terribly chopped by bullets and mostly abandoned. It seems that these attacks, like individual acts of suicide bombing, are the disorganized attempts made by frustrated Palestinians who lack a coordinated struggle.

Machsom (Checkpoint) Watch, an Israeli checkpoint observation project, emerged with the goal of reducing the harm to Palestinians as they attempt to cross these barriers. The organization reports having approximately 400 volunteer observers working in small teams across the Occupied Territories. Their volunteers are exclusively women, they say, because women's "quiet but assertive presence at checkpoints is a direct challenge to the dominant militaristic discourse that prevails in Israeli society. It demands accountability on the part of the security forces toward the civilian estate, something hitherto almost unheard of" (Machsom Watch 2004). The group publishes reports in a weekly e-mail digest that documents the extremely arbitrary nature of check-point enforcement and how much depends upon the personal discretion of commanding officers, some of whom do their best to accommodate the Pales-tinians, while others do their best to make them suffer (see Brown 2004; Nirgad 2004). Machsom Watch, like other human rights observers, such as the Chris-tian Peacemaker Teams in Hebron or the International Solidarity Movement throughout the Occupied Territories, has helped cultivate international attention and criticism of the use of these checkpoints.

Checkpoints have created a more circumscribed form of control, imprison-ing West Bankers and Gazans in their villages and towns and rupturing the social and economic fabric in which they live. Arbitrary and capricious vio-lence by soldiers against civilians at these locations is not uncommon. The logic expressed by official policy and by the soldier doing his job is that anyone could be a terrorist, so everyone must be approached that way until convinced otherwise. Consequently, every Palestinian suffers. Most Palestinians endure the checkpoints, many try to get around them, and a small handful attack them. Human rights groups have become aware of these places as locations of conflict and keep them under observation as much as possible. The immobility created by these checkpoints is similar to being kept under town arrest, and the prison metaphor is a common way to describe the closures.

Walls

In the fall of 2002, I stood atop a hill in the Tulkarm district of the West Bank with the mayor of the village of Qufeen. We were surrounded by olive and orange groves. Despite the rural, agricultural landscape, the setting was anything but tranquil because 70 meters in front of us the largest pieces of land-moving equip-ment I had ever seen were tearing through the trees and earth. They were busily clearing a path about 50 meters wide through the groves to build a wall. In some areas the wall is a high concrete structure with guard lookouts, cameras, and 50 meters of cleared security area. In other areas it is an electronic, barbed-wire fence with trenches on both sides and 50 meters of cleared security area.

Because the wall does not follow the pre-1967 border but instead has been built inside the West Bank, Palestinians see it as a way for Israel to confiscate more land and destroy more Palestinian resources and infrastructure. The mayor of Qufeen related that the project had already felled about 3,000 trees and the owners were not even allowed to take the wood because the Israeli contractors had sold it. As the machines creaked and clanked, the mayor said that the barrier itself would uproot about 600 dunums (approximately 150 acres) and that an additional 6,500 dunums (approximately 1,625 acres) with around 120,000 trees would be isolated on the other side of the barrier. In October 2003, in the northern West Bank, the Israeli Army declared the land between the barrier and the Green Line to be a closed military area, requiring Palestinians living in or visiting those areas to obtain a permit. Gates were built that allow permit holders to cross the barrier, but not everyone can get a permit. And sometimes the gates are closed even to those with permits. B'tselem (2007) reports that there are 73 such gates in the separation barrier, but only 38 are for Palestinians, and they are open for only part of the day. Pointing east and south, the mayor explained that they already had a Jewish settlement, Harmish, and its bypass road closing them in on two sides. When finished, the barrier, completing the circle, "will be like a rope around the neck."

The Israeli government's stated intention has been to build a barrier to prevent Palestinian attacks originating in the West Bank. The government of Yitzhak Rabin built a fence around Gaza back in 1994. Following an attack that killed 21 teenagers on the beach of Tel Aviv in June 2001, a campaign began to build a wall referred to as a "Wall for Life." The Ministry of Defense (2007) Web site explains: "The Security Fence is an operational concept conceived by the Israeli Defense Establishment in order to reduce the number of terrorist attacks whether in the form of explosive-rigged vehicles or in the form of suicide bombers who enter into Israel with the intention of murdering innocent babies, children, women and men." In addition to the fear of terrorism, Rabinowitz (2003) also points to the psychological need of Israelis to unilaterally define a border, given the much greater looming threat of a right of return for 1948 refugees as demanded by many Palestinians. Building a wall defines a border, at least psychologically, if not politically.

Building walls for security has coincided opportunistically with material benefit for settlers and settlements near or in the West Bank. Such opportunistic security building is a long-standing tactic in the conflict. Using simpler technology, Zionist settlers in Palestine began a movement to build 'wall and tower' settlements in 1936. By erecting prefabricated walls and towers in one day, the 'wall and tower movement' was able to 'pioneer' Jewish settlements in the hills of the Galilee, despite being under attack during what became know as the Great Revolt (1936–1939) of the Palestinian peasantry. These wall and tower colonies expanded the area of Jewish settlement and influenced, to Israel's benefit, the mapping of partition that came a decade later. Similarly, today's security/apartheid wall creates facts on the ground that expand the land of Israel.

The wall makes it much more difficult to enter Israel without going through a checkpoint. It does not, however, make it impossible to enter illegally—only impractical to do it on a daily basis. Workers who once snuck around a checkpoint early in the morning and returned at the end of the day, now travel long distances, stay in Israel for a week or two or more, and live hidden at construction sites and factories. One of my friends works and lives in hiding in Israel at a location that would be only 10 minutes by car from his home in the West Bank—if there were no wall or checkpoint. But with walls and checkpoints, his journey can take six or more hours, so he sees his wife and five children only about every other weekend.

A broad coalition, including Palestinian farmers, municipalities, and civil committees, accompanied by foreign and Israeli activists, have demonstrated to oppose the wall and stop bulldozers from destroying trees. They put up tents in the groves, tied themselves to trees, replanted uprooted trees, and marched and marched. In the summer of 2004, thousands of Palestinians, Israelis, and internationals from different organizations and political parties joined with children and farmers in a Freedom March Against the Wall, starting in Jenin and stopping in dozens of villages and towns along the wall's route. The Israeli Army sometimes broke up these gatherings, arrested demonstrators, and dispersed others with tear gas, sound bombs, and live ammunition fire. These demonstrations received publicity in Israel in January 2004, when it became known that Gil Na'amati, recently discharged from the Israeli Army and the son of a regional Labor Party activist, had been shot by an Israeli soldier and seriously injured while protesting at the wall in late December 2003 (*Ha'aretz* 2004). The event, caught on video by demonstrators, led to significant protests by civilians in front of the Israeli Defense Ministry building and by MP Shimon Peres, who said, "[T]his is a shocking incident that should be thoroughly and independently investigated so that it will not happen again" (ibid.).

In December 2003, the United Nations General Assembly sent the issue of the wall's construction to the International Court of Justice (ICJ) in the Hague for an advisory opinion. In June 2004, the ICJ said that it was illegal and should be torn down. Dozens of Palestinians who had lost land to the wall construction filed petitions. In 2004, the Israeli High Court of Justice ruled the route illegal, and a new route, closer to the Green Line, was approved (Harel 2004; Schiff 2003). The new route, however, still runs through the West Bank, not along the Green Line. Israeli Justice Minister Yosef Lapid urged at the time that the wall be moved closer to the Green Line, warning that the hearing "could be the first step toward turning Israel into the South Africa of today, and there is a danger that we will be exposed to international boycotts" (Susser 2004). Israel's attorney general also cautioned that the opinion "could lead to anti-Israel actions in international forums that could include sanctions" and recommended that Israel move the wall's route closer to the Green Line, according to the Israeli High Court of Justice's earlier decisions (Yoaz 2004). The Israeli Cabinet plan in February 2005 brought the proposed route closer to the Green Line, but still cut away about 7 percent of the West Bank, putting about 10,000 Palestinians on the Israeli side (Benn, Mualem, and Harel 2005).

Carceralization, Identity, and Violence

In Foucault's carceral society, particular subjectivities are created, notably the 'delinquent', who has not only committed bad deeds but whose very nature is pathologized. In Israel-Palestine, carceral architecture is intended not to reform the delinquent but to stop the terrorist. Israeli government spokespersons explain that the prisons, checkpoints, and walls are all designed with security in mind. In either case, injustices caused by prisons in the US or by the Occupation are more easily dismissed or forgiven by media pundits as unfortunate collateral damage when presented as part of a just war against crime or terror. However, to the targets of these actions, the pathological label imposed by oppressors is illegitimate, and the damage is not *collateral*. The carceralization of a society not only has an impact on its economy in terms of per capita income and gross national product but also produces widely shared experiences that can result in mobilization around collective actions.

Clearly, particular forms of Israeli identity are enacted at these locations. Like the 'wall and tower pioneers' of the 1930s, many Israelis believe that they are performing a heroic defense of their people against an Arab threat, against the Arabs' irrational hatred of Jews. However, mixed in with this nationalist ideal of protecting one's own is the base opportunism of occupation, the dispossession of Palestinians, the profits enjoyed by building contractors, and the possibility of cheaper housing for Israelis. Furthermore, Israeli entrepreneurs have created a multi-billion dollar export industry out of anti-terror technology tested on Palestinians, and Israel is a net exporter of military goods to the largest military producer in the world, the United States (Klein 2007). But security concerns and material gain cannot fully explain the excesses of violence. Perhaps, as Israeli journalist Yaron Ezrahi (1997: 226–227) suggests, these excesses of violence reveal a tragic aspect of Israeli identity, "a sign of a recovered masculinity, a repudiation of anti-Semitic stereotypes of the Jew as weak and impotent, a means of restoring Jewish pride, a symbolic revenge for past crimes against the Jews or as the instrument of a redemptive messianic Jewish mission."

For Palestinians, the prisons, checkpoints, and walls are one escalating system of collective jailing, a carceral society. All Palestinians in the Occupied Territories are now in administrative detention, but they are providing their own housing and food. The architecture of the Occupation is destructive of their livelihoods and communities, but it also produces particular identities, most obviously the identity of incarcerated victims vulnerable to Israeli aggression. Suffering such violence can have multiple effects. The killing and maiming of loved ones and the destruction of natural resources and community infrastructures are the most obvious costs of the violence directed toward the Palestinians, but the anxiety of trauma continues to manifest itself in behaviors and experiences such as insomnia, depression, violent outbursts, and dissociative disorders. One consequence is that fear can inhibit the organization of resistance to domination and exploitation, pushing some Palestinians to collaborate with Israel and many others to emigrate.

But using violence to secure the compliance or elimination of a population sometimes creates solidarity and communities of resistance. For example, the mothers of those 'disappeared' by the Argentine military became united in their grief and demonstrated in the Plaza de Mayo in Buenos Aires, demanding information about their missing loved ones and eventually calling for criminal prosecution of the perpetrators. To suffer and identify as the receiver of violence often motivates humans—following the negative side of Mauss's rule of the gift—to reciprocate with violence. To be a victim is to be an object, and that, in the minds of many humans, obligates one to seek retribution against oppressors and collaborators and thus attempt to make oneself back into a subject. Fanon (2005) describes the feelings of the colonized and the psychological necessity of striking back violently against the colonizer. Cycles of violence between groups such as Muslims and Hindus in India or the Hatfields and McCoys in Appalachia, while intended to intimidate, often only harden defiance on each side and perpetuate reprisal.

For most Palestinians in the Occupied Territories, resistance is pursued through *sumud*, which means being steadfast and refers to non-violent struggle in the form of vehemently remaining on their land and enduring the violence and the closures. For a handful of individuals, resistance takes the form of desperate, armed attack. According to Hass (2002: 20), since the al-Aqsa Intifada, Palestinians have lacked "a vanguard central power that could consciously work at transforming this vast individual capacity into a collective strategy of nonviolent—and thus far more effective—resistance." However, the struggle has been sustained for multiple generations, and recent evidence of increasing popular support for Hamas's political leadership suggests not only a rejection of Fatah's corruption but also a willingness to continue a slow burning war of attrition—which they dream of winning one day, some day—rather than concede defeat. That hope for redemption from exile or from prison does not easily go away, and that hope and that anger are formative of Palestinian subjectivity.

Occupation: From Palestine to Iraq

The occupation of Iraq is quite different from that in Israeli-Palestine. There are far fewer Palestinians, about 7 million (of whom only about half are in Israel-Palestine) compared to about 24 million Iraqis, and Palestine is much smaller at about 20,000 square kilometers compared to Iraq's more than 438,000 square kilometers. There is no oil in Palestine, but Palestine is of sacred value to all of the Abrahamic faiths. Palestinians are not divided by a Shia-Sunni split or by Kurdish-Arabic (and sometimes Farsi) language differences, as is Iraq. There are minorities of Christian Palestinians and a small number of Druze, but the political divide among Palestinians is ideological, not sectarian. As for similarities, the Israeli conquest of the West Bank and Gaza Strip, like the US invasion of Iraq, was a swift and decisive victory—at first. But the progress of their 'foreign' military administrations of people after the wars has been anything but swift and decisive. On the contrary, these examples show how occupations can cause more suffering than the wars that made them. More to the point, the use of prisons, checkpoints, and wall building is not unique to the Israeli Occupation, although these architectures may have been refined there. They are all clearly evident in Iraq, involving a much larger and more belligerent occupation, where they have also had tragic and counter-productive outcomes.

The issue of Iraqi detainees became notorious in May 2004 when Seymour Hersh (2004) published a story on abuse in the now infamous prison at Abu Ghraib. The snapshots taken by witnesses and participants not only led to the latter's prosecutions, but were soon spread all over the world's media. For many in the Middle East and for Sontag (2004), those photographs were evidence of the willful disregard of law by US leaders and the depraved decadence that constitute 'fun' for youth in American culture. Although the Abu Ghraib photos had a particularly American pornographic twist, they were not unlike the photos shot by Israeli border guards on the Green Line in that they were trophy snapshots—like the photos that amateur fishermen and hunters take of their kill. They were meant as memorabilia of a moment of victory, of a good time. More importantly, the exposé revealed the widespread use of detention and of 'softening' techniques, such as hooding and contortions of the body, which duplicated tactics used in the 1980s in the Occupied Territories.

The scandal at Abu Ghraib may result in US detention conditions being kept under closer scrutiny, but many detainees are turned over to Iraqi custody, where their treatment is far less scrutinized. According to the Iraqi Ministry of Human Rights, the number of detained Iraqis had grown to 37,641 by the end of March 2007, with US forces detaining 2,000 prisoners a month (Dehghanpisheh 2007). The Iraqi judicial system is not able to process all of the detainees brought in, so more detention facilities are being built. A former prisoner reported that guards at one prison were asking families for $15,000 to $20,000 to free their relatives (ibid.). Like Palestine, mass arrests, largely of innocent people, in Iraq have turned detention facilities into recruiting stations for insurgents (ibid.).

The situation at checkpoints in Iraq is terrible. One young veteran of the current Iraq War told me that US soldiers may fire on vehicles for the slightest of reasons, for example, if they see a car turning back from a checkpoint, which a driver may do merely to avoid a long delay, or if a driver fails to understand a soldier's command. Such reports are widespread (Hedges and al-Arian 2007), and there are high-profile cases of European and Iraqi officials being killed at checkpoints. The ACLU has obtained and released the files of 496 claims (479 from Iraq and 17 from Afghanistan) submitted to the US Foreign Claims Commissions by surviving Iraqi and Afghan family members of civilians killed or injured or who have suffered property damages due to actions by the US and its coalition forces. Of 496 files, 50 relate to deaths at checkpoints (ACLU 2007).

Wall building has also come to Iraq. The most famous example is the Green Zone, a 4-square-mile area of central Baghdad, completely surrounded by high, concrete blast walls and barbed wire, with entrances controlled by coalition troops, where the new Iraqi government, Western private military contractors, and the US and British embassies keep themselves as cut off as possible from the war outside. As sectarian violence has grown, wall building has grown. In

April 2007, an American military spokesperson said that the Adhamiya district of Baghdad, one of the few remaining Sunni areas on the eastern side of the city, would be surrounded by 3.5 miles of 'Bremer walls' to prevent insurgency from, and attacks against, its inhabitants. Bremer walls—12-foot-high portable reinforced concrete walls—are usually used for blast protection and are already ubiquitous in Baghdad. Also known as 'T-walls' because they are shaped like an upside-down letter T, they were named after the Coalition Provisional Authority's former director of reconstruction, Paul Bremer. How they got this name is curious, especially given the fact that these walls were developed and used in the 1990s by the Israeli military (Schell 2007). Like the walls of Berlin and Israel-Palestine, the Bremer walls have drawn criticism. Shiite leader Moqtada al-Sadr urged Iraqis to paint the concrete barriers with murals depicting the US military occupation: "I call on you to draw magnificent tableaux that depict the ugliness and terrorist nature of the occupier, and the sedition, car bombings, blood and the like he has brought upon Iraqis" (Agence France Presse 2007).

In these rather different settings—the Israeli Occupation and the US occupation of Iraq—similar patterns of carceralization are evident. In the name of security, prisons, checkpoints, and walls constrain and disable the functioning of education, commerce, and social welfare institutions. Masses of individuals are terrorized and humiliated, and some are injured or killed by military violence at these locations. Additional suffering is brought about by chronic economic frustration and material vulnerability. Such forms of violence bring tragic destruction directly to those on the frontline and rob many others of needed resources. These social technologies are used to weaken popular support for resistance and thereby coerce political concessions from resistance leaders. It may cause many Palestinians and Iraqis to flee their homes and abandon their lands to others. However, others who are subject to these military places and practices decide that their redemption—collective, if not individual—is bound up with reciprocating that violence. This is how carceral societies work. Endless violence might be desirable for war profiteers and militarists, but we should not be fooled into thinking that an occupation is reconstruction. Occupation is one big prison, where prisoners are left to feed themselves, and where survival requires some resistance.

Avram Bornstein is an Associate Professor in the Department of Anthropology, John Jay College of Criminal Justice and the Graduate Center of the City University of New York. His research and teaching focus on state violence and racism in Israel-Palestine and in the United States. In addition to numerous scholarly review and research publications, he is the author of the book *Crossing the Green Line between the West Bank and Israel* (2002), which documents the impact of military border closures on the work and customs of West Bank Palestinians in the 1990s.

References

ACLU (American Civil Liberties Union). 2007. "ACLU Releases Files on Civilian Casualties in Afghanistan and Iraq." 12 April. http://www.aclu.org/natsec/foia/29316prs20070412 .html (accessed 6 June 2007).

Agence France Presse. 2007. "Sadr Urges Iraqis to Daub Anti-US Messages on Security Walls." 30 April.

Azza, Fateh. 2003. *Ansar*. Pp. 20–64 in *Short Arabic Plays: An Anthology*, ed. Salma Khadra Jayyusi. Northampton, MA: Interlink Publishing Group.

Barth, Fredrik. 1969. *Ethnic Groups and Boundaries*. Boston: Little, Brown.

Benn, Aluf, Mazal Mualem, and Amos Harel. 2005. "Cabinet to Okay Pullout; Netanyahu to Vote No." *Ha'aretz*, 20 February.

Bornstein, Avram. 2001. "Ethnography and the Politics of Prisoners in Palestine-Israel." *Journal of Comparative Ethnography* 30, no. 5: 546–574.

_____. 2002. *Crossing the Green Line between the West Bank and Israel*. Philadelphia: University of Pennsylvania Press.

Bowman, Glenn. 2003. "Constitutive Violence and Rhetorics of Identity: A Comparative Study of Nationalist Movements in the Israeli-Occupied Territories and Former Yugoslavia." *Social Anthropology* 11, no. 3: 319–340.

_____. 2004. "About a Wall." *Social Analysis* 48, no. 1: 149–155.

_____. 2007. "Israel's Wall and the Logic of Encystation: Sovereign Exception or Wild Sovereignty?" *Focaal* 2007, no. 50: 127–135.

Brown, Alison. 2004. "The Immobile Mass: Movement Restrictions in the West Bank." *Social and Legal Studies* 13, no. 4: 501–521.

B'tselem. 1991. *The Interrogation of Palestinians During the Intifada: Ill-Treatment, "Moderate Physical Pressure" or Torture?* Jerusalem: B'tselem.

_____. 1992. *The Interrogation of Palestinians During the Intifada: Follow-up to March 1991*. Jerusalem: B'tselem.

_____. 2007. "Freedom of Movement." http://www.btselem.org/english/Freedom_of _Movement/Checkpoints_and_Forbidden_Roads.asp (accessed 13 June 2007).

Darwish, Mahmoud. 1980. *The Music of Human Flesh*. London: Heinemann.

Dehghanpisheh, Babak. 2007. "Prison Blues." *Newsweek*, 21 May.

Escobar, Arturo. 2004. "Beyond the Third World: Imperial Globality, Global Coloniality and Anti-Globalization Social Movements." *Third World Quarterly* 25, no. 1: 207–230.

Ezrahi, Yaron. 1997. *Rubber Bullets: Power and Conscience in Modern Israel*. Berkeley: University of California Press.

Fanon, Frantz. 2005. *Wretched of the Earth*. New York: Grove Press.

Foucault, Michel. 1979. *Discipline and Punish: The Birth of the Prison*. Trans. Alan Sheridan. New York: Vintage Books.

Gazit, Shlomo. 1995. *The Carrot and the Stick: Israel's Policy in Judea and Samaria, 1967–68*. Washington, DC: B'nai B'rith Books.

Ginbar, Yuval. 1993. *The "New Procedure" in GSS Interrogations: The Case of Abd A-Nasser 'Ubeid*. Jerusalem: B'tselem.

_____. 1998. *Routine Torture: Interrogation Methods of the General Security Service*. Jerusalem: B'tselem.

Golan, Daphna. 1992. *Detention without Trial: Administrative Detention in the Occupied Territories Since the Beginning of the Intifada*. Jerusalem: B'tselem.

Ha'aretz. 2004. "Kibbutz Member Seriously Injured by IDF Gunfire During Fence Protest." 5 January.

Hammami, Rima. 2004. "On the Importance of Thugs: The Moral Economy of a Checkpoint." *Middle East Report* 231: 26–34.

Al-Haq. 1989. *Perpetual Emergency: A Legal Analysis of Israel's Use of the British Defence (Emergency) Regulations, 1945, in the Occupied Territories*. Ramallah: Al Haq.

_____. 1990. *Punishing a Nation: Israeli Human Rights Violations During the Palestinian Uprising, December 1987–December 1988*. Boston: South End Press.

Harel, Amos. 2004. "IDF Moving Sections of Separation Fence Westward." *Ha'aretz*, 9 January.

Hass, Amira. 2002. "Israel's Closure Policy: An Ineffective Strategy of Containment and Repression." *Journal of Palestine Studies* 31, no. 3: 5–20.

Hedges, Chris, and Laila al-Arian. 2007. "The Other War." *Nation*, 6 August.

Hersh, Seymour M. 2004. "Torture at Abu Ghraib." *New Yorker*, 10 May. http://www.newyorker.com/archive/2004/05/10/040510fa_fact.

Hiltermann, Joost. 1992. *Behind the Intifada: Labor and Women's Committees in the Occupied Territories*. Princeton, NJ: Princeton University Press.

Hockstader, Lee. 2000. "Trophy Photos Betray Israeli Police Abuse." *Washington Post*, 19 September.

Human Rights Watch. 1991. *Prison Conditions in Israel and the Occupied Territories*. New York: Human Rights Watch.

_____. 1994. *Torture and Ill-Treatment: Israel's Interrogation of Palestinians from the Occupied Territories*. New York: Human Rights Watch.

_____. 1998. *Palestinian Self-Rule Areas: Human Rights under the Palestinian Authority*. New York: Human Rights Watch.

Israel News Agency. 2007. "Israel Defense Forces Ease Restrictions in West Bank." 1 January. http://www.israelnewsagency.com/palestineisraelsecurityidfhumanitarian48990107.html (accessed 17 August 2007).

Kelly, Tobias. 2006. "Documented Lives: Fear and the Uncertainties of Law during the Second Palestinian Intifada." *Journal of the Royal Anthropological Society* 12: 89–107.

Khalil, Mahmoud Lutfi Yaseen. 1988. *Al-Tajrabat al-a'taqaliah fi al-Sijin al-Israeliah* [Ordeal and Interdependence in an Israeli Prison]. Amman: Ibn Rushd House.

Klein, Naomi. 2007. "Laboratory for a Fortressed World." *Nation*, 2 July.

Machsom Watch. 2004. "About Us." http://www.machsomwatch.org/en (accessed 17 August 2007).

Mahmood, Cynthia Keppley. 1996. *Fighting for Faith and Nation: Dialogues with Sikh Militants*. Philadelphia: University of Pennsylvania Press.

Ministry of Defense. 2007. "Israel's Security Fence." http://www.seamzone.mod.gov.il/Pages/ENG/default.htm (accessed 10 June 2007).

Nakhleh, Khalil, and Elia Zureik, eds. 1980. *The Sociology of the Palestinians*. New York: St. Martin's Press.

Nasser, Jamal, and Roger Heacock, eds. 1990. *Intifada: Palestine at the Crossroads*. New York: Praeger.

Nirgad, Lia. 2004. *Horef B'Qalandia* [Winter in Qalandia]. Tel Aviv: Xargol Publishers.

Owen, Roger. 1989. "The West Bank Now: Economic Development." Pp. 43–56 in *Palestine under Occupation: Prospects for the Future*, ed. Peter Krogh and Mary McDavid. Washington, DC: Georgetown University.

Peteet, Julie. 1994. "Male Gender and Rituals of Resistance in the Palestinian Intifada: A Cultural Politics of Violence." *American Ethnologist* 2, no. 1: 31–49.

Rabinowitz, Dan. 2003. "Borders and Their Discontents: Israel's Green Line, Arabness and Unilateral Separation." *European Studies* 19: 2–17.

Rajub, Jabril. 1986. *Al-Zinzanah raqm 704* [Cell 704]. Jerusalem: Wakalat Abu 'Arafah lil-Sihafa.

Rosenfeld, Maya. 2004. *Confronting the Occupation: Work, Education, and Political Activism of Palestinian Families in a Refugee Camp*. Stanford, CA: Stanford University Press.

Roy, Sarah. 1991. "The Political Economy of Despair: Changing Political and Economic Realities in the Gaza Strip." *Journal of Palestine Studies* 20, no. 3: 58–69.

_____. 1995. *The Gaza Strip: The Political Economy of De-Development*. Washington, DC: Institute for Palestine Studies.

Said, Edward. 1978. *Orientalism*. New York: Vintage.

Saleh, Samir Abdallah. 1990. "The Effects of the Israeli Occupation on the Economy of the West Bank and Gaza Strip." Pp. 37–51 in Nassar and Heacock 1990.

Samara, Adel. 1989. "The Political Economy of the West Bank 1967–1987: From Peripheralization of Development." Pp. 7–31 in *Palestine: Profile of an Occupation*, ed. Toby Shelley and Ben Cashdan. London: Zed Books.

_____. 2001. *Epidemic of Globalization: Ventures in World Order, Arab Nation and Zionism.* Glendale, CA: Palestine Research and Publishing Foundation.

Sayigh, Yusif. 1986. "The Palestinian Economy under Occupation: Dependency and Pauperization." *Journal of Palestine Studies* 15, no. 4: 46–67.

Schell, Orville. 2007. "Baghdad: The Besieged Press." *Mother Jones*, 14 March.

Schiff, Ze'ev. 2003. "Fence Route Is Moved, Scrapping Two Enclaves." *Ha'aretz*, 30 December.

Seifert, Ruth. 1996. "The Second Front: The Logic of Sexual Violence in Wars." *Women's Studies International Forum* 19, no. 1/2: 35–43.

Semyonov, Moshe, and Noah Lewin-Epstein. 1987. *Hewers of Wood and Drawers of Water: Noncitizen Arabs in the Israeli Labor Market*. Ithaca, NY: International Labor Organization Press and Cornell University Press.

Sontag, Susan. 2004. "Regarding the Torture of Others." *New York Times Magazine*, 23 May.

Susser, Leslie. 2004. "Despite the Criticism at Home and Abroad, No Major Changes for Route of West Bank Fence." *Jerusalem Report*, 26 January.

Tamari, Salim. 1980. "The Palestinians in the West Bank and Gaza: The Sociology of Dependency." Pp. 84–111 in Nakhleh and Zureik 1980.

_____. 1981. "Building Others People's Homes: The Palestinian Peasants' Household and Work in Israel." *Journal of Palestine Studies* 11, no. 1: 31–66.

_____. 1990. "Revolt of the Petit Bourgeoisie." Pp. 159–189 in Nassar and Heacock 1990.

Weizman, Eyal. 2007. *Hollow Land: Israel's Architecture of Occupation*. London: Verso.

Yoaz, Yuval. 2004. "AG: ICJ Fence Ruling May Lead to Sanctions Against Israel." *Ha'aretz*, 20 August.

Chapter 6

WAR AND PEACE IN COLOMBIA

Lesley Gill

Most US citizens experienced the Cold War as 'peace'. Firefights never disrupted their communities. Neighbors and family members did not disappear and then return as mutilated corpses in highly visible public places. Muffled voices never relayed death threats over the telephone in the middle of the night. The Cold War touched most American lives only indirectly through the evening news, where televised images of the carnage in Vietnam (1964–1975), massacred Nicaraguans during the war against the Somoza dictatorship (1975–1979), or murdered Jesuit priests in El Salvador (1989) signaled a distant crisis. Yet for the Vietnamese, Nicaraguans, Salvadorans, and many others, the Cold War represented less a brush fire on the periphery of the industrial capitalist world than a bloody orgy of violence in which thousands died at the hands of the American military and the security forces trained by them (Gill 2004; McCoy 2006; McSherry 2005). Citizens of what used to be called the Third

Notes for this chapter begin on page 147.

World lived through or died in counter-insurgency 'dirty wars' that were not defined as war. Counter-insurgency wars relied on clandestine paramilitary forces and secret detention centers that operated outside lawful state action to target guerrilla insurgencies, civilian sympathizers, and critics of the status quo (McClintock 1992). They were promoted by the Reagan administration in the aftermath of Vietnam because they offered government officials the possibility of fighting a war without declaring one and of sidestepping public aversion to US intervention. There were no frontlines, and governments and the official security forces typically denied any participation in or knowledge of the horrific human rights violations.

When the Cold War fight against 'communists'—an enormously elastic category that could accommodate almost any critic—became obsolete, the simmering 'war on drugs' in the Andean region became, in the 1990s, a more important mechanism for mobilizing public support for intervention, especially US involvement in Colombia's decades-long civil war. For a brief moment, the 'narco-guerrilla' replaced the 'communist' as the new enemy, but the 'terrorist' quickly supplanted it in the aftermath of the 9/11 attacks on the United States, when George W. Bush capitalized on public fear and indignation to declare a 'war on terror'. Although the formal declaration of a war on terror and the subsequent invasions of Afghanistan and Iraq signaled a new era of unveiled imperialist power, the initial victories soon evaporated, and the United States found itself mired in unwinnable counter-insurgency wars. The morass in Iraq suggests similarities to Vietnam, but a closer analogy is El Salvador, as frustrated Pentagon officials have considered resurrecting the 'Salvador option'—a strategy from the Central American civil wars that used paramilitary assassination squads to hunt down insurgents (Hersh and Barry 2005).

The war on terror is global in scope and has no well-defined endpoint. Like counter-insurgent wars of the past, there are no frontlines, and the distinctions between combatants and non-combatants are not clear. 'Terrorists' are vaguely defined, and, like an earlier generation of 'communist' enemies, they are conceivably everywhere, lurking among the civilian population while waiting for the moment to strike. All of this raises questions about how we understand war: What is the difference between war and peace? Where does war begin, and where does it end? Answering these questions is difficult. Decades ago, in his famous 'military-industrial complex' speech, Dwight Eisenhower warned of the dangers posed to US society by ties between the government and military contractors. Nowadays, global instability, fueled by neo-liberalism and imperial conflict, generates new opportunities for defense contractors, arms dealers, and high-tech security firms. War is not simply the means for opening markets that can then be exploited in peacetime. War *is* a market, and the objective is to profit from endless violence through the creation of 'security' within fortified areas, such as Baghdad's Green Zone, surrounded by low-level conflict and disarray. There is little incentive for peace, as a durable disorder becomes the new stability.[1]

There is a considerable amount of scholarly literature that examines the disjunctures between war and peace (e.g., Godoy 2006; Hollander 1997; Scheper-Hughes and Bourgois 2004). Some scholars examine broader processes of militarization in which labor, resources, and social relationships are shaped in accord with military goals and to legitimize military action. Their work points to an understanding of war that moves beyond a discussion of combat to include the ways that societies prepare for war through the reorganization of institutions, the hardening of social hierarchies, and the promotion of ideologies that justify the use of violence (e.g., Enloe 1993; Lutz 2004). Other scholars have examined the relationship between the 'brute' violence of the state and the structural violence of poverty and exclusion to understand better the relationship between these social forces and to grasp how social inequalities give rise to political instability (e.g., Auyero 2000; Farmer 1997; Litwack 1998). These studies demonstrate that delineating the boundaries where war ends and peace begins is not a straightforward endeavor.

Other scholars have explored the routinization of terror (Taussig 1992), the banalization of brutality (Pécaut 2001), and everyday violence (Bourgois 2001) in contexts of ongoing war and instability. Despite the potential utility of these concepts, they paint an overgeneralized picture of violence and terror that leaves unexamined the social relations and institutional forms that generate fear at particular historical moments (Binford 2002). One is left with a sense that there is no escaping a continually regenerated cycle of terror. It becomes difficult to understand how the opposition of subordinate groups may attenuate fear and even re-establish a modicum of security for threatened people (Binford 2002), and to see how fear is tied to specific places and shaped by memories (Gordillo 2004; Riaño 2002).

In this chapter I examine the ragged edges of war and peace in Colombia, a country that is generally ignored in discussions of the war on terror, even though it receives the largest amount of US military aid in the Western hemisphere and remains mired in an intractable conflict that has displaced over two million people and has generated the second-largest internally displaced population in the world, after Sudan (HRW 2005a). Colombia allows us to examine the blurring of war and peace and the consequences for civilians. First, patterns of counter-insurgent terror established during the mid-twentieth-century turmoil known as 'La Violencia' made little distinction between civilians and combatants (Roldán 2002). The Cold War continued to obscure the differences, which remain unclear in the anti-terrorism perspective of the post-9/11 period. Second, scholars do not agree on how to describe the Colombian conflict, which has endured with varying degrees of intensity for over 40 years. Some contemporary observers see it as a civil war (Hylton 2006; Richani 2002), but others argue that because of the lack of popular support for warring groups and the diverse ways that violence affects regions and social groups, the conflict is less a civil war than a "war against society" (Pécaut 2001; see also LeGrand 2003).

This chapter focuses on the working-class city of Barrancabermeja in the conflicted Middle Magdalena region, a city that has been a focal point of the state's counter-insurgency war for decades. It demonstrates that daily life in Barrancabermeja is less a 'culture of fear' than a shifting kaleidoscope of uncertainty and vulnerability in which some people are more exposed to violence than others, and in which persistent instability heightens the demand for 'security' and obscures the boundaries between war and peace. The essay first explores how right-wing paramilitaries used terror to seize control of Barrancabermeja at the beginning of the twenty-first century. In Barrancabermeja and elsewhere in Colombia, paramilitaries with clandestine state support have carried out the disreputable acts of a dirty war—murders, assassinations, disappearances, and torture—that have allowed the Colombian state to fight powerful guerrilla insurgencies while denying any knowledge of or participation in widespread human rights violations (HRW 1996, 2001). Through a campaign of terror, they have expelled three guerrilla groups from the city, displaced civilians, and eliminated or severely weakened trade unions, opposition political parties, community groups, and human rights organizations that they accuse of supporting the insurgents. The essay then examines how surviving residents of Barrancabermeja experience an unsteady peace and an invisible war in which the paramilitaries have become the state itself. Finally, it considers how a small number of trade unionists and human rights defenders are expanding the limits of political possibility by challenging the widespread impunity that threatens to extinguish political alternatives and obliterate memories of the violent past.

War in the Twilight Zone

Barrancabermeja, with a population of 250,000, is an oil-refining center, the home of Colombia's only refinery and long a center of populist and left-wing labor activism led by the oil workers' union, Unión Sindical Obrera (USO). The paramilitary takeover in 2002 was a severe shock to activist labor and social organizations, from which they have yet to recover, and ruptured social life in a city known for its militant labor history. Throughout the 1980s and 1990s, the city served as a refuge for displaced peasants fleeing an intensifying dirty war in the countryside. Peasants uprooted from rural areas dominated by a particular insurgent group tended to settle in neighborhoods controlled by the same group in Barrancabermeja, where three guerrilla organizations shared power in the peripheral northeast and southeast sectors during the 1990s.[2] Yet the violent paramilitary siege of Barrancabermeja in 2000–2002 created a refugee exodus from the city. Terror shattered daily life, forcing both the recently displaced and many longtime residents to abandon their homes. Although some people thought that because of the strength of its trade unions, human rights groups, and social organizations, Barrancabermeja would never fall to the paramilitaries, the prospect of a paramilitary takeover had been building for some time.

Beginning in the late 1970s and early 1980s, the Middle Magdalena region became the scene of an escalating conflict, as regional elites came under growing pressure from rural guerrillas—especially those of the Revolutionary Armed Forces of Colombia (FARC), Colombia's largest and oldest insurgency—who kidnapped and extorted money from them. Cattle ranchers, merchants, representatives of the Texas Petroleum Company, and newly rich drug-traffickers-turned-landlords claimed that the state was not doing enough to protect them. As a result, they collaborated with sectors of the armed forces to finance and train paramilitary groups in the river town of Puerto Boyacá, which in 1982 became the epicenter of paramilitarism (Medina Gallegos 1990). Hit-and-run death squads, such as Death to Kidnappers (MAS), initially did more harm to unarmed peasants and trade union leaders than to the guerrillas, but the paramilitary capacity for terror changed, as profits from the cocaine traffic increased and an 'anti-subversive' political movement gained traction in the region. This movement received a boost in 1988 when a process of political decentralization initiated by the national government permitted the first direct election of mayors and councilmen. A number of politicians, committed to the campaign against the guerrillas and backed by disgruntled elites, managed to get elected to local political office and then aided and abetted the expansion of paramilitarism, even as the national government committed itself to a peace process with the guerrillas (Medina Gallegos 1990; Romero 2003).

The 'Puerto Boyacá paramilitary model' was subsequently extended to other parts of the country, and regionally based paramilitary entities morphed from roving death squads into standing armies whose commanders disputed territorial control with the guerrillas (Duncan 2006). They federated in 1997 under a national umbrella organization called the United Self-Defense Forces of Colombia (AUC). The AUC managed to centralize 18 different regional groups, or approximately 75 percent of the paramilitaries, under its command (Bejarano and Pizarro 2004: 110). It grew more lethal with the passage in 2000 of Plan Colombia, a $1.3 billion mostly military US aid program, approved under President Clinton, that strengthened the police and the military, the AUC's closest allies. Plan Colombia targeted the guerrilla-controlled coca fields in the southern provinces of Putumayo, Caqueta, and Meta for fumigation and displaced thousands of peasants who formed the support base of the FARC. Yet it left paramilitary-dominated areas in the north largely untouched, and there was little effort to wrest control of strategic cocaine trafficking corridors, like the Magdalena River, from the paramilitaries. Not surprisingly, the paramilitary blocs (*bloques*) consolidated their political power and territorial control in areas once ruled by the guerrillas (Hylton 2006).

In the Middle Magdalena region, two paramilitary armies affiliated with the AUC—the Central Bolívar Bloc (BCB) and the Peasant Self-Defense Forces of Magdalena Medio (ACMM)—succeeded in pushing the guerrillas out of longtime strongholds and occupying almost all of the river ports along the Magdalena River. The BCB then set its sights on Barrancabermeja, the region's principal port and the location of the state's only oil refinery, which offered potential profits from the illegal sale of gasoline and a strategic urban base from which to control the rural hinterlands. The AUC signaled its intention to take control of Barrancabermeja in 1998 with the massacre of 32 people in a neighborhood in the southeast sector that had been under the protection of the National Liberation Army (ELN).[3] The intent of the massacre was to sow terror among residents presumed to sympathize with the guerrillas and to demonstrate that the ELN could not offer any security or defense.

A number of factors paved the way for the subsequent paramilitary takeover of Barrancabermeja. A death squad operated by the navy during the 1980s and 1990s murdered many key trade unionists, journalists, and community leaders who opposed the paramilitary project (CINEP/CREDHOS 2004; HRW 1996). Moreover, by the 1990s, the guerrillas had lost legitimacy among the civilian population after attacks on police installations in crowded residential areas demonstrated an apparent disregard for civilian life. In addition, excessive 'taxes' levied by at least one guerrilla group—the FARC—eroded popular support for the insurgents. It was, however, police and military backing that enabled the paramilitaries to overwhelm the guerrilla militias when Barrancabermeja became subsumed in conflict between 2000 and 2002 (Loingsigh 2002). The police and the military allowed BCB forces to pass through roadblocks, ignored civilian pleas for help, and looked the other way as the paramilitaries committed gruesome atrocities. As one human rights defender explained, "When the paramilitaries came into Barranca, everyone knew that they stayed in the army battalion. And we knew what cars they used, where they ate, and even what prostitutes they had sex with. It was so obvious that sometimes we even told the authorities and gave them addresses, but they didn't do shit."[4] In the end, the massive violence finally overwhelmed the armed resistance and paved the way for the paramilitaries to occupy the city.

Between 2000 and 2003, over 1,000 people were murdered and 300 forcibly disappeared in Barrancabermeja and the surrounding municipalities (CINEP/CREDHOS 2004). During the first two months of 2001, one resident of Barrancabermeja died every 12 hours (Madero 2001). The paramilitaries perpetrated most of the murders and disappearances, and survivors were left feeling terrified, confused, and completely unprotected. A resident in the northeast sector decided to abandon his home after four neighbors were murdered in one day. Especially in those sectors under guerrilla control, the paramilitaries and the police made few distinctions between guerrillas and non-combatants—everyone was a 'subversive'. A human rights worker, for example, learned that paramilitaries clad in civilian clothing were positioned outside his home after his daughter returned from an errand and reported the presence of the strange men. Fearing that they would soon break in and kill him and his family, the man made a series of desperate phone calls to the police—but to no avail. The family finally managed to flee after a young guerrilla militiaman (*miliciano*), on his way to visit a neighbor across the street, spotted the paramilitaries and started to shoot at them.[5]

With the expulsion of the guerrillas and the weakening of the political opposition, the paramilitaries have extended their power beyond acts of violence against alleged subversives. The new lords of the city no longer operate as a mercenary army that carries out the distasteful acts of a dirty war under the protective wing of the state. They have in effect become the state itself. The paramilitaries have penetrated the official state apparatus and erected a mafia-like 'shadow state' in which organized crime fuses with the politics of counter-insurgency. They manipulate elections by openly or tacitly supporting certain candidates, while intimidating others and dictating to people how to vote. Because of their enormous power, aspiring candidates for political office seek out their support, albeit surreptitiously. Through their control of government office, the paramilitaries can thus tap into municipal treasuries, decide who will be awarded government contracts, and demand kickbacks. They monopolize the illegal cocaine traffic and the theft and sale of gasoline from the state oil company, while also operating a variety of legal businesses, such as the lottery, private security firms, and subcontracting agencies. Like the guerrillas before them, the paramilitaries suck wealth out of the local economy by imposing 'taxes' on merchants and demanding that the residents of certain neighborhoods make 'contributions' in exchange for 'protection'. Finally, they have divided the city into zones of control in collaboration with the state security forces, with whom they cut deals and make compromises as they negotiate the imposition of order with them.[6]

Even as they erected a criminal shadow state, the BCB entered demobilization negotiations with the government in 2002 and then in 2005 took advantage of the controversial Justice and Peace Law, which granted paramilitaries nearly complete impunity and laid a framework for their incorporation into the political process. The law offered the BCB's commander, Carlos Mario Jiménez (known as Macaco), a reduced prison sentence in exchange for demobilizing his troops, confessing all crimes, and dismantling the criminal operations. Macaco had amassed a fortune in the drug traffic through his affiliation with the North Valle cartel and had then purchased the BCB 'franchise' from renowned paramilitary Vicente Castaño in 1997, when the latter was looking for ways to expand the AUC throughout the country (*Semana* 2007b). On the eve of passage of the Justice and Peace Law, the BCB had established a presence in 11 Colombian provinces and had become one of the AUC's most powerful blocs. Yet in a series of public ceremonies, the BCB's 7,000 to 8,000 fighters began to surrender their weapons and hand over helicopters used by the group. By late 2005, nearly 30,000 paramilitaries from various paramilitary blocs had officially demobilized.

Despite the highly publicized demobilizations, the Justice and Peace Law completely ignored the difficult problem of dismantling the organizational and financial structures of the AUC and its affiliates. Even though it required paramilitaries to hand over arms and wealth acquired illegally, there was no mechanism to force them to do so, and few networks were completely broken up. With their wealth intact—especially proceeds from the cocaine traffic— paramilitary commanders continued to manage their criminal operations from jail, and new foot soldiers soon stepped into the vacuum left by the demobilizations, drawing salaries that far exceeded those available in Colombia's degraded informal economy (HRW 2005b). Not surprisingly, by the end of 2006, at least 70 'new' groups had emerged in the national territory. They counted within their ranks rearmed mercenaries who had participated in the demobilization process and former mid-level AUC commanders, who took advantage of a power vacuum created by the demobilizations to rise to the head of reconfigured paramilitary entities.[7] All of this made clear the connections between the 'old' and the 'new' generations of paramilitaries.[8]

Normal between Quotation Marks

Nowadays, everything looks 'normal' in Barrancabermeja. The oil refinery belches noxious fumes into the air, and its 200-foot flare burns 24 hours a day. The dull grind and clank of the refinery can be heard across much of the city at night, when the sky is aglow from the refinery's lights. Small boats equipped with outboard motors ferry passengers into and out of the bustling port, where *vallenato* music blares from riverside restaurants. Buses, motorcycles, and cars compete for space on downtown streets, and merchants and buyers clog the commercial district. If asked, many of the residents of Barrancabermeja's northeast and southeast neighborhoods will reply, "Todo está tranquilo" (Everything is fine). What they mean is that wholesale massacres no longer occur, and civilians do not die in firefights that erupt without warning on the streets. Yet Barrancabermeja is hardly at peace.

Because the near monopolization of the illegal economy provides them with an independent source of income, the paramilitaries do not need broad popular support to survive in Barrancabermeja. Although they can count on the backing of some sectors of the population, their rule is based less on consensus than on the threat and periodic exercise of brute force. One woman—a widow whose husband had been murdered by the FARC—described daily life under paramilitary control as worse than the guerrillas. "The guerrillas," she explained, "killed people for being police informers, and they didn't like it when teenage girls flirted with the soldiers. But people talked to them and helped them out so as not to have problems with them. They thought that this would keep the guerrillas on their side ... [but when] the paramilitaries took control, it got worse because they massacred everyone who collaborated with the guerrillas. There were more deaths, and there are still more deaths."[9] With the guerrillas vanquished, the paramilitaries no longer need to use massacres and indiscriminate terror to control the population. Instead, they employ more subtle means of domination through the use of death threats, selective assassinations, and disappearances to reinforce the status quo and to send a message about the consequences of challenging their power.

Many merchants and business owners were secretly happy to see the guerrillas expelled from the city. From their comfortable, centrally located neighborhoods, they had witnessed little of the terror that had enveloped the zones under guerrilla control, and, like urban Colombians elsewhere, they experienced the violence only indirectly on the television news. Even in poor, peripheral neighborhoods, a sector of the population was fed up with the guerrillas' heavy-handedness and at least initially welcomed the arrival of the BCB, even facilitating its entry into the city with information about the guerrillas and their sympathizers. And if they did not actively support the BCB, many people accepted it as the lesser evil—the latest group of armed overlords to dominate their neighborhoods—and adjusted to life under BCB rule. The paramilitaries rewarded them with jobs in road construction, park maintenance, transportation, and, of course, a range of illegal activities in the underground economy (Loingsigh 2002). Some urban residents therefore benefited from new authoritarian forms of clientelism, as the paramilitaries erected an apparatus of patronage and control in Barrancabermeja.

The paramilitaries have even set up development organizations, such as the Science and Technology Foundation for the Integral Development of Middle Magdalena Communities based in Bucaramanga, the provincial capital, that channel money into projects for supporters in the region. Indeed, when BCB leader Macaco testified in Medellín under the terms of the Justice and Peace Law, this organization, to which he was a large contributor, paid for three buses to take supporters from Bucaramanga and Barrancabermeja to demonstrate their support for the commander (*Semana* 2007a). According to a Barrancabermeja trade union leader, local people have few difficulties with the paramilitaries as long as the residents "do what they say. That means going from home to work, agreeing to participate in their marches and meetings, showing up when the *paracos* (paramilitaries) announce through the neighborhood councils that there will be a clean up [of trash], not complaining about the high cost of electricity and the absence of public services, and, above all else, not organizing other people who might challenge the power of the paramilitaries."[10]

Other residents who oppose the paramilitary project, or who did so at one time, live with a sense of menace. The paramilitary takeover has ruptured the institutional forms that represent their ties to each other and has undercut their ability to do anything about what happened and what continues to happen to them. In addition, paramilitary violence has hastened the privatization of public enterprises, the restructuring of private businesses, and the reorganization of labor relations, all of which form part of the neo-liberal economic model that the state has supported since the early 1990s, and this has aggravated unemployment and underemployment in the city (Gill forthcoming). Many trade unions, neighborhood councils, and human rights committees that once channeled popular demands to the state either no longer exist or are under the control of the paramilitaries. Speaking out against the abuses that one has suffered or the erosion of working conditions means risking the possibility of physical displacement or death. Residents are wary of the ever present—although often invisible—paramilitary threat. Recruited with offers of salaries superior to what they can earn in the informal economy, young men spy on meetings, report on suspicious activities, and watch the comings and goings of residents in order to prevent a return of the guerrillas. Dressed in civilian clothing, they blend into the local population and may even be the longtime neighbors of the people they monitor. All of this reinforces a deafening silence about disappearances, murders, and torture, in both the past and the present.

One woman, who discussed daily life in a northeastern neighborhood with me in the privacy of her home, made only oblique reference to "those people" (*esa gente*) when referring to the paramilitaries, and she repeatedly lowered her voice when describing the human rights violations perpetrated by them in her neighborhood. She explained that many of her neighbors maintained a resolute silence because of what might happen if they complained, and others have left the neighborhood for fear of paramilitary reprisals. A family across the street, she said in a hushed tone, lost a son; paramilitaries disappeared him because he was a guerrilla. But now, "they don't say anything," she whispered, putting a finger to her lips and glancing toward the door.[11]

A pervasive mistrust fuels the residents' silence and corrodes social relationships. One man, whose neighborhood was the scene of a 1998 paramilitary massacre, described daily life today as "normal between quotation marks." Unlike the weeks and months that followed the massacre, he says, "people sit outside [their homes] and talk to their neighbors now, but you always know that at any moment something can happen ... and when you walk past an unknown person, you always go on the defensive. It's not the same anymore. If somebody comes around asking if you know so-and-so, nobody will admit to knowing [the person] because you don't know who is asking or why they are looking for him."[12] Such pervasive mistrust arises not only from what has happened to people but also from what they have done—and been forced to do—to each other.

Residents of Barrancabermeja's impoverished northeast sector recall with deep bitterness how guerrilla *milicianos* switched sides and joined the paramilitaries because of threats to their own lives or the possibility of earning higher pay. The turncoats then fingered the guerrillas and anyone rumored to sympathize with them. "Many from the FARC switched to the other side," explained one elderly woman whose neighborhood had been under FARC control, "and it wasn't just the boys (*muchachos*). It was the commandants, too. This was the ugliest thing that happened at that time. It was really ugly."[13] The guerrillas-turned-paramilitaries became community enforcers, terrorizing neighbors and acquaintances, administering paramilitary 'justice', and forcing people to observe social norms, which included the prohibition of long hair, earrings, and bracelets for men, the public humiliation of prostitutes, and the repression of homosexuals. Although residents say that the paramilitaries eventually murdered these individuals because they knew too much, the betrayals left people feeling deceived and broken. They ruptured bonds of trust, divided people from each other, and provoked cynicism about the future. For some, the only solution was to turn inward and seek individual solutions for their troubles.

The fragmentation and individualization of social life, combined with the destruction or weakening of once vital organizations and the murder or displacement of community leaders, has resulted in paramilitarism becoming embedded within the fabric of society. As a result of the exclusions fostered by neo-liberal capitalism, many people have been forced to turn to the paramilitaries for assistance that they once provided to each other. The labor movement, led by Unión Sindical Obrera, the combative oil workers' union, can no longer mobilize large-scale opposition. A civic strike in 1999 was the last time that labor and community organizations had succeeded in shutting down the city. Not surprisingly, a loss of jobs, the erosion of social security protections, and the rising cost of privatized social services have pushed more and more Barranqueños into poverty. Many people find that their only economic option is to toil in the informal economy, where they are incorporated into new paramilitary-controlled patronage networks in which they have no rights (Gill forthcoming).

The paramilitaries' lack of accountability for the terror that they have wreaked on Barrancabermeja's poor neighborhoods makes it difficult for the victims of political violence to reconstruct their shattered lives. This is because widespread impunity empowers an unaccountable criminal state to continue violating the rights of ordinary people. Impunity also strengthens an emerging authoritarian 'democracy' in which violence undergirds elections and new forms of despotic political and economic clientelism, while erasing the possibility of alternatives. Consequently, many Barranqueños have accommodated to the new order, either for the rewards that collusion offers or for lack of effective alternatives, and they have remained silent because the institutional structures that might support struggles for justice and accountability are either weak or no longer exist. As one woman explained, "People who are alone and not organized have to remain quiet. But for an organization, it is different. Leaders with bodyguards make the accusations (*denuncias*)."[14] Indeed, despite the high level of repression, a number of trade unions and human rights organizations have survived the paramilitary takeover of Barrancabermeja, and their members continue to demand justice, propose alternatives, and struggle to lift the heavy blanket of impunity that suffocates their city. In the process, they must deal with the nominally democratic, official state, which is both predatory and protective, and they must negotiate the opaque boundaries between it and the para-state.

Fighting Impunity in the Para-state

On 13 February 2007, a local television news program interviewed a female politician who hoped to gain a spot on the ballot for the mayoral elections scheduled later in the year. The young host asked his guest what she would do if elected mayor of the city. She replied that one of her major proposals was to develop tourism, because, like the incumbent mayor, she believed that promoting the oil industry—and especially the imposing refinery—constituted a powerful way to draw visitors to Barrancabermeja and boost local businesses. This proposal for petro-tourism characterized Barrancabermeja as a world of order, security, and economic stability. Yet during the previous week, unions and human rights organizations had received death threats from a shadowy new paramilitary group that called itself the Black Eagles, and a former municipal slaughterhouse worker, who was displaced from the city in 2001, barely escaped with his life after soldiers dressed as civilians kidnapped him off the street of the provincial capital and accused him of being a FARC commander. Terrified and convinced that they intended to kill him, the man 'confessed' and told his captors that he would lead them to a guerrilla arms cache in Barrancabermeja. He then took them on a wild goose chase to a neighborhood where, he hoped, people would recognize him, and as they passed the home of his sister, he escaped by running through the house and fleeing across a ravine. With the help of a relative, he then contacted a local human rights organization, which gave him refuge in its offices.[15]

Depictions of Barrancabermeja as a peaceful setting for petro-tourists paint a surreal portrait of a city in which selective assassinations and disappearances continue to imperil the lives of residents and in which oil workers have paid a particularly high price for opposing the paramilitarization of the petroleum industry. With the widely heralded paramilitary demobilizations, the government can now suggest that attacks on activists and ordinary people are less the result of political conflicts than the lamentable byproduct of common criminality and the work of 'emergent bands of delinquents'. All of this obscures the ever-present threat of violence that stalks anyone who challenges the status quo. Yet a handful of unions and human rights organizations and their leaders point their fingers at government officials, the state security forces, and their paramilitary allies to denounce the ongoing murders, the constant intimidation, and the lack of accountability. By so doing, they chip away at the wall of impotence and hopelessness that thrives under conditions of impunity, and they connect some residents to broader collectivities that are crucial for repairing the tattered social fabric.

For example, the Popular Feminine Organization (OFP)—one of the most prominent and outspoken human rights organizations in Barrancabermeja—denounced the disappearance of Katherine González, the 20-year-old sister of one of the organization's employees, only a week after the mayoral candidate laid out her plans for petro-tourism. It then organized a protest caravan that traveled through the heart of Barrancabermeja's paramilitary-controlled neighborhoods, where activists—some traveling with bodyguards in armored cars—condemned the disappearance, excoriated the impunity that shielded the perpetrators, and asked residents to defy the paramilitaries and provide information about the young woman. They also blocked traffic on the main road out of the city and held nightly protest vigils to maintain the pressure. Approximately a month later, the young woman was dumped—bound and blindfolded, but alive—outside the bus terminal of another city in the early morning hours. Her release punctured the apparent invulnerability of the dark forces that control Barrancabermeja, even as the protests that surrounded her kidnapping raised the already high stakes for the OFP.

Not surprisingly, members of the OFP and activists of other union and human rights organizations live in constant insecurity. Worries about vulnerable family members, restrictions on their activities, and fears for their own safety hem in their daily lives, which are episodically disrupted by mortal threats. The paramilitaries view these individuals and their organizations as guerrilla sympathizers whose base-building work is intended to help the insurgents. They wage a low-intensity campaign of death threats, harassment, selective assassinations, and disappearances that attempts both to silence leaders and send a strong message to others about the consequences of challenging paramilitary power or associating themselves with the opposition.

Prior to an attack, the paramilitaries typically panic their targets with telephoned warnings and ominous letters faxed or e-mailed to offices or slipped under doors at night. In early February 2007, for example, two different entities claiming to represent demobilized paramilitaries began to harass social movement organizations in the city. One group e-mailed a threat to the offices of trade unions and human rights associations. The other group faxed a letter to the National Food and Beverage Workers Union (SINALTRAINAL) that singled out four leaders and included their nicknames, which suggested an alarming level of familiarity and proximity to the threatened individuals. The letter referred to the leaders as guerrilla terrorists, declared the men military targets, and then asked, "How do you prefer to die—torture, dismemberment, or a shot in the head Middle Magdalena style?"

The intention of these threats is to terrorize leaders and to throw them off balance by heightening feelings of vulnerability to a lethal, invisible enemy. They prompt suspicions about workmates, friends, and associates and incite rumors and speculation about imminent paramilitary 'social cleansing' operations. Going to work, coming home, and taking children to school become fraught with tension, as these everyday activities form part of a predictable routine that, if widely known, can jeopardize the security of an individual and his family members. Activists must vary their daily schedules or even abandon them completely at times. The threats also make the divides between dangerous 'no-go' areas of the city and places of relative safety, which have dictated the routines of opposition figures since the paramilitary takeover, more unstable, as individuals feel insecure everywhere. All of this fuels alarm and can isolate activists by aggravating cleavages between them and their constituencies, and by separating them from people who fear that associating too closely with targeted leaders will place their own lives at risk.

Activists address the threats, their own vulnerability, and the broad issue of impunity and human rights violations in a number of ways. Through ties to labor, religious, and human rights organizations in North America and Europe, they broadcast via e-mail and the Internet news of threats, disappearances, murders, and other human rights violations to an international audience, which is then called upon to pressure domestic and foreign policy makers to address the problems. Local activists thus circumvent the Colombian state and bring pressure to bear on it from a broader, international constituency (Gill 2007; Keck and Sikkink 1998; Tate 2007). At the same time, however, they confront the state directly in a high-risk effort to breach the alliance between the security forces and paramilitaries. They do so by demanding that the police and the military hold paramilitary perpetrators accountable for human rights violations, and then by denouncing them for complicity when they fail to act. By insisting that the state fulfill its duty to provide justice and protect citizens, activists place themselves in the difficult position of turning to the security forces whom they have long regarded as complicit in rights violations and asking them to safeguard people whom the police and the military regard as 'subversives', a label that legitimizes the use of lethal violence against them.[16] Activists confront this dilemma most directly in their own lives when they participate in a state-sponsored protection program that places their security in the hands of the Colombian state.

Since 1997, the Colombian state has operated a protection program for threatened leaders and activists from a number of union, civic, human rights, peasant, and opposition political organizations. Over 6,000 Colombians participated in the program in 2006, and over a third of these individuals were either trade union leaders or members of human rights organizations.[17] The program provides them with a series of 'hard' and 'soft' forms of support, depending on the level of risk established by either the police or the Departamento Administrativo de Seguridad (DAS, Administrative Department of Security). The hard support for the most gravely threatened individuals includes armored vehicles, bodyguards, bulletproof vests, and weapons, while the soft support consists of communication devices that link activists to an early warning system and financial assistance to move to safer locations. Because of the violence that continues to plague Barrancabermeja, it is not surprising that a number of activists receive a full range of hard security measures from the state, but it should also come as no surprise that the protection program is a constant source of tension, mistrust, and suspicion. Much of the conflict turns on the issue of bodyguards.

The struggle over bodyguards epitomizes the ambiguous, shifting boundaries between the official state and the shadowy para-state and underscores the security problems faced by unionists, human rights workers, and community leaders in a war in which the official state is both incapable of protecting them and suspected of conspiring to kill them. The DAS oversees the hiring and performance of all bodyguards in the Colombian state's protection program, but the agency is profoundly mistrusted because of a widespread belief that it maintains close ties to paramilitary organizations. The respected Colombian news weekly *Semana* (2006a) confirmed these fears in 2006, when it revealed that the DAS had drawn up a list of trade union leaders, academics, and government opponents and given it to a paramilitary bloc that operated on the north coast. The individuals on the list were then threatened, and several were either murdered or disappeared.[18]

The tensions between endangered leaders and the security forces begin with a risk evaluation that either the DAS or the police conduct before assigning protective security measures. Leaders complain that the risk assessments routinely underestimate the threat level and result in the provision of inadequate security or none at all. According to one trade unionist, "Over the years, there are people who have died in the protection program. There are also people who have been shot at and who have had to leave town on the run. Then the DAS or the police does a study of the risk level, and they assign an average level that doesn't come with bodyguards. And what is really idiotic is that sometimes they will give you a bulletproof vest, but the city is full of paramilitaries who shoot at your head."[19] One government official who oversees the protection program insists that because of the widespread mistrust of the DAS, individuals do not always provide enough information to do an accurate evaluation,[20] but the head of the program dismisses the complaints and argues that "everyone wants to have an armored car because [the cars] are status symbols." He claims that this is especially true for men who are accustomed to riding motorcycles and bicycles.[21]

Even when they are assigned bodyguards, many leaders will not accept personnel from the DAS because they believe that the agency will use the individuals to collect intelligence and then use the information to murder them or their family members. The protection program, however, permits participants to nominate their own bodyguards, and if the nominees pass muster with the DAS, the agency extends them a contract that lasts approximately six to eight months. Yet there are constant complaints that the DAS cancels these contracts without due cause, that it periodically refuses to provide airline tickets for bodyguards to travel on official business with their charges, and that it frequently leaves endangered individuals without protection. Indeed, when the DAS refuses to provide transportation for a bodyguard, threatened activists must either accept an unknown and untrusted guard from the DAS or travel alone. A trade union leader in Barrancabermeja who has been in the DAS's program for many years expressed his frustrations:

> Our guards are fired on the slightest pretext. The DAS kicked out my two bodyguards in 2006, even though I complained. It maintained the position that I had to accept the guards that the agency sent me, but the union has a very clear policy that we do not take any bodyguard that we do not know, because the DAS tries to use the guards to gather intelligence on us. Many times, but really very often, we have to travel alone because the DAS will not give the boys' tickets. It says that there is no money for the tickets. You call up the Ministry of Interior, and they tell you, "Oh, what a pity, we've run out of money. We can't. But if you want, we'll send you a man from the DAS as soon as you arrive in the airport." Obviously, we say no … So we have to travel alone, and we have to stay in other cities without protection because the DAS says that there isn't money for tickets.[22]

For organizations that either do not qualify for DAS protection or refuse to accept it, international accompaniment is another option. Two international, non-governmental organizations—the Christian Peacemaker Team and the Peace Brigades—provide volunteers to accompany threatened leaders of organizations and their members during meetings and public events and in the daily round of activities. Unlike the bodyguards of the DAS, the internationalists are unarmed and work only with organizations that eschew the use of weapons. The rationale behind international accompaniment is that because of the political relationships that the Colombian state maintains with other powerful states, especially the United States and the European Union, and because of the economic and military aid that it receives from them, government officials want to minimize the political cost of gross human rights violations and avoid the possible sanctions that might result if a foreigner witnessed a human rights crime. Similarly, the reasoning is that paramilitary leaders who are allied with the Colombian state do not want to draw the attention of powerful international states by committing atrocities in the presence of foreign observers. Consequently, those activists accompanied by foreigners—especially North Americans and Europeans—are less vulnerable to assault than others.[23]

Daily life is considerably more complicated and uncertain than this argument suggests, and there is never a guarantee that international accompaniment will have the desired effect. Yet many activists in Barrancabermeja embrace it, and some insist that they are still alive because of it. The deterrent value of accompaniment lies not only in the physical presence of a foreigner but also in the real threat of international consequences that transnational support networks can demonstrate. Foreign accompaniment has the added benefit of legitimizing struggles that are routinely silenced, misrepresented, and condemned by sectors of the dominant society (Mahoney and Eguren 1997), even as it brings activists face to face with the privileges of nationality, race, and class that make international escorts safer than they are. Yet the number of local activists and ordinary Barranqueños who want accompaniment is far greater than the number of internationalists able to support them, and many individuals must devise their own strategies to safeguard their lives.[24]

In the final analysis, activists—whether alone, protected by armed bodyguards, or accompanied by internationalists—face constant uncertainty, and nobody is ever completely sure where the boundaries between safety and danger are located. Yet as activists push up against the status quo and measure its strengths, they test its limits and may at times broaden the political space in which urban residents can rebuild ties to each other, act on their grievances, and speak out about the past. A demonstration, the condemnation of a disappearance, or the demand for better working and living conditions may provoke no response one day but elicit a lethal reprisal the next. A considerable amount of guesswork always shapes decisions and actions on a shifting political terrain where urban residents constantly measure the balance of power and assess what they can do with each other and by themselves, and gauge what is possible, impossible, and unimaginable.

Conclusion

War and peace are difficult concepts in Barrancabermeja. One cannot talk of a frontline nor can one locate a sharp boundary that delineates areas of security and tranquility from realms of mayhem and confusion. Disappearances can happen anywhere, assassins patrol the streets unimpeded, and trade unionists and human rights activists remain 'high-value' targets despite a veneer of urban normalcy. As in counter-insurgency struggles elsewhere, the difficulty of distinguishing combatants and non-combatants in Barrancabermeja has long generated apprehension and confusion. Moreover, as clandestine paramilitaries—once charged by the state to commit the despicable acts of a dirty war—have grown into a powerful shadow state that has penetrated government agencies and political parties, mass murderers increasingly control the state itself. The line between legality and illegality becomes more difficult to discern. Organized crime merges with the politics of counter-insurgency, and widespread impunity threatens to obliterate the crimes of the past and the present, while further empowering coercive entities to repress people who seek to hold the paramilitaries accountable and to expose the ties between them, state officials, regional landlords, and other power holders.

Much like the city of Medellín analyzed by Forrest Hylton, peace in Barrancabermeja is the "peace of the pacifiers" (Hylton 2008). The violent paramilitary takeover of Barrancabermeja has reconfigured the conditions of possibility for social, political, and economic change. It has exposed Barranqueños to varying degrees of threat and obliged them to create their own 'security' in a variety of ways. Some poor residents have established new, clientelistic relationships with paramilitary overlords in order to deal with the devastation of the social and economic networks that had once sustained them. Other have retreated behind a wall of silence or have fled the city. Still others, with protection provided by bodyguards, international accompaniment, and their own wits, continue to press for collective rights and an end to impunity.

This is what Colombian 'democracy' looks like. Although the country is often praised as Latin America's 'oldest democracy' because of its tradition of regular elections, parliamentary democracy has long co-existed with massive violence, an exclusionary political system, and economic policies that have concentrated wealth and power in the hands of a few. In this sense, Colombia resembles other low-intensity democracies, such as post–peace accord Guatemala, where criminal groups that interpenetrate the state bureaucracy carry out political crimes, enrich themselves through a range of illegal activities, and imperil the development of a truly democratic social order (Peacock and Beltrán 2003). War and peace dissolve into each other in these settings. The emergent 'order' requires impunity and repression to sustain it, and, as in the much broader 'war on terror' waged by the United States, civilians are the ultimate victims.

Acknowledgments

This chapter has benefited from the suggestions of Leigh Binford and Alisse Waterston. The research was supported by the National Science Foundation and American University.

Lesley Gill teaches anthropology at Vanderbilt University. She is the author of several books, including *The School of the Americas: Military Training and Political Violence in the Americas* (2004) and *Teetering on the Rim: Global Restructuring, Daily Life, and the Armed Retreat of the Bolivian State* (2000). She is currently conducting research on how political violence and neo-liberalism are reconfiguring work, trade unionism, and collective action among Colombian Coca-Cola workers.

Notes

1. Naomi Klein (2007) refers to this as part of the "disaster capitalism complex."
2. Three insurgent groups—the Revolutionary Armed Forces of Colombia (FARC), the National Liberation Army (ELN), and the Popular Liberation Army (EPL)—shared power on Barrancabermeja's impoverished periphery in the 1990s.

3. According to Amnesty International (1999): "Despite the fact that the Colombian armed forces maintain a heavy presence in close proximity to the districts where the attack took place and these units had only recently received intelligence reports indicating that paramilitary forces were planning a massacre in the city; despite the sound of gunfire and the reported cries for help of the victims and the appeals made to the security forces to pursue the paramilitary attackers, no action was taken by the security forces either to confront the paramilitary force ... or to track them down as they made their exit from the city."
4. Interview with human rights defender in Barrancabermeja, February 2007.
5. Interviews with residents of Barrancabermeja, February and March 2007.
6. The Colombian news weekly *Semana* (2006a, 2006b, 2006c) has done some of the best reporting on the embedding of paramilitarism in various regions of Colombia. See also Isacson (2005) on this topic. For a description of paramilitary control of Medellín, see Hylton (2007). For specific references to Barrancabermeja, see the comments of former AUC leader Carlos Castaño in Serrano Zabala (2007) and Aranguren Molina (2001: 255–257).
7. In 2008, President Álvaro Uribe extradited several key paramilitary leaders who were not abiding by the terms of the Justice and Peace Law. The mass extraditions came amid a highly publicized scandal in which some 60 congressional representatives—the majority of them from Uribe's ruling coalition—were linked to the paramilitaries.
8. Indepaz, a Colombian non-governmental organization, calculated the number of new groups based on information from the Organization of American States and the Colombian military and police. See http://www.indepaz.org.co (accessed 2 June 2007).
9. Interview with resident of Barrancabermeja, February 2007.
10. Interview with resident of Barrancabermeja, March 2007.
11. Interview with resident of Barrancabermeja, March 2007.
12. Interview with resident of Barrancabermeja, February 2007.
13. Interview with resident of Barrancabermeja, February 2007.
14. Interview with human rights defender, Barrancabermeja, February 2007.
15. Interview with former slaughterhouse worker in the office of the Popular Feminist Organization, Barrancabermeja, February 2007.
16. Godoy (2005: 622) makes a similar point about human rights workers in Guatemala.
17. Since 2001, the United States Agency for International Development has provided between 5 and 15 percent of the annual funding for this program. See http://www.mij .gov.co (accessed 2 April 2007).
18. See "The DAS Scandals," http://www.ciponline.org (accessed 17 April 2006).
19. Interview with union leader, 15 February 2007.
20. Interview with Gloria Gaviria, Ministry of Social Protection, Bogotá, Colombia, 13 April 2007.
21. Interview with Rafael Bustamante, Ministry of Interior, Bogotá, Colombia, 13 April 2007.
22. Interview with trade unionist, Barrancabermeja, March 2007.
23. See Mahoney and Eguren (1997) for more on the philosophy and practice of international accompaniment.
24. For this reason, activists frequently asked me to accompany them on routine activities.

References

Amnesty International. 1999. "Barrancabermeja: A City Under Siege." http://www.amnesty .org/library/print/ENGAMR230361999 (accessed 1 June 2007).

Aranguren Molina, Maurico. 2001. *Mi confesión: Carlos Castaño revela sus secretos* [My Confession: Carlos Castaño Reveals His Secrets]. Bogotá: Editorial Oveja Negra.

Auyero, Javier. 2000. "The Hyper-Shantytown: Neo-liberal Violence(s) in the Argentine Slum." *Ethnography* 1, no. 1: 93–116.

Bejarano, Ana Maria, and Eduardo Pizarro. 2004. "Colombia: The Partial Collapse of the State and the Emergence of Aspiring State-Makers." Pp. 99–118 in *States Within States: Incipient Political Entities in the Post–Cold War Era*, ed. Paul Kingston and Ian S. Spears. New York: Palgrave.

Binford, Leigh. 2002. "Violence in El Salvador: A Rejoinder to Philippe Bourgois's 'The Continuum of Violence in War and Peace: Post–Cold War Lessons from el Salvador.'" *Ethnology* 3, no. 2: 201–219.

Bourgois, Philippe. 2001. "The Power of Violence in War and Peace: Post–Cold War Lessons from El Salvador." *Ethnography* 2, no. 1: 5–34.

CINEP/CREDHOS. 2004. "Barrancabermeja, la otra versión: Paramilitarismo, control social, y desaparición forzada 2000–2003" [Barrancabermeja, the Other Version: Paramilitarism, Social Control, and Forced Disappearance, 2000–2003]. Noche y Niebla Caso Tipo No. 3. Bogotá: CINEP/CREDHOS.

Duncan, Gustavo. 2006. *Los señores de la guerra: De paramilitares, mafiosos y autodefensas en Colombia* [Warlords: Paramilitaries, Mafiosi, and Self-Defense Groups in Colombia]. Bogotá: Planeta/Fundación Seguridad y Democracia.

Enloe, Cynthia. 1993. *The Morning After: Sexual Politics at the End of the Cold War*. Berkeley: University of California Press.

Farmer, Paul. 1997. "On Suffering and Structural Violence: A View from Below." Pp. 261–283 in *Social Suffering*, ed. Arthur Kleinman, Veena Das, and Margaret Lock. Berkeley: University of California Press.

Gill, Lesley. 2004. *The School of the Americas: Military Training and Political Violence in the Americas*. Durham, NC: Duke University Press.

———. 2007. "'Right There with You': Coca-Cola, Labor Restructuring, and Political Violence in Colombia." *Critique of Anthropology* 27, no. 3: 235–260.

———. Forthcoming. "The Parastate in Colombia: Political Violence and the Restructuring of Barrancabermeja." *Anthropologica*.

Godoy, Angelina Snodgrass. 2005. "La Muchacha Respondona: Reflections on the Razor's Edge between Crime and Human Rights." *Human Rights Quarterly* 27: 597–624.

———. 2006. *Popular Injustice: Violence, Community and Law in Latin America*. Palo Alto, CA: Stanford University Press.

Gordillo, Gastón. 2004. *Landscape of Devils: Tensions of Place and Memory in the Argentinean Chaco*. Durham, NC: Duke University Press.

Hersh, Michael, and John Barry. 2005. "The Salvador Option." *Newsweek*. http://www.msnbc.msn.com/id/6802629/site/newsweek/ (accessed 19 May 2007).

Hollander, Nancy Caro. 1997. *Love in a Time of Hate: Liberation Psychology in Latin America*. New Brunswick, NJ: Rutgers University Press.

HRW (Human Rights Watch). 1996. "Colombia's Killer Networks: The Military-Paramilitary Partnership and the United States." New York: Human Rights Watch.

———. 2001. "The 'Sixth Division': Military-Paramilitary Ties and U.S. Policy in Colombia." New York: Human Rights Watch.

———. 2005a. "Colombia: Displaced and Discarded. The Plight of Internally Displaced Persons in Bogotá and Cartagena." New York: Human Rights Watch.

———. 2005b. "Smoke and Mirrors: Colombia's Demobilization of Paramilitary Groups." New York: Human Rights Watch.

Hylton, Forrest. 2006. *Evil Hour in Colombia*. London: Verso.

———. 2007. "Remaking Medellín." *New Left Review* 44: 71–90.

———. 2008. "Medellín: The Peace of the Pacifiers." *NACLA Report on the Americas* 41, no. 1: 35–42.

Isacson, Adam. 2005. *Peace or "Paramilitarization?* International policy report. Center for International Policy, Washington, DC.

Keck, Margaret E., and Kathryn Sikkink. 1998. *Activists Beyond Borders: Advocacy Networks in International Politics*. Ithaca, NY: Cornell University Press.

Klein, Naomi. 2007. *The Shock Doctrine: The Rise of Disaster Capitalism*. New York: Metropolitan Books.

LeGrand, Catherine. 2003. "The Colombian Crisis in Historical Perspective." *Canadian Journal of Latin American and Caribbean Studies* 28, no. 55–56: 165–209.

Litwack, Leon. 1998. *Trouble in Mind: Black Southerners in the Age of Jim Crow*. New York: Knopf.

Loingsigh, Gearóid. 2002. "The Integral Strategy of the Paramilitaries in Colombia's Magdalena Medio." Unpublished manuscript. Bogotá, Colombia.

Lutz, Catherine. 2004. "Militarization." Pp. 318–331 in *A Companion to the Anthropology of Politics*, ed. David Nugent and Joan Vincent. Malden, MA: Blackwell.

Madero, Régulo. 2001. "Human Rights Violations: Manifestations of a Perverse Model of Governance." http://www.colhrnet.igc.org/newsletter/y2001/spring01art/regulo101.htm (accessed 30 May 2007).

Mahoney, Liam, and Luis Enrique Eguren, eds. 1997. *Unarmed Bodyguards: International Accompaniment for the Protection of Human Rights*. West Hartford, CT: Kumarian Press.

McClintock, Michael. 1992. *Instruments of Statecraft: U.S. Guerrilla Warfare, Counterinsurgency, and Counterterrorism, 1940–1990*. New York: Pantheon.

McCoy, Alfred W. 2006. *A Question of Torture: CIA Interrogation, from the Cold War to the War on Terror*. New York: Metropolitan Books.

McSherry, J. Patrice. 2005. *Predatory States: Operation Condor and Covert War in Latin America*. Lanham, MD: Rowan and Littlefield.

Medina Gallegos, Carlos. 1990. *Autodefensas, paramilitares, y narcotráfico en Colombia: Orígen, desarrollo, consolidación* [Self-Defense Groups, Paramilitaries, and Drug Traffic in Colombia: Origin, Development, Consolidation]. Bogotá: Editorial Documentos Periódicos.

Peacock, Susan C., and Adriana Beltrán. 2003. "Hidden Powers in Post-Conflict Guatemala: Illegal Armed Groups and the Forces behind Them." Washington Office on Latin America, Washington, DC.

Pécaut, Daniel. 2001. *Guerra contra la sociedad* [War against Society]. Bogotá: ESPASA.

Riaño, Pilar. 2002. "Remembering Place: Memory and Violence in Medellín, Colombia." *Journal of Latin American Anthropology* 7, no. 1: 276–309.

Richani, Nazih. 2002. *Systems of Violence: The Political Economy of War and Peace in Colombia*. Albany, NY: SUNY Press.

Roldán, Mary. 2002. *Blood and Fire: La Violencia in Antioquia, Colombia, 1946–1953*. Durham, NC: Duke University Press.

Romero, Mauricio. 2003. *Paramilitares y autodefensas, 1982–2003* [Paramilitaries and Self-Defense Groups, 1982–2003]. Bogotá: IEPRI.

Scheper-Hughes, Nancy, and Philippe Bourgois, eds. 2004. *Violence in War and Peace*. Malden, MA: Blackwel.

Semana. 2006a. "Como se hizo el fraude" [How Fraud Happened]. 8 April. http://www.semana.com (accessed 10 April 2006).

_____. 2006b. "Memorias de un para" [Recollections of a Paramilitary]. 19 March. http://www.semana.com (accessed 20 August 2006).

_____. 2006c. "El 8.000 en la costa" [8,000 on the Coast]. 10 August. http://www.semana.com (accessed 20 August 2006).

_____. 2007a. "Hoy conocimos a Macaco" [Today We Meet Macaco]. 13 June. http://www.semana.com (accessed 13 June 2007).

_____. 2007b. "El Intocable?" [The Untouchable?]. 10 June. http://www.semana.com (accessed 10 June 2007).

Serrano Zabala, Alfredo. 2007. *La batalla final de Carlos Castaño: Secretos de la parapolítica* [The Final Battle of Carlos Castaño: Secrets of the Parapolitica]. Bogotá: Editorial Oveja Negra.

Tate, Winifred. 2007. *Counting the Dead: The Culture and Politics of Human Rights Activism in Colombia*. Berkeley: University of California Press.

Taussig, Michael. 1992. *The Nervous System*. New York: Routledge Press.

Chapter 7

THE CONTINUUM OF VIOLENCE IN POST-WAR GUATEMALA

Beatriz Manz

State violence in Guatemala reached genocidal proportions in the 1980s. The most targeted populations were rural Mayan communities. While officially peace was achieved at the end of 1996, everyday violence has reached epidemic proportions. This chapter reflects on the violence continuum and the social devastation it has wrought. The violence is rooted in a society that historically has been deeply divided along ethnic and rigid class lines and that has been fundamentally unjust, discriminatory, and abusive toward the oppressed population. The challenge then is much greater, and the likelihood of continued violence that much more likely, when the underlying grievances have not been and are unlikely to be addressed because those in power do not have the will to bring about the necessary changes.

Notes for this chapter are located on page 162.

Consider a scene that has become all too common in Guatemala. There is a mound engulfed in red fiery flames and acrid smoke while some 200 people (including children) intently watch the blaze in the town square. Some people stand on top of vehicles in the back to get a better view. The mound consists of the bodies of two human beings who have been burned alive, a gruesome example of today's popular vigilante justice, *justicia a mano propia*. Lynchings have become common in Guatemala today. In a country of 12 million, murders accounted for 5,338 deaths in 2005, according to the police—a 23 percent increase in one year. In the first six months of 2006, Amnesty International (2006) reported that 299 women were killed. Women are subjected to violence at alarming rates: over 1,000 women were killed between 2005 and June 2006, and other crimes are rising as well.[1]

Violence in the Post-war Period

After decades of state-sponsored violence inflicted on historically subordinated populations, Guatemala reached peace accords in 1996. However, signing a peace accord and ending the armed conflict have proven far different from achieving stability and a semblance of peace. Two decades ago, Americas Watch had already correctly pointed out the disjunction between what something is called and the reality on the ground by naming one of their reports *Creating a Desolation and Calling it Peace* (Americas Watch 1983). The fabric of society, even the fabric of small communities, was shredded during the ferocious internal armed conflict. The legacy of state terror is everywhere. The militarization of daily life—especially in rural communities—deformed previous human relations. The violence during the most recent conflict left a deep mark in the post-war period, most notably in the form of vigilante 'justice' and gangs (*maras*), which are a new and very serious phenomenon (Moser and McIlwaine 2001; Snodgrass-Godoy 2006).

The Guatemalan Army pulverized communities, inflicting more than 600 massacres, 200,000 deaths, the displacement of 1.5 million people, and tens of thousands of disappearances, most significantly in the 1980s.[2] The exhaustive documentation of atrocities conducted by the UN-sponsored Commission for Historical Clarification (Comisión para el Esclarecimiento Histótrico, CEH) concluded that the Guatemalan military had committed genocide, the term associated with the most horrific of war crimes. "The CEH concludes that agents of the State of Guatemala, within the framework of counterinsurgency operations carried out between 1981 and 1983, committed acts of genocide against groups of Mayan people" (CEH 1999: 41). "Ethnic cleansing," one observer noted, "was practiced on a scale beyond even that of Bosnia," compelling Mayan populations to live "under a ghastly form of state terrorism" (Kinzer 2001: 61). The savagery exceeded the violence in "El Salvador, Nicaragua, Chile, and Argentina combined" (ibid.). With this level of atrocities, it should not be surprising that the current interval of peace is so palpable and delicate. "This peace process is not irreversible," an official with the United Nations Verification Mission in

Guatemala (MINUGUA) warned. "If Guatemala doesn't have a period of social peace so that these changes can take hold, things could begin to fall apart. There is still the danger of a return to the past" (Kinzer 2001: 62). On the sixth anniversary of the peace accords, MINUGUA (2002) issued a press release listing some still unmet commitments: "It is impossible to ignore that discrimination and poverty, principal causes of the internal armed conflict, still have not been eradicated ... It is impossible to ignore the persistent high levels of impunity, and that the defenders of human rights and labor and social leaders have to continue operating in the current climate of threats and intimidation. It is impossible to ignore that the population in general has to continue suffering the effects of violence and of a constant insecurity."

In addition to the deaths, displacements, refugee crisis, and general economic and social devastation, the mayhem included a variety of army-instituted practices, most notably the maintenance of the one-million-strong Civil Defense Patrols (PAC).[3] This required regimentation made the militarization of daily activities a standard routine, involving training, 24-hour shifts, controls, and checkpoints. Residents were required to obtain permission to leave their villages and were encouraged to inform (to the military) on fellow citizens. These divisive strategies ruptured communities and provoked fear (not just of the military) as well as distrust and a sense of betrayal among one's fellow villagers. The tactics engendered a deep sense of uncertainty embedded in the traumas surging from the vulnerabilities in people's everyday life. The level of control and fear permeated many aspects of common communal practices. The PACs—rural paramilitary organizations—were forced to serve the army by conducting patrols, surveillance, and intelligence; informing on fellow villagers; and carrying out punishment and murder as directed by the army. This new, unpaid extraction of labor, vigilance, and intelligence subordinated and often transformed, or actually shattered, the customary norms of village life—a perverse transformation that continues to affect these communities in the post-war period. The army gave extraordinary power to local cliques, who often used that power in violent ways. As Primo Levi (1988: 67) observed, "[P]ower is like a drug ... the dependency and need for ever larger doses is born." Once savored, power becomes addictive and, when coupled with a culture of impunity, even more seductive and overpowering. Yet military commanders and local henchmen can appear to be "terribly and terrifyingly normal," as Hannah Arendt (1964: 276) chillingly noted.

This network of army collaborators, willingly (or unwillingly, in order to survive), became complicit in atrocities and abuse of power at the local level. The after-effect of the invasive military penetration is palpable throughout post-war Guatemalan society in the form of recrimination, vengeance, and a tendency to resolve disputes through direct violence—individually or collectively. The Catholic Church report on the human rights violations during the counter-insurgency war emphasized the long-term effects of the militarization of the society: "The large number of people deformed by [or educated in] violence through the civil patrols and the practice of forced recruitment indicates the danger that militarization will have long-term repercussions" (REMHI 1999:

176). Moreover, decades of routine violence and impunity have "influenced value systems and behavioral patterns and [have enabled] perpetrators to acquire expertise and perpetuate power networks" (ibid.).

Meanwhile, community ties and social structures have been difficult to repair. Alarmingly, one gets the sense of a pervasive feeling of defeatism and mistrust, which translates into lower expectations of cohesion, certainty, and confidence in a better future, as well as feelings of despair and, worse yet, the desire for revenge. War and post-war violence spirals down in frustration and cycles of reprisals. Indeed, violence leaves on its victims more than physical scars. "Violence can never be understood solely in terms of its physicality—force, assaults, or the infliction of pain—alone," Scheper-Hughes and Bourgois (2004: 1) have incisively noted. "Violence also includes assaults on the person-hood, dignity, sense of worth and value of the victim. The social and cultural dimensions of violence are what give violence its power and meaning." A society where devaluing human life has become a habit, where problem solving through violence has become a normal impulse, is a society in crisis with imminent social cohesion unlikely. The fatigue of daily havoc and the ordinariness of violence render them almost imperceptible and makes them part of the social landscape. Denoting all violent acts as common crimes and violence as a customary occurrence obscures the magnitude of this social malaise.

Resignation and cynicism, leading to the perception "Es el destino" (It is fate), are common outcomes. The belief "that nothing can be done about it" is evident in the lack of political participation (nearly 50 percent of the citizens abstained from voting in the 2007 elections) and in the exodus to the United States. Despite all the risks and tremendous obstacles they face, once they have emigrated Guatemalans feel a sense of liberation and assess optimistically their chances to improve their condition. Many villagers who participated in the vibrant rural cooperative movement in the 1960s and 1970s have lost faith in cooperative action, even though the cooperatives brought prosperity and advantages, especially in isolated villages. One peasant told me, "I have now found a way to live individually. I have my family. It's better to make my cooperative at home."[4]

People also tend to be disenchanted because they see that 'their moment' of possibility has passed. As Guatemalan anthropologist and Jesuit Ricardo Falla so eloquently writes in reference to Rigoberta Menchú's presidential campaign,[5] that moment was "the great hope of a very radical change" (Falla 2007). Failure fueled "great frustration" which left a residue of deep resignation and feelings of impotence. Falla continues, "That height of enthusiasm will not be repeated until a third generation following the one that lived that moment" take its place in history. The internal mobilization of the Mayan people in the 1970s and 1980s was a "spark of enthusiasm that could be seen in the eyes of young people, and that spark led them to act, to commit themselves, even to give their lives—it was combustible," Falla (ibid.) asserts. "That spark was a premonition, a certainty: we can win." But that moment of hope for millions of people resulted in genocide. Falla continues, "Now people don't see that. Even if Rigoberta were to win the presidency, we feel we will win nothing ... There are no possibilities of change ... There is not now the possibility of great hope."

"The loser's fear," Garretón (1992: 14) observed, "is pervaded by a sense of defeat, a perception of the overwhelming power of the enemy, a feeling of failure or weakness that cannot be blamed on others, and a sense of having lost the opportunity for personal or collective realization." A sense of defeat in the recent past takes a similar form—a sense of impotence—about the future as well: "It combines fear of terror or repression with terror of the future—namely, a new situation that will be fraught with unknown dangers" (ibid.).

One former insurgent combatant, who spent 16 years in the guerrilla ranks, expressed that sense of resignation when asked about how he saw the future: "We will end our lives as we are. There is no hope for a better life because there won't be any." He continued, "We also don't have dreams like the one we had before. We'll struggle for our lives, for the family, as much as possible." As a guerrilla, he had thought that the struggle was just, necessary, and possible, but he now felt that the fight to attain greater social and political change was pointless. "I no longer want to fight for the people, to be thinking the way I did before. I believed that everything was going to be accomplished."[6] His words, no doubt, give comfort, at least for the time being, to those who did not and do not want social change in the country.

The sense of hopelessness and resignation is evident in practical terms at the local level, where it is manifested in less cooperation, less collective action, and more individualism. Although the PACs were officially dissolved as part of the peace accords in 1996, the lingering effects of violence cast a dark, pervasive shadow, leaving deep scars and shattering families in irreparable ways. Recovery and social cohesion are daunting tasks. Overcoming mistrust in this highly polarized society is possible only if the causes that led to genocide are explicitly addressed and acknowledged, and if the fundamental schisms that separate the population in question from their persecutors are redressed.

The concept of reconciliation in the case of Guatemala seems to be a misnomer. The elites, the military, and the majority of the population—the poor and the Mayans—were never "conciliated" to begin with (Simpson 1998: 491). To create a society with the semblance of harmony and respect would require major and fundamental changes in the very core of social relations, rather than focusing solely on the period of the most recent conflict. What is that historic core? Since the creation of the country, that core has been based on political and economic exclusion and discrimination, racism, spatial segregation, and a long-standing and extreme exploitation. The contempt for the native population dates back to the initial encounter of a small powerful elite, which came to control and dominate the overwhelming majority. Bartolomé de las Casas ([1552] 1974), who witnessed the brutality to which the native population was subjected at the hands of his fellow Spaniards, wrote in the mid-1500s about the abuse that brought laborers to collapse: "It should be told that the Indians of this land, when they weary and sink down, fainting under the heavy loads they are made to carry, are buffeted and kicked by the Spaniards, who break their teeth with blows from their sword hilts" (ibid.: 101). The natives did not receive the most basic human considerations, according to de las Casas. They were hungry and miserable, and were not given time to rest. The Spaniards treated them "with such rigor and inhumanity that they seemed the very ministers of Hell, driving them day and night with beatings, kicks, lashes, and blows, and calling them no sweeter name than dogs" (Goodpasture 1989: 10). Catholic priests who accompanied the Spanish colonization (in de las Casas's term the "destruction" of the discovered lands and peoples) were alarmed by the cruelty and harshness that accompanied conversion to Christianity: "By what right or justice do you wage such detestable wars on these people who lived mildly and peaceful in their own lands?" (Goodpasture 1989: 12). These descriptions were not confined to the period of the Mayans being colonized by the Spaniards. Rather, references to cruelty—overwork, death by hunger and disease, and torture for those suspected of rebelling against the status quo—appear and reappear, almost as a habit, with violence as normality, into the contemporary period.

Progress toward an inclusive and just society is daunting. Injustice and privation are the norm for the vast majority, interrupted only by periods of increasing or decreasing violence and levels of scarcity, while well-being and unchecked access to privileges and unlimited resources are the standard for the small number of elites. The state's requirement to suppress periods of bottom-up dissent and the degree to which the disenfranchised are unwilling to accept their subordinate status guide the level of violence. What ensues is the ever-mounting suffering that is a result of unachievable expectations in economic and social change. One observer correctly points out that "the state relinquished for many years its role as mediator between different social and economic interests, opening thereby a vacuum that led to a direct confrontation between those who received the benefits, defenders of that established order, and those who were forced to claim their aspirations" (Kinzer 2001: 61).

The violence in Guatemala today is exemplified most dramatically in the prevalence and acceptance of public lynchings. In her excellent book, *Popular Injustice: Violence, Community, and Law in Latin America*, Angelina Snodgrass-Godoy (2006) analyzes this gruesome phenomenon. She argues that "under authoritarianism, the institutionalized practices of state terror produced a functional inversion of the law in Guatemala, a system that justified (indeed, mandated) violence in the name of order and cast the formal law itself in a role of near irrelevance. In the postwar period, practices known as *mano dura* have prolonged this perverse marriage of violence and law, with devastating effects on democracy as a whole" (ibid.: 41). The widespread sense that the laws have not and do not function has led many ordinary people affected by criminal activities to take matters into their own hands to solve the pervasive problem. "One key component of *mano dura* across the region," Snodgrass-Godoy continues, "is support for private acts of vigilantism, locally known as *justicia a mano propia*, or 'justice by one's own hand.' These include lynchings, as well as the murky work of 'social cleansing' squads, usually carried out under cover of darkness" (ibid.: 57).

The character of the violence has changed, as rural communities would be quick to admit. Compared to the years when the army would massacre entire villages, there are no genocidal practices being undertaken today. The new fear and insecurity is nonetheless distressing and a cause of continuous anxiety. "[T]he decline in state killing and the cessation of the armed conflict have been accompanied by what, to many, would appear to be a flourishing of new forms of violence," observes Snodgrass-Godoy (2006: 44–45). "This new wave of terror is usually referred to as *delinquencia* (delinquency) or common crime. And although the government's human rights record has improved, there is still ample cause for concern: in 2003, reacting to the wave of office break-ins, death threats, and attacks on human rights defenders, Amnesty International declared that the country was experiencing a 'human rights meltdown,' the worst human rights crisis since the era of state-sponsored genocide" (ibid.). It takes a big toll on a population to live with heightened anxiety and constant surveillance of their surroundings.

Paramilitary groups and former members of the military are actively engaged in criminal activities, ranging from personal vendettas and settling scores to corruption, kidnappings, rapes, thefts, shootings, and drug trafficking. Thus, the formal ending of war and the transition from military dictatorship to elected civilian government did not in itself bring about much needed changes and practices. As one scholar observes, "individuals can readily get caught up in self-deluding mentalities used to justify violence even when they do not accept the larger political project that leads to this behavior that fuels the culture of violence. In such an environment, we might see the persistence of violent behaviors and mentalities among police, even when the regime changes from authoritarian to democratic" (Davis 2006: 187).

The Legacy of the War

The consequences of suffering, devastation, and massive displacement are far from being addressed. The social dilemma resulting from the genocidal violence, which resulted in destruction, mistrust, and tensions within the communities, is further exacerbated by poverty. The devastating economic legacy of the war acts as a counterweight on the broader political and social change in the country. During the war years, over a million rural people were displaced from their homes. Given the dismal economic conditions, the displacement is continuing today with migrations to the United States, which are estimated to be as high as one million. In 2005, these migrants sent $3 billion in remittances to relatives in Guatemala. Already by 2002, remittances were over seven times the value of coffee exports and more than triple that of tourism, approaching the value of all of Guatemala's merchandise exports.

The CEH (1999: 17) summarized this situation best: "The anti-democratic nature of the Guatemalan political tradition has its roots in an economic structure that is marked by the concentration of productive wealth in the hands of a minority." This structure, the commission pointedly concluded, forged "a system of multiple exclusions, including elements of racism" and "a violent and dehumanizing social system" (ibid.). This system of social exclusion and repression is deeply rooted in the political-economic configuration of a society that compels the disenfranchised population to live under dreadful and increasingly untenable physical and emotional distress. What we are seeing are the ramifications of state terror in a historically oppressive society recently decimated by civil war.

What are the prospects for economic improvement for those mired in degrading poverty? Some argue that the impact of globalization and trade agreements (such as the Central American Free Trade Agreement and its recent revisions) will increase the likelihood of development, democracy, and respect for human rights. This may be a dubious assumption. There is a strong counter-argument that globalization and inadequate trade agreements will weaken the economy and further polarize the society.

Where do academics fit into all this? In considering levels of responsibility in cases of mass terror, there is the "atrocity triangle,"[7] composed of victims, perpetrators, and observers. The observer or proverbial bystander—a part often played by the academic—does not need to witness human rights violations directly. Nowadays, violence that is inflicted in distant geographic regions implicates us all in some way, given the globalized world in which we live. Global bystanders should not evade responsibility by claiming a conflict of interest and recusing themselves in order to avoid participating in the jury and ethical judgment. When it comes to human rights, we live in a world without borders and therefore have a far broader moral burden of accountability.

Are all bystanders equal? Some, especially those in the United States, carry greater responsibility. US academics occupy a privileged position and should be willing to expose human right abuses, injustice, degrading poverty, and exploitation. If we want to be relevant, anthropologists should shape the public debate, reframe the issues and perceptions, and provide new insights. In a globalized world, our subjects and our audience are not disconnected, as Clifford Geertz (1988) noted. Our audience should not just be informed, he asserted, they need to be implicated. Likewise our subjects need to be informed.

In the 'hard' sciences, researchers share findings about a problem and present research results as to the causes of the problem and, even better, if they find solutions for it. In our discipline, those steps have the maligned name of 'activism', and their practitioners become denigrated and shunned. Have we ever heard of a 'cancer cure activist'? Why do we tend to be so timid about finding solutions for those who suffer and live in human-made scarcity and injustice? What specific results are we providing? Why are we not advocates? Why do we not make a concerted effort to improve human lives? Ricardo Falla remarks, "I would suggest a criterion to be used for judging the integration of research and action—the furtherance of justice in the world ... Justice here is to be understood broadly and in a variety of dimensions, covering economic, social and cultural relations" (Falla, Rios, and Alvarez 2000: 45). Falla sees research and social action reinforcing each other, and he and his co-authors expand this notion further: "The motivation for the research should be the desire to solve great problems of justice such as poverty, violence, the destruction of the environment, the spread of AIDS, discrimination against women, and political corruption" (ibid.: 47). The authors suggest that social research today should include high levels of dialogue between different researchers and social and political leaders, especially across national borders in this age of globalization.

Finally, where is the United States today in relation to Guatemala? Where is the country that conceived the CIA's 'Operation Success' in 1954 and unilaterally decided that it was time for regime change in Guatemala (see Gleijeses 1991; Immerman 1982; Schlesinger and Kinzer 1982)? It was not the US that suffered the devastation, political chaos, and social suffering that followed the intervention. For 50 years Guatemala has endured anti-democratic regimes, economic hopelessness, and terror. Amnesty International states that the "prevailing climate of impunity" and the violations are "so severe," Guatemala can be referred to as undergoing a "human rights melt-down" (Amnesty International 2002: 5–6).

The world has changed since the end of the Cold War. The United States is the undisputed superpower, and this puts American citizens and especially US academics in a quandary. Millions of people are experiencing the tyranny of global monopolies as never before. Many ex-colonies are now supplying a new type of wretched labor for the powerful countries. It may not be slave plantation work, but it is back-breaking nonetheless, with disheartening living conditions and few prospects for a better and more dignified life for future generations. Are we to accept this extreme imbalance of power and its dreadful consequences? Should American anthropologists be concerned about economic globalization, social conditions, injustice, exploitation, and military interventions in other countries? Should we be attempting to counter these trends in a more public role, or should we stay at the sidelines and accept the current state of world affairs? Why not think of a 'global human rights alliance'? Is there a discipline better suited than anthropology to take the lead? The US government has had a long and direct involvement in Guatemala's internal affairs. The head of the UN's CEH pointedly incriminated the United States: "Up until the mid-1980s, there was strong pressure from the U.S. government and U.S. companies to maintain the country's archaic and unjust economic structure."[8] The US interventions date to at least the 1950s, and during the period of mass terror, as Aryeh Neier points out, "the United States embassy in Guatemala was effectively a public relations mouthpiece for the armed forces" (Manz 2004: xiv). Moreover, Jeane Kirkpatrick, the US ambassador to the United Nations "said of the regime committing genocide that it 'offered new powers of self-government and self-defense to the Indians,'" claiming that the genocidal regime "included a strong effort to end human rights abuses by government forces" (ibid.). The US State Department was quite aware of the historical practices of human rights abuses in that country. While not admitting publicly to the inhumane treatment meted out by pupils trained in US military academies and by recipients of US military aid, government officials were making clear in internal memos the excesses and impunity of the Guatemalan government forces: "[P]eople are killed or disappeared on the basis of simple accusations."[9]

Dilemmas of Building a New Society

Ultimately, recovery is daunting for the victims of war, and memory has a long and debilitating persistence. The legacy of genocide is present in everyday lives. To build a new society from the wreck of the past is difficult and in the best of cases will take time, as we have seen in various parts of the world. Justice should be the ultimate goal and a prerequisite for recovery, but as South African Judge Goldstone points out: "That ideal is not possible in the aftermath of massive violence ... There are simply too many victims and too many perpetrators" (Minow 1998: ix). However, the oft-taken path of pretending that nothing has happened or that the country has turned a new page is not a legitimate solution. Mayans have suffered human rights violations for centuries and are unlikely to forget, but that does not prevent the government from pretending that nothing happened: "Some countries simply forget the past and attempt to induce a national amnesia in its people" (ibid.: x).

The repression—in which millions were harmed and to which they are still being subjected today—should not go unchallenged. Perpetrators and bystanders should know that "there are no tidy endings following mass atrocity," as Judge Goldstone points out (Minow 1998: x). Survivors of mass terror need to know that their society acknowledges what happened to their loved ones and to them and will take action to address the psychological harm and fear that they experience.

Analyzing the psychological impact of the violence on women, Judith Zur (1996) noticed that "outbursts of anger are extremely rare," yet the anger and anxiety engendered often comes from circumstances where "the perpetrators of some of the worst atrocities were village men whom the bereaved women continue to see almost daily and toward whom they have to be mute and deferential because of the authority they still retain" (ibid.: 311). These circumstances of unchanged dominance by murderers, torturers, and rapists are distressingly common and devastating. How do victims face this anger and pain on a day-to-day basis and have faith that the horrible past is not still present? How can they have confidence that the past will not repeat itself in the future?

Chilean writer Ariel Dorfman (1991: 59) poses some key questions that are fitting for Guatemala: "[H]ow can those who torture and those who were tortured co-exist in the same land? How to heal a country that has been traumatized by repression if the fear to speak out is still omnipresent? And how do you reach the truth if lying has become a habit?" Clearly, the challenge is daunting. Is there a path between "too much memory and too much forgetting" (Minow 1998: 4)? Dorfman (1991: 59) ponders this dilemma: "How do we keep the past alive without becoming its prisoner? How do we forget it without risking its repetition in the future? Is it legitimate to sacrifice the truth to ensure peace?" I differ with Minow's (1998: 147) conclusion that "[b]etween vengeance and forgiveness lie the path of recollection and affirmation and the path of facing who we are, and what we could become." In the case of Guatemala, it will take considerably more than the path she suggests. One would wish it were less complex.

The United Nations Verification Mission in Guatemala warned about the dangers of ignoring the economic and social injustice and the vast unmet demands and expectations of the population: "If Guatemala doesn't have a period of social peace so that these changes can take hold, things could begin to fall apart. There is still the danger of a return to the past" (quoted in Kinzer

2001: 62; see also Jonas 2000; MINUGUA 2002). One of the leading Latin American social psychologists, Ignacio Martin-Baró, a professor and Jesuit priest assassinated in El Salvador in 1989, made a linkage between economic structures and social violence: "Structural violence cannot be reduced to an inadequate distribution of available resources which impede the satisfaction of the basic necessities of the majority," however significant that is. "Structural violence includes an ordering of the oppressive inequality, through the use of legislation which hides behind the mechanisms of the social distribution of wealth and establishes a coercive force obligating the people to respect them." The elite—who enjoy privilege, access to the resources of the society, and the protection of the state apparatus—seeks at all social costs to maintain the status quo and deny basic well-being and human dignity to the majority. "The system therefore closes the cycle of violence, justifying and protecting those structures that privilege the few at the cost of the many ... Violence is already present in the social order" (Instituto de Estudios Centroamericanos and El Rescate 1990: 10–11).

The words of Eleanor Roosevelt resonate today as we wonder whether it is possible to believe in universal human rights or to ignore the plight of people in distant villages in countries such as Guatemala. She remarked at the United Nations on 27 March 1953: "Where, after all, do universal human rights begin? In small places, close to home, so close and so small that they cannot be seen on any maps of the world. Yet they are the world of the individual person: The neighborhood he lives in; the school or college he attends; the factory, farm, or office where he works. Such are the places where every man, woman, and child seeks equal justice, equal opportunity, equal dignity without discrimination. Unless these rights have meaning there, they have little meaning anywhere."[10] The ghosts of Guatemala walk in the twilight here as well as there.

Acknowledgments

This chapter is a revised version of the paper presented in the "War" panel at the annual meeting of the American Anthropological Association, San Jose, CA, on 17 November 2006. I would like to thank Jeff Jordan, a Berkeley graduate student, and Miriam Meux, an undergraduate student at Berkeley for their assistance.

Beatriz Manz, who was born in Chile, is Professor and Chair of Comparative Ethnic Studies and Professor of Geography at the University of California, Berkeley. An anthropologist, her research has focused mainly on Guatemala's rural Mayan population. Her publications include *Paradise in Ashes: A Guatemalan Journey of Courage, Terror, and Hope* (2004), *Refugees of a Hidden War: The Aftermath of Counterinsurgency in Guatemala* (1988), and "Terror, Grief, and Recovery: Genocidal Trauma in a Mayan Village in Guatemala" (2002). Her research has been supported by, among others, the John D. and Catherine T. MacArthur Foundation. She is currently looking at the undocumented population in the United States as well as producing a special report for the United Nations High Commissioner of Refugees on violence in Central America.

Notes

1. "Guatemala's Femicide and the Ongoing Struggle for Women's Human Rights," Center for Gender and Refugee Studies (CGRS), University of California Hastings College of the Law, September 2006, 1.
2. For more information on the human rights situation in the 1980s, see Americas Watch (1982, 1984a, 1984b, 1985), Amnesty International (1981, 1982, 2002), CEH (1999), Hale (1997), and REMHI (1999).
3. For recent literature on conditions in Guatemala, see Americas Watch (1984b, 1986), Falla (1994), Jonas (1991), Manz (1988, 1995, 1999, 2002), Nelson (1999), Schirmer (1998), Smith (1990), Taylor (1998), Wilson (1995), and Zur (1998).
4. Interview with a former member of the cooperative of Santa Maria Tzejá.
5. Menchú, the K'iche' Maya 1992 Nobel Peace Prize winner, ran for president in 2007 and received only 3 percent of the vote.
6. Interview with K'iche' combatant from Santa Maria Tzejá.
7. The term is used in Stanley Cohen's book *States of Denial* (2001).
8. "Guatemalan Regime Blamed for War Atrocities," *Los Angeles Times*, 26 February 1999, A1.
9. Mr. Vaky to Mr. Oliver, Secret Memorandum, Department of State, Policy Planning Council, Washington, DC, 29 March 1968. See http://www.gwu.edu/~nsarchiv/NSAEBB/NSAEBB11/docs/05-01.htm (accessed 17 September 2007).
10. Remarks made at the United Nations, 27 March 1953, Eleanor Roosevelt National Historic Site, Hyde Park, New York. See http://www.nps.gov/archive/elro/who-is-er/er-quotes/.

References

Americas Watch. 1982. *Human Rights in Guatemala: No Neutrals Allowed*. New York: Americas Watch Committee.

———. 1983. *Creating a Desolation and Calling it Peace: May 1983 Supplement to the Report on Human Rights in Guatemala*. New York: Americas Watch Committee.

———. 1984a. *Guatemala: A Nation of Prisoners*. New York: Americas Watch Committee.

———. 1984b. *Guatemalan Refugees in Mexico, 1980–84*. New York: Americas Watch Committee.

———. 1985. *Little Hope: Human Rights in Guatemala, January 1984 to January 1985*. New York: Americas Watch Committee.

———. 1986. *Civil Patrols in Guatemala*. New York: Americas Watch Committee.

Amnesty International. 1981. *Guatemala: A Government Program of Political Murder*. London: Amnesty International Publications.

———. 1982. *Massive Extrajudicial Executions in Rural Areas under the Government of General Efrain Rios Montt*. London: Amnesty International Publications.

———. 2002. *Guatemala's Lethal Legacy: Past Impunity and Renewed Human Rights Violations*. London: International Secretariat.

———. 2006. *Guatemala: No Protection, No Justice—Killings of Women*. London: Amnesty International Publications.

Arendt, Hannah. 1964. *Eichman in Jerusalem: A Report on the Banality of Evil*. New York: McGraw-Hill.

CEH (Comisión para el Esclarecimiento Histórico). 1999. "Guatemala Memoria del Silencio [Guatemala Memory of Silence]. Conclusions and Recommendations." Guatemala City: United Nations Office for Project Services.

Cohen, Stanley. 2001. *States of Denial: Knowing about Atrocities and Suffering*. Cambridge: Polity.

Davis, Diane. 2006. "The Age of Insecurity: Violence and Social Disorder in the New Latin America." *Latin American Research Review* 41, no. 1: 178–197.

de las Casas, Bartolomé. [1552] 1974. *The Devastation of the Indies: A Brief Account*. Trans. Herma Briffault. New York: Seabury Press.

Dorfman, Ariel. 1991. *Death and the Maiden*. London: Nick Hern Books.

Falla, Ricardo. 1994. *Massacres in the Jungle: Ixcán, Guatemala, 1975–1982*. Boulder, CO: Westview Press.

———. 2007. "Rigoberta Menchú: A Shooting Star in the Electoral Sky?" *Envio*, no. 312 (July). http://www.envio.org.ni/articulo/3606.

Falla, Ricardo, Madeline Rios, and Rodney Alvarez. 2000. "Research and Social Action." *Latin American Perspective* 27, no. 1: 45–55.

Garretón, Manuel Antonio. 1992. "Fear in Military Regimes." Pp. 13–16 in *Fear at the Edge: State Terror and Resistance in Latin America*, ed. Juan E. Corradi, Patricia Weiss Fagen, and Manuel Antonio Garretón. Berkeley: University of California Press.

Geertz, Clifford. 1988. *Works and Lives: The Anthropologist as Author*. Stanford, CA: Stanford University Press.

Gleijeses, Piero. 1991. *Shattered Hope: The Guatemalan Revolution and the United States, 1944–1954*. Princeton, NJ: Princeton University Press.

Goodpasture, H. McKennie, ed. 1989. *Cross and Sword: An Eyewitness History of Christianity in Latin America*. New York: Orbis Books.

Hale, Charles R. 1997. "Consciousness, Violence, and the Politics of Memory in Guatemala." *Current Anthropology* 38, no. 5: 817–838.

Immerman, Richard H. 1982. *The CIA in Guatemala: The Foreign Policy of Intervention*. Austin: University of Texas Press.

Instituto de Estudios Centroamericanos and El Rescate. 1990. *The Jesuit Assassinations: The Writings of Ellacuría, Marín-Baró, and Segundo Montes, with a Chronology of the Investigation*. Kansas City, MO: Sheed and Ward.

Jonas, Susanne. 1991. *The Battle for Guatemala: Rebels, Death Squads, and U.S. Power*. Boulder, CO: Westview Press.

———. 2000. *Of Centaurs and Doves: Guatemala's Peace Process*. Boulder, CO: Westview Press.

Kinzer, Stephen. 2001. "Guatemala: The Unfinished Peace." *New York Review of Books*, 21 June, 61–63.

Levi, Primo. 1988. *The Drowned and the Saved*. New York: Vintage International.

Manz, Beatriz. 1988. *Refugees of a Hidden War: The Aftermath of Counterinsurgency in Guatemala*. Albany: State University of New York Press.

———. 1995. "Fostering Trust in a Climate of Fear." Pp. 151–167 in *Mistrusting Refugees*, ed. E. Valentine Daniel and John C. Knudsen. Berkeley: University of California Press.

———. 1999. *De la memoria a la reconstrucción histórica* [From Memory to Historical Reconstruction]. Guatemala City: AVANCSO.

_____. 2002. "Terror, Grief, and Recovery: Genocidal Trauma in a Mayan Village in Guatemala." Pp. 292–309 in *Annihilating Difference: The Anthropology of Genocide*, ed. Alexander Laban Hinton. Berkeley: University of California Press.

_____. 2004. *Paradise in Ashes: A Guatemalan Journey of Courage, Terror, and Hope*. Berkeley: University of California Press.

Minow, Martha. 1998. *Between Vengeance and Forgiveness: Facing History after Genocide and Mass Violence*. Boston: Beacon Press.

MINUGUA (United Nations Verification Mission in Guatemala). 2002. "Comunicado de MINUGUA sobre el sexto aniversario de la firma de la paz [MINUGUA Communiqué on the Sixth Anniversary of the Signing of the Peace Accords]." Guatemala City, 29 December.

Moser, Caroline, and Cathy McIlwaine. 2001. *Violence in a Post-conflict Context: Urban Poor Perceptions from Guatemala*. Washington, DC: World Bank.

Nelson, Diane. 1999. *The Finger in the Wound: Ethnicity, Nation, and Gender in the Body Politic of Quincentennial Guatemala*. Berkeley: University of California Berkeley.

REMHI (Recovery of Historical Memory Project). 1999. *Guatemala: Never Again!* Maryknoll, NY: Orbis Books.

Scheper-Hughes, Nancy, and Philippe Bourgois. 2004. *Violence in War and Peace: An Anthology*. Oxford: Blackwell.

Schirmer, Jennifer. 1998. *The Guatemalan Military Project: A Violence Called Democracy*. Philadelphia: University of Pennsylvania Press.

Schlesinger, Stephen, and Stephen Kinzer. 1982. *Bitter Fruit: The Untold Story of the American Coup in Guatemala*. New York: Doubleday.

Simpson, Michael A. 1998. "The Second Bullet: Transgenerational Impacts of the Trauma of Conflicts within a South African and World Context." Pp. 487–511 in *International Handbook of Multigenerational Legacies of Trauma*, ed. Yael Danieli. New York: Plenum Press.

Smith, Carol, ed. 1990. *Guatemalan Indians and the State, 1540–1988*. Austin: University of Texas Press.

Snodgrass-Godoy, Angelina. 2006. *Popular Injustice: Violence, Community, and Law in Latin America*. Stanford, CA: Stanford University Press.

Taylor, Clark. 1998. *Return of Guatemala's Refugees*. Philadelphia, PA: Temple University Press.

Wilson, Richard. 1995. *Mayan Resurgence in Guatemala: The Q'eqchi' Experience*. Norman: University of Oklahoma Press.

Zur, Judith N. 1996. "From PTSD to Voices in Context: From an 'Experience-Far' to an 'Experience-Near' Understanding of Responses to War and Atrocity across Cultures." *International Journal of Social Psychiatry* 42, no. 4: 305–317.

_____. 1998. *Violent Memories: Mayan War Widows in Guatemala*. Boulder, CO: Westview Press.

Chapter 8

MOTHER COURAGE AND THE FUTURE OF WAR

Paul E. Farmer

> I won't let you spoil my war for me. Destroys the weak, does it? Well, what does peace do for 'em, huh? War feeds its people better.
>
> — Bertolt Brecht, *Mother Courage and Her Children*

What Is It Good For?

War is good for something or someone, or it would not have persisted for millennia as a major staple of human interaction. "That war pays," notes Alisse Waterston in introducing this volume, "is an old saw." But what are the wages of war? Whom does it pay, and who pays for it? How does it pay? Most importantly, what are the real costs of war and conflict?

Notes for this chapter begin on page 180.

My guess is that Bertolt Brecht wrote his famous play in order to ask and answer some of these questions. And the answers are revealed, over time, to his unlikely protagonist, a Swedish market woman and mother seeking to keep her head above water during the course of a seventeenth-century conflict, whose purposes were unclear then and were even more so by 1939 when Brecht created Mother Courage.[1] Mother Courage's ability to answer these and other questions comes only as she loses her three children in quick succession. The lines cited above, in which she claims that war pays more than peace, come just as she, a shrewd businesswoman even in the worst of times, has reaped a few of the meager and transient spoils of war. But the play is titled *Mother Courage and Her Children* because, by the end, the audience or reader knows that the affective costs of losing one's children—and all victims of war are someone's children—are simply too high to calculate.

Today, when we ask questions about the costs of war, we are offered disparate quantitative answers. When I recently accessed a Web site regarding the cost of war, I read that the war in Iraq, entering its sixth year, has cost the United States, up to that point, over $503 billion or $275 million per day (National Priorities Project 2008), compared to an estimated and inflation-adjusted $549 billion for the 12-year war in Vietnam (Weisman 2006) and $5 trillion for what some have termed 'the good war'—World War II (Stiglitz and Bilmes 2008a). But Nobel laureate Joseph Stiglitz and Harvard economist Linda Bilmes have recently called Iraq the "Three Trillion Dollar War," after mining information not readily available to the public:

> From the unhealthy brew of emergency funding, multiple sets of books, and chronic underestimates of the resources required to prosecute the war, we have attempted to identify how much we have been spending—and how much we will, in the end, likely have to spend. The figure we arrive at is more than $3 trillion. Our calculations are based on conservative assumptions. They are conceptually simple, even if occasionally technically complicated. A $3 trillion figure for the total cost strikes us as judicious, and probably errs on the low side. Needless to say, this number represents the cost only to the United States. It does not reflect the enormous cost to the rest of the world, or to Iraq. (Stiglitz and Bilmes 2008a; see also Stiglitz and Bilmes 2008b)

They go on to note that "even in the best case scenario," the US government will spend on the Iraq war twice what it spent during the course of World War I, 10 times what was disbursed during the first Gulf War, and a third more than was spent in prosecuting the war in Vietnam.

But what do these figures really mean? Brecht wrote at least nine plays as contributions to the combat—the war—against fascism and Nazism. Following his vision, it would seem that the challenge of 'costing' the war is far more complex than whatever procedures were used to offer the figures cited above. First, these assessments are of costs to one nation, already a very powerful and wealthy one by the time of World War I. Imagine what the costs of World War II represent to, say, the Russians, who lost an estimated 27 million people and had a far weaker economic base. Imagine also the costs to European Jews. Anthropologists know that the true cost of armed conflict emerges not simply by tallying treasure spent, but by drawing on qualitative methodologies and locally relevant yardsticks. War also wreaks, to use modern parlance, 'collateral damage' upon civilians and their institutions, including health care, education, housing, telecommunications, and transport. War is costly in personal, affective terms. Physical and psychological damage is done to combatants, families, and communities. Damage is done even to a sense of where one fits into the world after peace treaties are signed and reconstruction begins. War spoils the meanings of things in complex and enduring ways that we are ill-equipped to measure. In short, although experts can offer only crude calculations of the cost of war, everyone who has thought about it, and certainly everyone who has endured it, knows that war costs too much. No doubt, that is why the rhetoric of war always ennobles sacrifice.

This chapter is linked to others in this collection that seek to estimate the social costs of war and related conflicts. Economists can help lead the way, but as Mother Courage's travails suggest, the misery provoked by armed conflict has no end. Hers was the Thirty Years' War, but do wars ever really have a clear beginning and an end? As Beatriz Manz (2004) reports from Guatemala, costs continue to mount long after overt hostilities draw to a close. This is what Carolyn Nordstrom (2004: 224) means when she reminds us that "violence has a tomorrow."

So much has been written about war that I initially had some hesitation about contributing to this volume. What could I add that had not been said before by someone more directly involved or better informed? Alisse Waterston called on us "to make a clear and powerful statement concerning what [you] know about war: its precursors, its causes, its aftermaths, its effects on human lives and on the future of humankind." A more accurate assessment of the true costs of war is one goal of this effort, but improving metrics is not for me, in any case, purposeful enough. As a physician-anthropologist (and parent) concerned with the hopelessly utopian project of ensuring that more of us humans reach our full potential and life expectancy, I am less interested in current discussions about the ways in which war might become less brutal in the third millennium and more interested in steps that might be taken to abolish it. I state this in spite of understanding that not all wars are similar and in spite of sympathy for and even gratitude to those who fight back, sometimes with force, against genocide, atrocity, and the unjust economic and social arrangements that almost always underlie armed conflict.

Other contributors to this volume lay out the political economy of war and teach us more about why such a destructive endeavor persists in an era in which alternatives to war must be found. They address the need to determine how national boundaries are set; how regional resources—oil and other sources of energy, mineral wealth, land, water, access to ports, labor—are to be shared; and how the right to an identity as a person can be ensured. Other contributors seek to expose common myths about wars and why we fight them. Even though I have long worked in places riven by violence, there are other contributors to this volume who know more about war zones.

In the end, I decided to write something that I (compared with the other contributors) might perhaps be better qualified to describe. It is not easy to say something new about war, and in this chapter I have three modest goals. The first is to draw on my experience as a physician-anthropologist and offer glimpses of the myriad ways in which war not only ends lives—which is, after all, one of the primary goals of war—but also damages them in slow-burning ways that can, as in the case of Mother Courage, reach from one generation into the next. The second goal is to reveal some of the mechanisms by which conflicts of all sorts are described in misleading terms. From the Thirty Years' War to 'the good war', from the conflicts in Guatemala, Vietnam, and Haiti to the current war in Iraq, each has been described, even long after the cessation of hostilities, in ways that could only be called altogether discrepant. But which versions are closer to truth? And how are multiple, inconsistent versions of the costs and consequences of war sustained—and why? The third goal is to speak to my peers about the ways in which anthropology, like other resocializing disciplines, might help to curb such dishonesty, reveal the true complexities and costs of war, and, by exposing war for what it really is, help lessen the damage of war in both the short and the long term.

I recommend *Mother Courage and Her Children* as a text offering great insight into war. In this chapter, however, I want to write about another mother. This mother is truly courageous, a Haitian refugee who was initially detained at the US base in Guantánamo, Cuba, and whose oldest son is also fighting in a war, the one being waged by the US in Iraq. There is a gruesome symmetry in this circumstance: if Iraq is the current US administration's best-known failure, its policies in Haiti—also disastrous—are perhaps its least-known failure.

From Haiti to Iraq: Mother Courage and Her Haitian Son

Most historians of war report that conflicts involving armies are built in part on lies and half-truths. At this late date, the lie regarding weapons of mass destruction in Iraq has been exposed in a raft of articles and books (see Danner 2006; Hersh 2004; Massing 2004), some of them written by scholars. For comparison's sake, I note that it was not until 1982 that we could read the first scholarly assessment of the CIA's involvement in the 1954 coup in Guatemala, the event that sparked another thirty years' war—the Guatemala civil war—which lasted from 1960 to 1996 (Immerman 1982). As Manz (2004) and others have shown, this disastrous and unequal civil war, which included genocidal sprees against indigenous people, continues to take lives more than a decade after peace was declared.

Let me return to the costs of war as calculated on the eve of the invasion of Iraq. This story is well documented, if less well known. When one of President George W. Bush's chief economic advisers, then head of the National Economic Council, hazarded an estimate of $200 billion to prosecute the war in Iraq, the riposte from then Secretary of Defense Donald Rumsfeld was swift—"baloney" (Bilmes and Stiglitz 2008). His own estimate, supported by the director of the Office of Management and Budget, was $50 to $60 billion, costs that would be shared by other members of 'the coalition of the willing'. Rumsfeld's deputy, Paul Wolfowitz, went further: the costs of post-war reconstruction in Iraq would be 'self-financed' through oil revenues from a more efficient post-Saddam Iraq (Alden, Swann, and Dinmore 2005). "The tone of the entire administration was cavalier," observe Stiglitz and Bilmes (2008a) crisply, "as if the sums involved were minimal." How did the administration—whether through chicanery or misjudgment, which matters little now—get away with such errors? Why is the true cost of this war still no more clearly recognized by the US public than it was by Rumsfeld and Wolfowitz in 2003? Stiglitz and Bilmes (ibid.) hazard a guess: "Most Americans have yet to feel these costs. The price in blood has been paid by our voluntary military and by hired contractors. The price in treasure has, in a sense, been financed entirely by borrowing. Taxes have not been raised to pay for it—in fact, taxes on the rich have actually fallen."

Most Americans may have not begun to feel the costs, but others, not all of them Americans, have felt them directly. As always in war, the numbers are contested. We know how many US troops have lost their lives—over 4,100 so far—and have less exact estimates (but increasing accounts) of how many have been damaged physically or psychologically (see Grady 2006).[2] Even less clear are the numbers of Iraqi dead. When a team from a US research university published, in a prestigious medical journal, a community-based study of 'excess' civilian mortality in Iraq a year into the war, the number they reached—over 100,000 between March 2003 and September 2004—caused a huge stir in the press (Roberts et al. 2004). The study and its authors were denounced by the architects of the war and their allies, who claimed that the large figure should be taken with a grain of salt due to "concerns about the methodology."[3] Yet subsequent inquiry suggests that the study was sound (Al-Rubeyi 2004; Horton 2006), while the responses from the powerful and their spokespersons were not.[4] Popular journalism is diverse enough to include some critical and even self-critical voices, although it took the debacle of the missing weapons of mass destruction to instill a sense of shame in a cheerleading, war-happy press (Borjesson 2005).

In its time, the Vietnam War generated no small number of disputes regarding civilian deaths, and excellent studies of mainstream press reporting on the first Gulf War have recently been published (MacArthur 2004). But if sorting through discrepant accounts is the analytic task, few places prepare an anthropologist (or US citizen) better than does Haiti, which gave me the interpretive grid that I have used to contemplate not only the rest of the world, including my own country, but also war and violence, regardless of the scale. And Haiti is tied as surely to my own country as it is to Iraq, as the experiences of Yolande Jean and her son reveal.

I will start with Yolande and her son, whom I will call 'Joe', since he is still in Iraq. I met Joe because of a 1991 military coup in Haiti, where I had been working since graduating from college less than a decade previously. Joe was 10 years old in 1991. His parents were poor but were able to read and write, and were interested in teaching others to do so (an estimated 60 percent of Haitian adults do not know how to read). They became deeply involved in a mass-literacy movement that had taken root in Haiti around the time of that country's first democratic elections in December 1990. Seven months after a landslide victory brought a liberation theologian to the presidency and also brought more resources to bear on Haiti's stubborn poverty, a violent military coup terminated democratic rule in Haiti. I have detailed elsewhere (Farmer 2006) the ways in which the US government was involved in this coup, a pattern that was to be repeated in 2004. The ensuing repression was fearsome. Refugees streamed out of the cities and into the hills; over the border into the Dominican Republic, where they were unwelcome; and onto the high seas.

Fleeing was not an obvious option for a young couple with two small boys. On 27 April 1992, Yolande, Joe's mother, was arrested and taken to Recherches Criminelles, the police station that served as the headquarters of Colonel Michel François, the alleged boss of Haiti's death squads. During the course of her 'interview' (to use the official euphemism for torture), Yolande, who was visibly pregnant with her third child, began to bleed. On her second day in prison, she miscarried. She did not receive medical attention.

Yolande later told me that she decided at that moment that if she survived detention, she would leave Haiti. She was released from prison the following day. Shortly thereafter, she entrusted her sons to a kinswoman and headed for northern Haiti. Her husband remained in hiding; she would not see him again. She told me: "I took the boat on May 12, and on the 14th [the US Coast Guard] came to get us. They did not say where they were taking us. We were still in Haitian waters at the time ... We hadn't even reached the Windward Passage when American soldiers came for us. But we thought they might be coming to help us ... there were sick children on board. On the 14th, we reached the base at Guantánamo" (Farmer 2006: 224). Yolande's initial instinct—that the US soldiers "might be coming to help us"—was soon corrected. "They burned all of our clothes, everything we had, the boat, our luggage, all the documents we were carrying," she related. US television had displayed images of Haitian boats burning, but both the Coast Guard and the media described the fires as the destruction of unseaworthy vessels, with no mention of personal items. When asked what reasons the US soldiers gave for burning the refugees' effects, Yolande replied, "They gave us none. They just started towing our belongings, and the next thing we know, the boat was in flames. Photos, documents. If you didn't have pockets in which to put things, you lost them. The reason that I came through with some of my documents is because I had a backpack and was wearing pants with pockets. They went through my bag and took some of my documents. Even my important papers they took. American soldiers did this. Fortunately, I had hidden some papers in my pockets" (ibid.).

Haiti was full to overflowing with people just like Yolande Jean. Soon the US military base on Guantánamo was full to overflowing as well. On 24 May 1992, President George H. W. Bush issued Executive Order 12807 from his summer home in Kennebunkport, Maine. Referring to the Haitian boats, he ordered the Coast Guard "to return the vessel and its passengers to the country from which it came ... provided, however, that the Attorney General, in his unreviewable discretion, may decide that a person who is a refugee will not be returned without his consent." As attorney Andrew Schoenholtz (1993: 71) of the Lawyers Committee for Human Rights wryly observed, "Grace did not abound; all Haitians have been returned under the new order."

I will not go through Yolande's whole story, which I have recounted elsewhere (Farmer 2005), but she clearly had her sons on her mind every day. Despite being one of the tiny number of those on Guantánamo deemed to be political refugees, she was not processed through to the United States because she was found to be infected with HIV. She learned that she would not be sent back to Haiti, but neither would she be released to the United States. "Where will I go?" she asked. The answer came in the form of no answer: she and hundreds of others would simply linger in the legal limbo that is Guantánamo, established as a US military base in the early twentieth century and subject to neither Cuban nor US laws. Thus, Guantánamo had a meaning for Haitians long before the enclave became synonymous with arbitrary and indeed illegal detention.

Many 'boat people' from Haiti were lost at sea, and none were welcome anywhere. In the same edition that announced "Boat with 396 Haitians Missing; Cuba Reports 8 Survivors," the *Orlando Sentinel* wrote of "what could be a huge problem for the state: an explosion of Haitian migrants to South Florida." The story, which ran on the front page, continued by noting, "Many fear that tens of thousands of refugees could sail for Miami around Inauguration Day, Jan. 20, because of President-elect Bill Clinton's pledge to give Haitians a fair hearing for political asylum in the United States." The plight of Haitian refugees had become enough of a cause célèbre during the 1992 US elections to spur candidates Clinton and Gore, in their official platform, to call for an end to the forced repatriation of Haitian boat people and the detention of HIV-positive refugees on Guantánamo (Clinton and Gore 1992). On 28 January, however, Clinton began backpedaling, stating that he would continue his predecessor's policies. On learning of this, a number of Guantánamo detainees began a hunger strike.

Yolande, unlike Brecht's fictitious Mother Courage, decided to act on principle. Distrustful of the US military doctors and even her own lawyers, she encouraged the other detainees to refuse to eat. This is what she said happened next:

> Before the strike, I'd been in prison, a tiny little cell, but crammed in with many others, men, women, and children. There was no privacy. Snakes would come in; we were lying on the ground, and lizards were climbing over us. One of us was bitten by a scorpion ... there were spiders. Bees were stinging the children, and there were flies everywhere: whenever you tried to eat something, flies would fly into your mouth. Because of all this, I just got to the point, sometime in January, [that] I said to myself, come what may, I might well die, but we can't continue in this fashion.
>
> We called together the committee and decided to have a hunger strike. Children, pregnant women, everyone was lying outside, rain or shine, day and night. After fifteen days without food, people began to faint. The colonel called us together and warned us, and me particularly, to call off the strike. We said no.
>
> At four in the morning, as we were lying on the ground, the colonel came with many soldiers. They began to beat us—I still bear a scar from this—and to strike us with nightsticks ... True, we threw rocks back at them, but they outnumbered us, and they were armed. Then they used big tractors to back us against the shelter, and they barred our escape with barbed wire.

Yolande was arrested and placed in solitary confinement in a place called Camp Bulkeley. Her version of the story did not make it into the *New York Times*, which reported only that "at least seven Haitian refugees protesting their detention here by refusing food have lost consciousness" (Farmer 2006: 233). No mention was made of any retribution by the strikers' warders. Even the lawyers for the Haitian detainees, who reached the base in the middle of the strike, seemed a bit annoyed by their clients' actions. "[T]he hunger strike took us all by surprise," said one, "especially given the fact that the litigation team is in the middle of settlement negotiations with the Department of Justice" (ibid.: 233–234). The Haitians, it seems, were no longer impressed by all the legal wrangling. On 11 March 1993, 11 prisoners attempted to escape to Cuba but were recaptured. Two of the detainees tried to commit suicide, one by hanging.[5]

Brecht's Mother Courage was confident that she was a survivor. Yolande, less sure, had already decided to pursue her hunger strike until her release from Guantánamo. Her letter to her sons was widely circulated in the community of concern that was taking shape in response to the situation on Guantánamo. It was read out loud at a New York demonstration by the American actress Susan Sarandon:

To my family:

Don't count on me anymore, because I have lost in the struggle for life. Thus, there is nothing left of me. Take care of my children, so they have strength to continue my struggle, because it is our duty.

As for me, my obligation ends here. [Joe] and Jeff, you have to continue with the struggle so that you may become men of the future. I have lost hope; I am alone in my distress. I know you will understand my situation, but do not worry about me because I have made my own decision. I am alone in life and will remain so. Life is no longer worth living to me.

[Joe] and Jeff, you no longer have a mother. Understand that you don't have a bad mother, it is simply that circumstances have taken me to where I am at this moment. I am sending you two pictures so you could look at me for a last time. Goodbye my children. Goodbye my family. We will meet again in another world.

The Haitians' advocates, including a handful of celebrities like Sarandon, several human rights organizations, and Haitian refugee groups in the eastern United States, stepped up pressure on the US government. And then something surprising happened. Federal Judge Sterling Johnson of New York, although a Bush appointee, heard the case and ruled against the policy crafted by that administration. The more depositions he heard, the more convinced he became that the detention of the HIV-positive Haitians represented "cruel and unusual punishment" in violation of the Eighth Amendment of the US Constitution. In his 1993 ruling on the case, he described Haitians detained in Camp Bulkeley in these words: "They live in camps surrounded by razor barbed wire. They tie plastic garbage bags to the sides of the building to keep the rain out. They sleep on cots and hang sheets to create some semblance of privacy. They are guarded by the military and are not permitted to leave the camp, except under military escort. The Haitian detainees have been subjected to pre-dawn military sweeps as they sleep by as many as 400 soldiers dressed in full riot gear. They are confined like prisoners and are subject to detention in the brig without hearing for camp rule infractions" (cited in Annas 1993: 590).

On 26 March 1993, Judge Johnson ordered that all detainees "with fewer than 200 total T-lymphocytes" be transferred to the United States. It was the first time that such laboratory tests had ever been mentioned in a judicial order. A Justice Department spokesman complained that "there are aspects of Judge Johnson's decision that we would find it difficult to live with." The first of these, noted the spokesman, "would be the judge's very expansive view of the rights of aliens, who came into American hands purely out of our own humanitarian impulses to rescue them at sea" (Friedman 1993: A12). Decades earlier, Judge Johnson had been a JAG (Judge Advocate General) officer on Gitmo, as the base is termed in military argot. Perhaps this gave him a perspective on the way humanitarian impulses are expressed in an extra-legal environment.

Although I was never permitted to go to Gitmo, I later got to know Yolande fairly well and visited her and other Haitian refugees in New York and Boston. When I first met Joe, he was about 12, and his brother, 10. They were, to me, the children of a courageous mother whom I wished to interview. I wanted to get her story out, and I did my best. Yolande's story was carried in the *Boston Globe* and in several Harvard publications. I wrote about her experience in a book published in 1994. But then a decade went by, and I confess I did not think much about Yolande or Joe. I continued to work in Haiti and elsewhere, and argued on behalf of sick and afflicted Haitians in the US who were threatened with deportation.

After the events of 11 September 2001, Gitmo once again exploded in the world's consciousness.[6] Now everyone knows that Gitmo is the place where prisoners are held at the US military's pleasure, with no jurisdiction to appeal to. But the earlier use of Gitmo as a staging area for Haitians not deemed deserving of refugee status had been forgotten. It was as if the travails of Yolande Jean had been erased from the public memory. I noted this erasure, but did nothing. Having written about Gitmo and having seen my account, like others, flushed down the public *oubliette*, I did not know what else I could add.

Toward the end of 2005, I received a message from Joe, Yolande's older son. It was in fact more than a message: he sent me, via a close friend of his, a check in the amount of $250. Joe said he wished to support our work in Haiti and to help us serve the destitute sick there. I was grateful for the contribution, for we certainly needed the help in Haiti. What struck me most, though, was that it came from Fallujah. Joe had joined the Marines and been sent to Iraq. I wrote back to him at once. We stayed in touch through e-mail and once in a while by phone. For a year, we corresponded regularly, at least once a week, but did not talk much about the war or his daily reality. He took great pains to let me know that by the time I began inquiring anxiously about his safety, he no longer went out on missions "beyond the wire," but was responsible for supplying another group of Marines out on patrol. He did not say much, over e-mail, about his activities, noting only how relieved he felt when his "guys" returned safely to the forward-operating base in Fallujah. More often than not, he would tell me that I was the one who needed to be careful, since he knew about the ongoing violence and instability in Haiti. But I guessed that being in Iraq was both a great outward and internal struggle for him. I felt that Joe must be distressed by what he was hearing about Gitmo, and I had to assume he was thinking about his own mother's experience there. Once, when I sent him a care package, I weighed carefully what sort of books to include: something light, I thought; some videos and escapist novels. "No," he responded by e-mail, "send me things about Haiti. Like I told you, I want to go back to Haiti one day and work with you." And so I sent him one of my own books about Haiti, with some concern that he might find my detailed description of his mother's stay at Gitmo harrowing or upsetting. He did not say one way or another, but after he read it, he asked me to send a copy to a friend of his. "He's Native American," wrote Joe. "He'll like it." I sent the book.

After a year of brief but regular e-mails, our connection deepened. We made plans to meet for a meal when Joe was next on leave. I was in Haiti when Joe e-mailed me one Monday in 2007. It was nighttime in Fallujah, and he was leaving just then for the States. He would call me as soon as he landed, he wrote. I forgot to ask when exactly that would be, and so started to worry right away. The most dangerous part, I thought, would be getting in and out of Baghdad. My phone rang on Saturday, and shortly thereafter I got to enjoy a long reunion with Joe and to see his brother briefly. During the course of a leisurely meal that included what I reckoned to be the first red wine he had had in a while, Joe explained that the main reasons he was planning to stay in Iraq were to be able to look after his mother, who he knew might fall gravely ill at any time; to send his brother to a proper college; and eventually to buy a home and have a family. "I want to look forward, not back," said the irrepressibly optimistic Joe.

Some things we did not discuss, including the fact that Joe, like many others serving in Iraq, is not yet a US citizen. I felt too uneasy to ask what Joe thought about the war in Iraq. We never discussed US policies in Haiti, nor did we discuss his mother's harrowing experience on Gitmo. But we did discuss his younger brother's plans. Whenever money was tight, Jeff thought about joining the military too. "Do that only as a last resort," advised Joe. "I'll find the money for you to finish college." Yet in spite of the many things we left unspoken, there was so much left to talk about that we called each other often during Joe's leave, and I found his departure more distressing than I had expected. As of this writing, Joe is still in Fallujah.

So what, exactly, is this story about and what might it reveal about the causes and consequences of war and conflict? First, and obviously enough, it is a story about connections. I let Joe and his family fall out of my life for a decade. Joe's generosity brought us back together. Returning to the theme of *Mother Courage and Her Children*, Joe's mother made a very different set of choices than did Brecht's character. Following the 1991 coup and during her illegal internment on Guantánamo, Yolande's leadership and convictions led directly to the release of the detainees and to the reunification of what was left of her family. She never believed that war paid better than peace, and she was willing to take risks to make her point.

Next come other connections of the kind best revealed by linking personal narrative to the study of history and political economy. Such connections seem at first glance impersonal, since they are invariably about the use or misuse of power, including the ability to wage war. The intimate links between my country and Haiti—the Western hemisphere's two oldest republics—over the past two centuries make a shameful story from an American point of view. And the connection between our country and Iraq will cause us grief, I fear, for generations. Fallujah, where Joe is based, is already a proverb for brutality. Just over a year ago, one US colonel deployed in Anbar province explained his approach to counter-insurgency: "[F]ix Ramadi, but don't destroy it. Don't do a Fallujah."[7] Fallujah, a city of roughly 435,000 people, was reduced to rubble in offensives launched after the 2004 US presidential elections seemed to the Republicans to have filled their accounts with 'political capital', and it is to this bloodbath that the US officer referred.

In addition, this story also reveals the strange ways in which war creates opportunities (as Mother Courage might argue). Like Joe, many young men and women enlist in part for economic reasons. In fact, as the need for volunteers to serve in Afghanistan and Iraq has grown, military recruiters have targeted young people in low-income communities and communities of color precisely because joining the army or the marines can be pitched as a route for social mobility in places where few, if any, opportunities exist, and as a way to acquire job training, college scholarships, and signing bonuses (Savage 2004; Singer n.d.).

But what about our military base so peculiarly located in Cuba? That is a story about connections, too, as Jonathan Hansen (2007) recently illustrated in a talk given about Gitmo at Harvard University:

A bay, a harbor, a hideout, a home, a military base, a sanctuary, a prison; an outpost on the threshold of nations where neither Cuban, nor U.S., nor international law applies. Guantánamo blurs the categories of modern political representation. Paradoxically, by doing so, it brings them into sharp relief. The history of Guantánamo illuminates the artificial and yet necessary distinctions that construct and sustain the modern world. This project is a tale of that world: on the one hand, of the interaction of nation-states and of national interest with international law; on the other hand, of individuals caught up in the system of states, trying to negotiate the tangle of allegiances and affiliations which that system imposes. Guantánamo Bay has been there all along—when the Taino Indians met Columbus, when Caribbean pirates preyed on the shipping of newly consolidated states, when Spain clashed with Britain, when the U.S. defeated Spain, when Kennedy confronted Castro, when George W. Bush set out to vanquish terror. To know Guantánamo is to know ourselves—as citizens, as a country, as individuals in a world of states.

Gitmo is a place outside the reach of American constitutional protections, so you might think of it as a place of disconnection. But that very disconnection connects us to that place and to what is done there now, in 2008, when Guantánamo continues to serve as a detention center for men (and some teenagers) captured in Iraq, Afghanistan, and other places from which we 'render' our enemies to unlimited imprisonment. Guantánamo is a place where responsibility can be denied. Like all such denials—about the fate of Haitian refugees, about the price tag on war, about the reasons for prosecuting it in Iraq—this act will not hold up forever. Many Americans are shamed and disquieted by the things done in their name in this place outside the law.

As I noted earlier, if Iraq is the best known of the current US administration's foreign policy blunders, Haiti is its best-kept dirty secret. Between 2000 and 2004, the US administration, once again displeased with Haiti's left-leaning president, Jean-Bertrand Aristide, who had been re-elected by a landslide, orchestrated an aid embargo on his government. Other kinds of aid continued, however, as groups such as the International Republican Institute funneled funds to various sectors of what is called 'civil society'—in the eyes of the people I serve in Haiti and elsewhere in Latin America, this phrase invariably designates the minority of those who are not poor—in order to weaken the elected government. Similar tactics were being used in Venezuela, but the government there was better defended and vastly wealthier than that of Haiti. Mainstream US news sources paid almost no attention to the sabotage in Haiti until its aims—which culminated in the kidnapping of a sitting, elected head of state—were accomplished. Finally, in March 2006, investigative reporters at the *New York Times* released a long and devastating report about the precise mechanisms by which the Haitian government had been overthrown in late February 2004 (Bogdanich and Nordberg 2006).[8] After the coup came a long interregnum of lawlessness, as in post-invasion Iraq. One news report in December 2005 named Port-au-Prince the kidnapping capital of the world (de Montesquiou 2005).

The abduction of Haiti's president has recently been the subject of two informative books (see Hallward 2008; Robinson 2007). Reading them is a good antidote to the effrontery of American officials. Donald Rumsfeld, soon to be replaced as secretary of defense, dismissed allegations of kidnapping as "ridiculous" (recalling, in tone and in credibility, his previous dismissal of a colleague's Iraq war-cost estimate as "baloney"). Our former secretary of state insisted that the Haitian president was flown "to a destination of his choice ... So this was not a kidnapping" (US Department of State 2004). Regardless of your views on the individual probity of the US administration's cabinet members, it seems unlikely that the Haitian president would choose as his destination the Central African Republic, a country he had never visited, one that had had its own coup d'état a few months earlier and was known for general lawlessness (the BBC had just dubbed Bangui, the capital of said republic, as "the world's least safe place to live").[9]

Haitians know a lot about kidnapping, of course. Almost all of them are descendants of people kidnapped from Africa. Toussaint Louverture, the Haitian general who led the world's first successful slave revolt, was invited at the dawn of the nineteenth century to a parley with French forces and was given the assurances that are usual in such negotiations between the heads of opposed armies. Instead of a parley, what occurred was a kidnapping: Louverture was chained and put on a boat bound for France, where he later died, apparently of tuberculosis, in an Alpine prison.

'Extraordinary rendition', the latest term for kidnapping, fits well with an age that has seen habeas corpus treated as an option, not a constitutional right (Sadat 2006). When the president of our nation's oldest neighbor, Haiti, is 'rendered' all the way to Central Africa, the justifications offered by those responsible amount to no more than dismissals and character assassination (Hallward 2008).[10] The same sense of justice, accountability, and respect for public opinion ushered us into an apparently unending war in Iraq. The arrogance of power underwrites the connection between Joe's Haiti and his Iraq.

Finally, Joe's story, like his mother's and that of the country in which both of them were born, raises questions about the kind of world we want to live in, the kind of world we want to leave to our children. Does honest analysis of war and conflict make any difference at all? Pierre Bourdieu thought so. "To subject to scrutiny the mechanisms that render life painful, even untenable," he wrote, "is not to neutralize them; to bring to light contradictions is not to resolve them. But as skeptical as one might be about the efficacy of the sociological message, we cannot dismiss the effect it can have by allowing sufferers to discover the possible social causes of their suffering and, thus, to be relieved of blame" (Bourdieu 1993: 944; trans. by author). To the end, and despite all that he had witnessed and written, Bourdieu believed in what is essentially an Enlightenment ideal—that we can lessen social suffering if we understand how it is generated and sustained over time, across generations.

Conclusions: 'Mother Courage' and the Fight to Abolish War

As a physician, teacher, anthropologist, and parent, I meet no one who favors war. And yet war is of prime interest to societies both rich and poor and a major source not only of death and conquest but of profit. Fifty years after the beginning of the nuclear era of 'mutually assured destruction', war remains a growth industry. All of us who have written for this volume would like to share Waterston's Enlightenment optimism regarding the possibility that these essays might make a difference; that they might improve US foreign policy (whether toward Haiti or in the Middle East); that they might help to shut down Guantánamo and other extralegal limbos; that they might stop practices such as torture and extraordinary rendition; that they might even contribute to the utopian goal of abolishing war.

But there is of course cause for pessimism. Although the stories of Joe and his mother are singular in their detail, the underlying wish—to abolish war—is as old as war itself. It is as old as the grief of parents who bury their children. There is cause for pessimism, too, if the goal of our writing is suasion through enlightenment, through offering details about the causes and consequences, the true costs of war. After all, arguments against war have been laid out persuasively enough before. Take, for example, what is often called the Russell-Einstein Manifesto, issued in London on 9 July 1955, in which two of the greatest minds of the last century insisted: "We have to learn to ask ourselves, not what steps can be taken to give military victory to whatever group we prefer, for there no longer are such steps; the question we have to ask ourselves is: what steps can be taken to prevent a military contest of which the issue must be disastrous to all parties?" Einstein and Russell had nuclear weapons in mind. The 'overkill' that such weapons promised was insane, they wrote (again and again). And they spoke of bonds between families and generations as a force that might rein in the ambitions of bellicose statesmen: "The abolition of war will demand distasteful limitations of national sovereignty. But what perhaps impedes understanding of the situation more than anything else is that the term 'mankind' feels vague and abstract. People scarcely realize in imagination that the danger is to themselves and their children and their grandchildren, and not only to a dimly apprehended humanity. They can scarcely bring themselves to grasp that they, individually, and those whom they love are in imminent danger of perishing agonizingly. And so they hope that perhaps war may be allowed to continue provided modern weapons are prohibited" (Russell and Einstein 1955). Today's "modern weapons" are weapons of mass destruction. The threat of such weapons was brandished to justify the most recent invasion of Iraq—a false pretext that served as a prelude to a bloody war with more or less conventional weapons during which hundreds of rash decisions have made through arrogance and incompetence.[11]

The testimonies of those who prosecute, participate in, or survive wars are countless, a rich literature. The title of Ernst Friedrich's 1924 photographic collection, *War Against War*, is inspiring. Many are stirred, as Bertolt Brecht was, to give war artistic form so as to reveal to a broad audience the stupidity and cruelty of war. Brecht's Mother Courage was a Swedish woman caught up in the informal economy of the war—selling food, articles of daily use, and just about anything in the mad optimistic belief that "war feeds its people better." But war is a machine that invariably devours its young. Toward the end, a peasant woman assures Mother Courage's doomed daughter, "There's nothing we can do. Pray, poor thing, pray! There's nothing we can do to stop this bloodshed, so even if you can't talk, at least pray. He hears, if no one else does" (Brecht 1991: 105).

But who knows what God hears?

Nonetheless, there are certainly some things we can do, as physicians, scholars, parents, and kin. Medical practitioners like myself and other members of the global health community can document the myriad ways "in which complex political emergencies are undermining health service provision and threatening human rights" and can "learn lessons from previous conflicts to help guide our response to current and future ones" (Zwi 2004: 033). This is, in fact, what my colleagues and I have tried to do with regard to the violence, political and structural, that has recently plagued the poor majority of Haiti (Farmer 2004a; Farmer and Smith Fawzi 2002; Farmer, Smith Fawzi, and Nevil 2003). Others have called on health care professionals to take an even more active role in critiquing policies and actions of governments that undermine the foundations of medicine and public health by disregarding human rights and that promote war and violence, resulting in massive casualties and suffering (Wilks 2006; Yamada et al. 2006).

Scholars from other disciplines can also contribute to such efforts. Within anthropology, voices have spoken out individually and collectively against the war in Iraq and against the use of torture on enemy combatants by the current US administration.[12] Concerns have also been raised regarding evolving roles for anthropologists in 'the global war on terror' (González 2007, 2008; Rylko-Bauer 2008).[13] Increasingly, anthropologists are turning their attention to the study of the military and militarization (especially in the US), and exploring the ways in which anthropological knowledge can and has been used—and abused (AAA 2007b; Ben-Ari 2006; Gusterson 2007; Price 2007a, 2007b).

Finally, there is a nascent movement among ordinary citizens—and among the scholars who are the typical readers of a journal such as this one—to fight back against war and injustice. It took just such a movement to end the slave trade in the nineteenth century. It took similar movements to push for universal enfranchisement in the United States and to abolish apartheid in South Africa. Sometimes movements such as these are founded on 'mother courage' in the best sense of the term. I have never had much opportunity to follow blogs, but it happens that there is one called "Mother Courage: Musings of a Marine Mother." Allow me to cite from a recent posting by this mother:

> George W. Bush's Fourth of July speech to the usual hand-picked audience, this time the West Virginia National Guard, plumbed new depths of inanity, propaganda and the dumbing-down of U.S. history. I fired off several angry letters to the usual suspects—none were published though plenty of sentiments similar to mine were—then saw this riposte written by Marty Kaplan in Thursday's *Huffington Post* ...
>
> "'There are many ways for our fellow citizens to say thanks to the men and women who wear the uniform and their families. You can send a care package. You can reach out to a military family in your neighborhood ... You can car pool' [a quotation from President George W. Bush]. Instead of sending them a care package, how about sending them home? Instead of car pooling, how about an energy policy that prevents our country from financing the very nations who hold our economy hostage, let alone the terrorists they quietly harbor?" ...
>
> Not surprisingly, my favorite line: "Instead of sending [the troops] a care package, how about sending them home?"
>
> Pass it on. (Anton 2007)

I do not know that we can stop war. I cannot be sure that the best analysis in the world, the best plays imaginable, or even a painting as beautiful as *Guernica* will stop the insanity—profitable to a few but devastating to the majority—that is war. I do not know how much I can do as a physician either, besides patching up some of the wounds, stanching the bleeding, and making sure that blood is stocked and safe for transfusion.

But I do know this: we can marshal the evidence against war, and we can pass it on.

Acknowledgments

Special thanks to Howard Zinn for encouraging all of us, years ago and with great personal authority, to address the difficult topic of the abolition of war at a time when many (even among the ranks of those opposed to the war in Iraq) regard such exercises as unimportant or hopelessly utopian. I write as a physician-anthropologist and am grateful for the insights of peers from both groups: Gino Strada, Barbara Rylko-Bauer, Alisse Waterston. I am, of course, deeply in debt to Yolande Jean and her son, 'Joe'. I am especially grateful to Meryl Streep (whose rendering of Mother Courage I will never forget) and to Zoe Agoos, Brian Concannon, Ophelia Dahl, Melissa Gillooly, and (as ever) Haun Saussy. This chapter is dedicated to the memory and gentle pacifism of Roz Zinn.

Paul E. Farmer, MD, PhD, is the Maude and Lillian Presley Professor of Medical Anthropology in the Department of Social Medicine at Harvard Medical School, Associate Chief of the Division of Social Medicine and Health Inequalities at Brigham and Women's Hospital, and a co-founder of Partners In Health, a non-profit organization that provides health care to and undertakes research and advocacy on behalf of the destitute. Along with his colleagues at these organizations, Dr. Farmer has pioneered novel, community-based treatment strategies for infectious diseases (including HIV/AIDS and multidrug-resistant tuberculosis) in resource-poor settings. His most recent book is *Pathologies of Power: Health, Human Rights, and the New War on the Poor* (2005).

Notes

1. The play was provoked, say Brecht's biographers, by the German invasion of Poland in September 1939.
2. The Department of Defense notes that as of 22 March 2008, there have been 29,496 soldiers wounded in action, which does not include those evacuated from the 'theatre' for other medical reasons. See Department of Defense table, "Global War on Terrorism, Casualties by Military Service Component—Active, Guard, and Reserve," http://siadapp.dmdc.osd.mil/personnel/CASUALTY/gwot_component.pdf (accessed 31 March 2008).
3. Press briefing of the Prime Minister's Official Spokesperson in London, 29 October 2004, http://www.number10.gov.uk/output/Page6496.asp (accessed 17 March 2008).
4. Two years later, Burnham et al. (2006) published a figure of over 650,000 Iraqi civilian deaths from the start of the war until July 2006. As of this writing, the most recent figures from the Iraq Family Health Survey Study Group (2008) estimate 151,000 civilians in the same time period. Clearly, the numbers debate rages on. See also the report by Amnesty International (2008), "Carnage and Despair: Iraq Five Years On."
5. The similarities with recent hunger strikes and suicides on Guantánamo, during what has been dubbed 'the global war on terror', are striking but not supernatural.
6. For more on the use of the US base at Guantánamo as a detention site for those rendered there as terrorist combatants, see Danner (2004), Hersh (2004), Human Rights Watch (2006), Margulies (2007), and Miles (2006, 2007).

7. "Behind Success in Ramadi: An Army Colonel's Gamble," *USA Today*, 1 May 2007, 1–2.
8. For a more detailed history of these events, see Farmer (2004a, 2004b), Farmer and Smith Fawzi (2002), Farmer, Smith Fawzi, and Nevil (2003), and Kidder (2003).
9. "Brazzaville—'World's Worst City,'" *BBC News*, 3 March 2003, http://news.bbc.co.uk/1/hi/world/africa/2815105.stm.
10. See also "Did He Go or Was He Pushed? America's Debate on Haiti," *Economist*, 6 March 2004.
11. Take, for example, the momentous decision made by a Bush appointee, Paul Bremer, to abolish the Iraqi army, without warning, consultation, or coordination. What would become of these soldiers, armed as they were and suddenly unemployed? Was there a well-thought-out plan for addressing things as simple as what to do with a huge number of young men suddenly out of work and how to disarm them? It would seem, as the American proverb goes, that the right hand had no idea what the left hand was doing. Violent chaos ensued. Michael Gordon (2008) reported in the *New York Times*: "'Anyone who is experienced in the ways of Washington knows the difference between an open, transparent policy process and slamming something through the system,' said Franklin C. Miller, the senior director for Defense Policy and Arms Control, who played an important role on the National Security Council in overseeing plans for the postwar phase. 'The most portentous decision of the occupation was carried out stealthily and without giving the president's principal advisers an opportunity to consider it and give the president their views.'"
12. At its annual meeting in November 2006, members of the American Anthropological Association (AAA) passed two resolutions calling for a "complete end to all U.S. military operations in Iraq and full U.S. compliance with the United Nations Convention against Torture" (AAA 2006).
13. See also the AAA's Executive Board Statement on the involvement of anthropologists in the US military's Human Terrain System project, deployed in Afghanistan and Iraq (AAA 2007a).

References

AAA (American Anthropological Association). 2006. "Anthropologists Weigh In On Iraq, Torture at Annual Meeting." Press release, 11 December. http://www.aaanet.org/pdf/iraqtorture.pdf (accessed 1 April 2008).

———. 2007a. "American Anthropological Association's Executive Board Statement on the Human Terrain System Project." Press release, 6 November. http://www.aaanet.org/pdf/upload/EB-Resolution-on-HTS.pdf (accessed 1 April 2008).

———. 2007b. "AAA Commission on the Engagement of Anthropology with the US Security and Intelligence Communities." Final report, 4 November. Available at http://www.aaanet.org/pdf/Final_Report.pdf (accessed 1 April 2008).

Alden, Edward, Christopher Swann, and Guy Dinmore. 2005. "Wolfowitz Nomination a Shock for Europe." *Financial Times*, 16 March. http://www.ft.com/cms/s/0/33aa58b6-965b-11d9-8fcc-00000e2511c8.html (accessed 17 March 2008).

Al-Rubeyi, Bushra I. 2004. "Mortality Before and After the Invasion of Iraq in 2003." *Lancet* 364, no. 9448: 1834–1835.

Amnesty International. 2008. *Carnage and Despair: Iraq Five Years On*. 17 March. http://www.amnesty.org/en/library/info/MDE14/001/2008/en (accessed 17 March 2008).

Annas, George J. 1993. "Detention of HIV-Positive Haitians at Guantanamo: Human Rights and Medical Care." *New England Journal of Medicine* 329, no. 8: 589–592.

Anton, Donna. 2007. "Mother Courage: Musings of a Marine Mother." 12 July. http://www.donna-anton.com/wordpress/ (accessed 17 March 2008).

Ben-Ari, Eyal. 2006. "Review Essay: The Military and Militarization in the United States." *American Ethnologist* 31, no. 3: 340–348.

Bilmes, Linda J., and Joseph E. Stiglitz. 2008. "The Iraq War Will Cost Us $3 Trillion, and Much More." *Washington Post*, 9 March. http://www.washingtonpost.com/wp-dyn/content/article/2008/03/07/AR2008030702846.html.

Bogdanich, Walt, and Jenny Nordberg. 2006. "Mixed U.S. Signals Helped Tilt Haiti Toward Chaos." *New York Times*, 19 January.

Borjesson, Kristina, ed. 2005. *Feet to the Fire: The Media after 9/11, Top Journalists Speak Out.* Amherst, NY: Prometheus Books.

Bourdieu, Pierre. 1993. *La Misère du monde.* Paris: Seuil.

Brecht, Bertolt. 1991. *Mother Courage and Her Children.* Trans. Eric Bentley. New York: Grove Press.

Burnham, Gilbert, Riyadh Lafta, Shannon Doocy, and Les Roberts. 2006. "Mortality after the 2003 Invasion of Iraq: A Cross-Sectional Cluster Sample Survey." *Lancet* 368, no. 9545: 1421–1428.

Clinton, William J., and Al Gore. 1992. *Putting People First: How We Can All Change America.* New York: Times Books.

Danner, Mark. 2004. *Torture and Truth: America, Abu Ghraib, and the War on Terror.* New York: New York Review Books.

_____. 2006. *The Secret Way to War: The Downing Street Memo and the Iraq War's Buried History.* New York: New York Review Books.

de Montesquiou, Alfred. 2005. "Kidnappings Plague Residents Across Haiti." Associated Press, 26 December.

Farmer, Paul. 2004a. "Political Violence and Public Health in Haiti." *New England Journal of Medicine* 350, no. 15: 1483–1486.

_____. 2004b. "Who Removed Aristide?" *London Review of Books* 26, no. 8: 28–31.

_____. 2005. "Pestilence and Restraint: Guantánamo, AIDS, and the Logic of Quarantine." Pp. 51–90 in *Pathologies of Power: Health, Human Rights, and the New War on the Poor.* Berkeley: University of California Press.

_____. 2006. *The Uses of Haiti.* 3rd ed. Monroe, ME: Common Courage Press.

Farmer, Paul, and Mary Kay Smith Fawzi. 2002. "Unjust Embargo Deepens Haiti's Health Crisis." *Boston Globe*, 30 December, sec. A:15.

Farmer, Paul, Mary Kay Smith Fawzi, and Patrice Nevil. 2003. "Unjust Embargo of Aid for Haiti." *Lancet* 361, no. 9355: 420–423.

Friedman, Thomas L. 1993. "U.S. to Release 158 Haitian Detainees." *New York Times*, 10 June, A12.

González, Roberto. 2007. "Towards Mercenary Anthropology?" *Anthropology Today* 23, no. 3: 14–19.

_____. 2008. "'Human Terrain': Past, Present, and Future Applications." *Anthropology Today* 24, no. 1: 21–26.

Gordon, Michael R. 2008. "Five Years In: Fateful Choice on Iraq Army Bypassed Debate." *New York Times*, 17 March.

Grady, Denise. 2006. "Struggling Back from War's Once-Deadly Wounds." *New York Times*, 22 January.

Gusterson, Hugh. 2007. "Anthropology and Militarism." *Annual Review of Anthropology* 36: 155–175.

Hallward, Peter. 2008. *Damming the Flood: Haiti, Aristide, and the Politics of Containment.* London: Verso Press.

Hansen, Jonathan M. 2007. "Guantánamo Bay: An American Story." Talk given at the David Rockefeller Center for Latin American Studies, Harvard University, 26 April.

Hersh, Seymour M. 2004. *Chain of Command: The Road from 9/11 to Abu Ghraib.* New York: HarperCollins.

Horton, Richard. 2006. "Iraq: Time to Signal a New Era for Health in Foreign Policy." *Lancet* 368, no. 9545: 1395–1397.

Human Rights Watch. 2006. "By the Numbers: Findings of the Detainee Abuse and Accountability Project." http://hrw.org/reports/2006/ct0406/ct0406web.pdf (accessed 25 June 2007).

Immerman, Richard. 1982. *The CIA in Guatemala: The Foreign Policy of Intervention.* Austin: University of Texas Press.

Iraq Family Health Survey Study Group. 2008. "Violence-Related Mortality in Iraq from 2002 to 2006." *New England Journal of Medicine* 358, no. 5: 484–493.

Kidder, Tracy. 2003. "The Trials of Haiti." *The Nation*, 27 October.

MacArthur, John R. 2004. *Second Front: Censorship and Propaganda in the 1991 Gulf War.* Berkeley: University of California Press.

Manz, Beatriz. 2004. *Paradise in Ashes: A Guatemalan Journey of Courage, Terror, and Hope.* Berkeley: University of California Press.

Margulies, Joseph. 2007. *Guantánamo and the Abuse of Presidential Power.* New York: Simon and Schuster.

Massing, Michael. 2004. *Now They Tell Us: The American Press and Iraq.* New York: New York Review Books.

Miles, Steven H. 2006. *Oath Betrayed: Torture, Medical Complicity, and the War on Terror.* New York: Random House.

_____. 2007. "Medical Ethics and the Interrogation of Guantanamo 063." *American Journal of Bioethics* 7, no. 4: 5–11.

National Priorities Project. 2008. "The War in Iraq Costs." http://www.nationalpriorities. org/costofwar_home (accessed 17 March 2008).

Nordstrom, Carolyn. 2004. "The Tomorrow of Violence." Pp. 223–242 in *Violence*, ed. Neil L. Whitehead. Santa Fe, NM: School of American Research Press.

Price, David. 2007a. "Buying a Piece of Anthropology. Part 1: Human Ecology and Unwitting Anthropological Research for the CIA." *Anthropology Today* 23, no. 3: 8–13.

_____. 2007b. "Buying a Piece of Anthropology. Part 2: The CIA and Our Tortured Past." *Anthropology Today* 23, no. 5: 17–22.

Roberts, Les, Riyadh Lafta, Richard Garfield, Jamal Khudhairi, and Gilbert Burnham. 2004. "Mortality Before and After the 2003 Invasion of Iraq: Cluster Sample Survey." *Lancet* 364, no. 9448: 1857–1864.

Robinson, Randall. 2007. *An Unbroken Agony: Haiti, from Revolution to the Kidnapping of a President.* Philadelphia, PA: Basic Civitas Books.

Russell, Bertrand, and Albert Einstein. 1955. "The Russell-Einstein Manifesto." 9 July. http://www.pugwash.org/about/manifesto.htm (accessed 8 April 2008).

Rylko-Bauer, Barbara. 2008. "Applied Anthropology and Counterinsurgency." *Society for Applied Anthropology Newsletter* 19, no. 1: 1–5.

Sadat, Leila N. 2006. "Ghost Prisoners and Black Sites: Extraordinary Rendition under International Law." *Case Western Reserve Journal of International Law* 37, no. 2/3: 309–342.

Savage, Charlie. 2004. "Military Recruiters Target Schools Strategically." *Boston Globe*, 29 November. http://www.boston.com/news/nation/articles/2004/11/29/military_recruiters _pursue_target_schools_carefully?mode = PF (accessed 7 April 2008).

Schoenholtz, Andrew. 1993. "Aiding and Abetting Persecutors: The Seizure and Return of Haitian Refugees in Violation of the U.N. Refugee Convention and Protocol." *Georgetown Immigration Law Journal* 7, no. 1: 67–85.

Singer, Merrill. n.d. "Desperate Measures: A Syndemic Approach to the Anthropology of Health in a Violent City." In *Global Health in the Time of Violence*, ed. Barbara Rylko-Bauer, Linda Whiteford, and Paul Farmer. Santa Fe, NM: School for Advanced Research Press. Forthcoming.

Stiglitz, Joseph, and Linda Bilmes. 2008a. "The Three Trillion Dollar War: The Cost of the Iraq and Afghanistan Conflicts Have Grown to Staggering Proportions." *The Times*, 23 February. http://www.timesonline.co.uk/tol/comment/columnists/guest_contributors/ article3419840.ece (accessed 17 March 2008).

_____. 2008b. *The Three Trillion Dollar War: The True Cost of the Iraq Conflict.* New York: W.W. Norton.

US Department of State. 2004. "Interview on NPR with Juan Williams." 8 March. http://www.state.gov/secretary/former/powell/remarks/30245.htm (accessed 17 March 2008).

Weisman, Jonathan. 2006. "Projected Iraq War Costs Soar: Total Spending Is Likely to More Than Double, Analysis Finds." *Washington Post*, 27 April, A16.

Wilks, Michael. 2006. "Guantánamo: A Call for Action." *British Medical Journal* 332: 560–561.

Yamada, Seiji, Mary C. Smith Fawzi, Gregory G. Maskarinec, and Paul E. Farmer. 2006. "Casualties: Narrative and Images of the War on Iraq." *International Journal of Health Services* 36, no. 2: 401–415.

Zwi, Anthony. 2004. "How Should the Health Community Respond to Violent Political Conflict?" *PLoS Medicine* 1, no. 1: e14:033–036. http://www.plosmedicine.org (accessed 1 April 2008).

INDEX

Quarrel, causes, 20

Rapid Deployment Forces (RDF), 61
Reconstruction, repurchase, 5–6
Religious war, 42–43
Remarque, Erich, 15
Revolutionary Armed Forces of Colombia
    (FARC), guerilla organization, 64
    control, 140
    impact, 134–135
    murder, 138
Reyna, Stephen, 19, 50
Roosevelt, Eleanor, 161
Rumsfeld, Donald (Iraq war cost estima-
    tion), 168–169
Russell-Einstein Manifesto, 177–178

Schultz, George, 51–52
Science and Technology Foundation for the
    Integral Development of Middle Mag-
    dalena Communities, 139
Sciences, evolution, 7–8
Second Intifada (al-Aqsa Intifada), 109, 113,
    119–120
Seven Years' War, battle, 55
Sharon, Ariel, 111
'Shock and awe' campaign (Rumsfeld),
    93–94
Situation
    focus (Badiou), 73–74
    global flows, impact, 75
Small wars, 52
Small Wars Center of Excellence, setup, 52
Social development, militaristic/non-milita-
    ristic trajectories, 40
Social existence, war (presence), 34–36
Social forces, evolution, 7
Social infrastructure/programs, decline, 81
Social/national services (failures), profiteer-
    ing (linkage), 75–76
Societal recovery, impairment, 8
Society
    political-economic configuration, 157
    war, impact, 39–40
Socio-cultural phenomena, division, 36
Soldier as a System (SaaS) concepts, devel-
    opment, 89
Sovereignty
    cash, requirement, 79
    construction. *See* Fractures
    fractures, 76–77
Sponsel, Leslie, 46
States, experiment, 79
Sudanese Liberation Army (SLA), anti-Khar-
    toum guerrilla movement, 63

Sudan's People's Liberation Army (SPLA),
    success, 63
Supertroop, usage, 89
Systematic murder, 17
Systemic crises, 56, 59–60
Szafranski, Richard, 52

Terror
    global war, 42–43, 62
    scope, 132
    routinization, 133
Terrorist leaders, impact, 46
Todays, explanation, 15
Torture, official reason, 114–115
Trade to GDP ratios, increase, 57t
Transaction lines, extra-legal dollar flow, 75
Transnational corporation (TNC), operations
    (maintenance), 67
Treaty of Westphalia, 42
Tribal zones, 40–41
Trumbo, Dalton, 15
Truth (hiding), journalism (impact), 16

United Nations Verification Mission in Gua-
    temala (MINUGUA), 152–153
    warnings, 160–161
United Self-Defense Forces of Colombia
    (AUC), umbrella organization, 135
    impact, 137
United States
    anthropology, debates, 13
    CEH incrimination, 159
    economy, functionality (degree), 57–60
    global warring, 60–64
    military, global involvement, 60–61
    vulnerability, 19
Unmanned aerial vehicles (UAVs), 94–95
Ury, William, 46

Value/values, 75–76
Vasquez, Jose N., 16, 87
Vietnam War, civilian deaths (disputes), 169
Vigilante justice. See *Justicia a mano propia*
Violence
    experience, 72–73
    monopoly, loss, 54
    ontological reality, 73
Virtual reality, 87
    extended edits, commentary (inclusion),
    99–100
    future, 100–102
    military edits, 98–99
    systems, experience, 90–91
    training, 101
    video, watching (problems), 98

Printed in the United States
131057LV00005B/123/P

9 781845 456221